the
Power of
Mother
Love

Transforming Both
Mother and Child

the
Power of
Mother
Love

Brenda Hunter, Ph.D.

WaterBrook
PRESS

COLORADO SPRINGS

THE POWER OF MOTHER LOVE
PUBLISHED BY WATERBROOK PRESS
5446 North Academy Boulevard, Suite 200
Colorado Springs, Colorado 80918
A division of Bantam Doubleday Dell Publishing Group, Inc.

All Scripture quotations are taken from
The Holy Bible, New International Version (NIV)
© 1973, 1978, 1984 by International Bible Society,
used by permission of Zondervan Publishing House.

ISBN 1-57856-001-2

Printed in the United States of America

1998—First Edition

1 3 5 7 9 10 8 6 4 2

To little Austin,
my first grandbaby,
whose birth has brought me great joy
and strengthened my resolve to defeat cancer.
Truly, the timing of your birth was part of God's design.

Contents

Acknowledgments

This book was written during a time of extreme stress and personal suffering. I wondered at times if I would ever finish it or ever say what I wanted to communicate to other women. So when I admit that I could not have produced this book alone, I am not being modest. I am simply telling the truth.

Since that was the case, I want to thank my husband, Don, for his daily prayers and practical support, for all the dishes he washed and the housework he did, so that Holly, Kristen, and I could work together. What a man! I also want to thank my wonderful daughters who made room in their demanding lives to give me the word processing and editorial help I so desperately needed. We have worked together on nine books so far. In addition, I am grateful to my editor, Liz Heaney, for her empathy and intelligent editorial support. Liz kept my feet to the fire by asking penetrating questions I needed to answer. But she was always kind. I needed both her push and wise human understanding. I also want to thank WaterBrook for their forbearance when I missed my deadline and for caring more about this woman than about her book. In addition, I am grateful that a number of women willingly shared their motherhood experiences with me. Their stories made this book richer and deeper.

Finally, I want to thank the Lord for sending Austin to hold, diaper, and sing to sleep during this painful season of my life. My baby grandson kept the joy flowing and strengthened my hope. Just as God knew he would.

Preface

Years ago when I became a mother, I began an inner journey that has revolutionized my life. I began a journey to my heart. As I cared for my two daughters, I came to see that my children—with their love, neediness, and daily demands—were shaping me in ways I but dimly perceived. Only as they grew to adulthood did I come to understand how mother love had transformed me. Because of my daughters I have become more patient, hopeful, accepting, and less perfectionistic.

I, in turn, have shaped my children's lives, molding their sense of self, their values, and their conscience, as well as their feelings about intimacy. In short, I have touched their very souls. Such is the wonder and power of mother love.

Yet thirty years ago I had no idea I was embarking on such a profound and cataclysmic passage. After the early magical days as a new mother, I often felt exhausted and overwhelmed by the daily demands of caring for my babies. Like many other mothers, I wondered if surrendering to my children meant losing myself. Some days I felt a sense of melancholy that my life was not nearly as productive as I longed for it to be. Who had energy for anything after feeding two clamorous infants, changing their diapers, and running a million errands? I sometimes felt a nagging sense of guilt that I wasn't teaching college students (after all, I had a graduate degree in English), writing the great American novel, or steering important committees. Instead, I was struggling just to clean the house or take a shower—not to mention maintain a marriage. Then, too, I was aware of the cultural drumbeat which has only gotten louder since the late sixties—a drumbeat that says *a woman's worth is her work.* Long before this mantra signaled the birth of a national movement, I left my babies and went to work, teaching first at a local university and later at an area high school. But that didn't satisfy me either, especially when I started to see the fallout from my daily absences.

When I finally allowed myself to see my children's growing sense of emotional insecurity, I made a decision that radically altered my life. I decided that rearing them would become my most important *work.* And that choice has made all the difference. Because I chose to surrender to mother love, I can honestly say that rearing my children has given me deep and lasting fulfillment, as well as quiet joy. Oh, it hasn't always been easy, and there have been days, particularly when they were teenagers, when I threatened to become a Cistercian nun and see my family through a grill on weekends. But I've loved being a mother and believe this is the part of womanhood that feminism forgot. And it's also what most women in our culture wish to affirm in the latter part of this century.

Most of us want to become mothers, and we find tremendous gratification in rearing our children. But it's not easy to do this in our achievement-driven, materialistic culture. That is why I've written this book: to share my expertise as a mother and psychologist, to extol the power of mother love.

The subject of the mother-child bond has, over a lifetime, become my passion. As a young mother, I learned invaluable lessons from my children. Then as a fortysomething mom of teens, I decided I wanted to understand what psychology said about child development. Hence, I got a Ph.D. in developmental psychology from Georgetown University at the age of forty-nine, specializing in the mother-child bond. And during my fifties I have worked as a therapist, almost exclusively with women. My years as a therapist have only underscored my conviction that our earliest bond with our mother is paramount, shaping all other intimate attachments as well as our sense of self.

From my vantage point as a psychologist and seasoned mother, I have written this book to encourage you, dear readers, to affirm those of you who have given your hearts and time to mothering, and to suggest to those beginning this journey that as you surrender to mother love you will find you're becoming the women you were meant to be. In mothering your children well, you will become your best selves and experience a deep sense of meaning and purpose that no job or career could ever give you.

And what if you've been running from your children in your heart and in your life? Then I invite you to ponder why and—like me— make a midcourse correction. Not only will this make an enormous difference in your children's lives, but you will find the fulfillment you long for.

At a time when our culture urges us to seek our worth in careers, exotic vacations, and possessions—things that take us *away* from our children—I invite you to come *home.* To your children, to your best self, to your heart. And in the process, I urge you to reflect upon what is truly important in life—on what lasts.

I have spent these last few months thinking deeply about what lasts. Why this subject and why now? During the writing of this book I was diagnosed with breast cancer. In fact, I had a lumpectomy, followed three weeks later by a mastectomy, during the last month of pushing hard to get this manuscript out the door. What an experience!

This life-threatening disease has shaken me to my very core. I've had moments of absolute terror and sleepless nights, convinced that every ache and pain signaled my last breath. In the process, I've confronted my mortality as never before. This has caused me to dig deeper into the meaning of life. And it has solidified a conviction that I believe is the central message of this book: Our ability to experience the power of mother love is one of God's greatest gifts to us as women. So I invite you to join me on the motherhood journey and listen to the many voices that echo throughout these pages—mine and those of other mother-warriors. May their wit and wisdom bring strength to your soul and a lightness to your step. Come. Let's enjoy the journey together.

Brenda Hunter, Ph.D.
Vienna, Virginia

PART ONE

THE POWER OF MOTHER LOVE

IN A MOTHER'S LIFE

One night, as I hovered in a fragile state between sleeping and waking, I envisioned mother love as a jet stream encircling the globe. In villages, towns, and cities around the world, mothers push and groan, giving birth to babies who will someday carry their dreams. Most will love their children with unreasoning passion and go to inordinate lengths to protect and sustain them as they grow.

Yet even as mother love shapes lives and cultures, it, like the jet stream, can be threatened by other winds that would disrupt its course—winds that seek to discredit the bond that mothers have always had with their children; winds that attempt to diminish the power that children have in influencing their mothers' lives and psyches. Winds of fear. Winds of change.

I was troubled when I thought of these lesser forces. But even in my sleepy state I became aware of a mightier wind, undergirding and supporting this jet stream of mother love: the wind of God. This mightiest of winds, the Holy Spirit, not only gave each star its course but set our world in motion and created the original human family. And it is the wind of God which ensures that mothers everywhere will continue to love and protect their children until time as we know it ceases to exist.

Comforted, I slept, though all around my Virginia farmhouse winds howled fiercely in those hours just before dawn . . .

CHAPTER 1

The Power
of Mother Love

My baby has a little heart," said my daughter Kristen. Her voice was soft and tender as she stood in the kitchen of my hundred-year-old Virginia farmhouse, stirring a pot of soup. "Although I'm only twenty-five days pregnant, the books say that my little baby already has a heart."

Hugging my daughter, whom I call Krissy, I lifted her soft blond-brown hair off her neck and whispered in her ear, "Yes, and in the not too distant future your little baby will have a mother who has made room in her heart for him."

Ah, the power of mother love. How it stretches and swells across generations, uniting mother and child, fleshing out the expectant mother's identity and femininity, shaping the personality and life of her child, and changing society in ways our culture has chosen to ignore. Mother love is ultimately a love song, a siren's call, luring women to new ways of being . . . to sacrifice and being turned inside out . . . to fulfillment.

Mother love transforms a woman, forever changing the way she defines herself. From the moment a woman first discovers she carries *life* in her womb, mother love begins its alchemy. From then on a woman can no longer simply think in terms of herself—*her* body, *her* success, *her* marriage, *her* future. She must make room in her heart and life for another person, a child she will love passionately and feel deeply responsible for throughout her life.

As a psychologist and mother in her midfifties, I am watching my daughter make room in her life and her psyche for her first child. It wasn't easy for Kristen to decide to have a baby. She worked at a well-known think tank in downtown Washington, D.C., and had dreams of graduate school. She had her own goals to consider as she and her husband, Greg, talked about having a family. As a child of divorce, Kristen also needed to feel secure in her marriage before she embarked on this new journey.

During the time she and Greg were discussing the timing of their first child, Kristen had a dream. "In my dream," she later told me, "I held a tiny son and nursed him." She felt that God had given her the dream to encourage her. Not only has this dream framed my daughter's nascent feelings about mother love, it has proven instrumental in helping her postpone a personal agenda for a more encompassing family agenda. Daily I watch her grow and change.

When she and Greg went to see her physician for her three-month checkup, like most first-time mothers, Kristen was anxious, wondering if her baby was developing on schedule. Her obstetrician was warmly reassuring. "Would you like to hear your baby's heartbeat?" she asked as she moved the hand-held Doppler across Kristen's abdomen. Locating the heartbeat, she smiled and said, "It sounds great. Your baby's heartbeat is strong and steady. Now isn't that reassuring? Let's listen some more." Kristen and Greg sat mesmerized, surrounded by the stereophonic sound of their unborn baby's beating heart. *Thump, thump, thump, thump, thump, thump.* The sound of their baby's heart was loud, fast, regular. Kristen cried softly as she listened. What can be more exciting for a pregnant woman than to hear the strong, steady beating of her unborn baby's heart? This is part of the enchantment of becoming a mother.

GROWING A NEW HEART

For many women, becoming a mother means breaking down the walls they have erected to protect a vulnerable self. In an interview after she had adopted her son, Parker, talk-show host Rosie O'Donnell eloquently described her experience of becoming a mother: "It's like you grow another heart, like someone kicks down a door that was sealed shut, and the whole world—sunshine, flowers—falls through. . . . I have such joy that I didn't think was possible."[1]

Growing a new heart—how apt and wonderful this image is, for this is essentially what needs to happen if a woman is to become a sensitive, empathic mother. For mother love to be a positive force in a child's life, a woman must move beyond her need for control and her fears of vulnerability. She must grow, as it were, a new heart.

When my own daughters were born in the late sixties, I had no idea how motherhood would change me. I had not yet learned the ways of mother love. For instance, I didn't know that I would need to sharpen my communication skills and develop sensitivities I had never even thought of before. Nor did I dream that I would have to make peace with my own mother to be able to create healthy intimacy with my children. And I had not begun to understand that my soft, winsome babies would teach me how to love and care for them as they grew to womanhood.

Sadly, for the first few years of their lives, I saw these wonderful and beautiful little girls as accessories in my life. I was not willing to put their needs and development ahead of my own. My work—teaching literature to college students—was more important to me than caring for the unending needs of my children. While most of the women I knew were content to put their children's needs ahead of their own, I felt restless, driven to perform and achieve. I did not yet understand that this compulsion grew out of my own deprived infancy and early childhood. It took a tragic, unwanted divorce and five years as a single mother to sensitize me to my children's needs, to take me beyond my self-absorption, to enable me to surrender to the power of mother love.

During the early and painful months after I became a single mother, I stumbled across a verse in the Old Testament that I didn't fully comprehend at the time: "I will give you a new heart and put a new spirit in you; I will remove from you your heart of stone and give you a heart of flesh" (Ezekiel 36:26). Although I recoiled at the idea of the "heart of stone," I did understand that God was about to grow a new heart in me. I have since learned that a "heart of stone" is a wounded heart. But even the wounded heart must find a way to heal, to go beyond self-interest and self-protection, if a new mother is to give her child the warmth and affection and emotional availability he so desperately needs. Growing a new heart, then, is a metaphor for what happens to us once we give birth.

As our children develop and mature over the years, something curious happens: They begin to hear our voices in the deepest recesses of their beings. In their hearts. Psychologists call this process *internalization*. What this means is that our children internalize the image of mother that we give them. Jeanne Hendricks, a writer and the mother of four grown children, wrote the following about internalization:

> My children tell me that at those times when I was no more than a photograph on the dresser two thousand miles away, I talked in their consciences. I showed up in their habits and decisions. I was there in a front row seat. What an assignment!
>
> In everything from the high chair routine to the bridal parties, I had been teaching something . . . and I had the inside track. Because I was "Mom," I was different; *I walked in their hearts* [italics mine] whether I wanted to or not. It was critically important that I went in the right direction,

that I used my own devotion to package God's love for them.[2]

When we become mothers, we grow a new heart and eventually "walk around" in our children's hearts, whether we're aware of this or not. Fortunately, this process occurs over all the years our children are growing up in our presence. Otherwise, we might become overwhelmed by the enormity of the challenge that mothering poses.

MEMORIES OF DISTANT PAST

As I watch Kristen begin to embrace mother love, I am reminded of how nine months of pregnancy can prepare a woman for loving the child she carries in her womb and will soon carry in her arms. A daughter's pregnancy also affects her mother. As I talk with Kristen, I realize that I am on an inward journey. On the one hand, I'm deeply interested in all she shares. On the other hand, I find myself thinking about things I haven't thought about in years. Her words evoke a distant past. This, too, is part of what it means to be a mother.

The year was 1967, and I was twenty-five, two years younger than Kristen is now, when I learned that I was pregnant for the first time. I was a graduate student in English at the University of Buffalo. I called my busy husband, David, a third-year medical student, to tell him our wonderful news. We were going to have a baby! What joy! How we had hoped for, and planned for, this child. Conception had not been easy. In fact, David had been on call at the hospital every third night, and he was sometimes exhausted when he was home. We worried about having sex during that magical time of ovulation. To encourage me to relax, my gynecologist, a jovial, balding man, said, "Don't worry. Women are like rabbits. They ovulate every time they get around a man." Whether he was right or not, I didn't know. But as the months passed and I failed to conceive, my anxiety grew.

About this time my mother came to visit with her second

husband, an itinerant evangelist. Although my husband and I were lapsed churchgoers, we asked my stepfather if he would pray that we would have a baby. Willingly he intoned a sweet and intimate prayer to the Lord one morning as we four lingered over coffee. Within weeks his prayer was answered. To say that David and I were thrilled is an understatement. Thirty years later I can still summon those vibrant and powerful memories from days when life was full of hope and expectancy. Recently I remembered:

> It is summer and I see myself sitting on the dock at Lake
> Sacandoga, wearing a two-piece navy and red bathing suit,
> talking to my husband. We have come to visit friends, Lou
> and Elaine, who are in the cottage with Elaine's parents.
> Suddenly, I feel something move in my belly. I place my
> husband's hand on my abdomen and say, "Can you feel it?
> The flutter? Can you feel our baby move?" He nods, and we,
> who would later witness the tragic end of our seven-year
> marriage, are profoundly one at that moment. And for the
> first time I feel the stirrings of mother love. The "quickening"
> has occurred. I carry life in my belly, and I somehow intuit I
> will never be the same.

Mother love. What is it about mother love that has inspired mothers and their children across the centuries? What was it about Nancy Hanks that inspired her son Abraham Lincoln to say after he became president: "All that I am or ever hope to be I owe to my mother"?[3] Or caused basketball legend Shaquille O'Neal to gush, "In the Greek stories, a guy named Oedipus was so in love with his mother that he married her. Of course, I can't marry my mother, but whenever I get married, I'll marry someone like her"?[4] Now that's a devoted son. So devoted is Shaquille, whose name means "Little Warrior," that he bought his mother a seventeen-room house just forty-five minutes from his own opulent spread.

THE LEGACY OF LOSS

While well-loved children may later reward their mothers with time or even houses and cars, what about those children who lose their mothers to death? How do they handle life without them?

When I was in graduate school, reviewing the psychological research on early maternal loss and subsequent depression, I learned that the loss of a mother in childhood is always devastating and may produce long-lasting, low-grade chronic depression. When a child loses his mother, he loses his primary comforter, his most intimate companion, his anchor in life.

In the fall of 1997, the world watched as Princes William and Harry attended the funeral of their mother, the late Princess Diana. What was most touching to me was watching the boys walk behind their mother's casket in the company of their uncle, the Earl of Spencer; their father, Prince Charles; and their grandfather, Prince Philip. All the key men in Diana's life. Resting on top of the casket were three white floral arrangements. The lilies in the middle from Diana's brother were flanked by tulips from fifteen-year-old Prince William and a small arrangement of roses from twelve-year-old Prince Harry with a card stuck in the middle. On the envelope, young Harry had written in a wobbly hand the word *Mummy.*

The world grieved with these two young princes who had lost their warm, affectionate mother. Many expressed concern on television and in print about the impact of Diana's loss on the boys' lives and hearts. And well they might. While all children can be helped to mourn the loss of a mother, so powerful is this loss that it can become the most profound and influential event in a child's life. Tolstoy, the great Russian writer, lost his mother as an infant. As an old man of eighty, he wrote in his journal:

> Yes, yes my Maman, whom I was never able to call that
> because I did not know how to talk when she died. She is my
> highest image of love—not cold, divine love, but warm,

earthly love, maternal. Maman, Maman, hold me. Baby me!
All this madness, but it is true.[5]

THE VULNERABLE BOND

Mother love is powerful, but like any force or power that has the ability to shape human lives as well as the course of society, it has its highly
vocal detractors. For more than three decades, feminists have railed
against the high and perilous cost of mother love. For some, mother
love has been cast in terms of individual rights and economics. In her
book *The Politics of Parenthood,* University of Pennsylvania professor
Mary Frances Berry, herself single and childless, stated that "despair"
motivated her to write her book. Why is she so despairing? She believes that defining women as mothers "leads to a devaluing of their
individual rights."[6] Children, Berry says, tie women down and prevent
them from realizing their full economic potential. She makes short
shrift of those women who embraced the women's movement and its
call for autonomy and individual rights in the sixties only to complain
in the seventies and eighties that "work without love and family was
unfulfilling."[7] According to Berry, women cannot experience any lasting joy apart from professional status and accomplishments.

Recently, the assault on mother love has taken a new turn. While
earlier feminists viewed children as an albatross around a mother's
neck to be tolerated, now some feminists question the wisdom of having children at all. We are in the early stages of a growing, worldwide
movement that seeks to define the self-actualized woman as "childless
by choice." In her book *Beyond Motherhood,* psychoanalyst Jeanne
Safer writes of herself and other women who have chosen *not* to have
children:

> Nobody will ever send me a Mother's Day card—one of
> those Crayola-decorated creations made by dedicated, not
> fully coordinated small hands. I will never search my

newborn's face for signs of my khaki eyes or my husband's aquamarine ones, or sing a lullaby. No child of mine will ever smile at me, or graduate, or marry or dedicate a book to me. I will leave no heir when I die.[8]

Lest we feel sorry for her, Safer adds: "I chose this fate. I made a conscious decision not to have a child."[9] Sadly, she doesn't realize her loss. Nor does the media, which greeted the publication of Safer's book with a frenzy of publicity; to the press, Safer simply heralded the advent of a new trend.

WOMEN OPT FOR MOTHER LOVE

Despite voices that insist children are a time-consuming, costly, and risky business—one forty-two-year-old, married, childless professional said, "They may run amok and break your heart"—most women continue to opt for mother love. Whether they are responding to a biological imperative or a desire to nurture children as their mothers nurtured them, nothing can finally deter or destroy the power of their love. Since the first woman, Eve, bore the first child, Cain, most women have willingly borne children and cared for them with great joy and no little personal cost.

I was moved by a story in the *Washington Post* of a resident in obstetrics and gynecology who chose to give her baby life, even though it cost her own.[10] Clementina Geraci, thirty-four, had been diagnosed with breast cancer and undergone a mastectomy and chemotherapy. Upon the advice of her doctor, she waited six months after chemo to get pregnant. Then in her first trimester she learned that her cancer had spread. As a physician, she understood her medical options better than most: She could fight her cancer aggressively and have an abortion, or she could take less hazardous drugs and give birth to her first child. She chose to carry her baby to term. One friend said of Tina, "It was a goal of her life to have a child. She really saw this as her one chance. She was a risktaker. She was hoping to beat the cancer, too."[11]

Unfortunately, even with her fighting spirit, Tina did not defeat the cancer, which had metastasized throughout her spine, liver, and brain by the time she gave birth. But this feisty mother who wore a black beret to cover her balding head, spent the last days of her life holding her four-month-old son, Dylan, and making videotapes for him to watch when he grew up. On the tapes Tina told her son about his Italian grandparents, her favorite music, and her dreams for him. And she read bedtime stories, including Dr. Seuss's *Green Eggs and Ham.* And Tina's husband? He said this about his wife and son: "I'll just tell Dylan what she was like—how much she loved him, how much she wanted to be with him but couldn't, how much she loved music and art and literature and exploring the world. I'll encourage him to do those things, too."[12]

According to a close friend of Tina's, she had no regrets. She said she'd do it all over again. What a woman . . . and what a mother.

THOSE WHO GO TO GREAT LENGTHS

Fortunately, most of us never have to confront the terrible choices Tina Geraci faced. But even when we don't face life-threatening illnesses, some of us go to great lengths to bear a child. Cindy Heaney, thirty-five, who lives in Boise, Idaho, is one of these moms. Cindy, who is married to a Christian Education pastor, says her "mother hormone" clicked in when she hit thirty. But she and her husband failed to conceive a child. Thankfully, they learned of a study conducted by the University of Washington in Seattle, so Cindy began her frequent trips to Seattle, staying with her sister for months at a time. She took a fertility drug ($180 per day) that she calls a "purified Perganol" and went to the university almost daily to track the results. It took her six months to conceive her first child, a daughter now two-and-half-years old, and seventeen days to conceive her second child, a son. Cindy loves being a mom and says her greatest surprise is "how wonderful motherhood is. I really love these children like I love myself."

Rachael Love, a thirty-nine-year-old mother of a twenty-one-month-old, adopted son, Stan, is another mother who struggled for years with the pain of infertility. Rachael, who works part-time as an editor in the publishing industry, lives in Ypsilanti, Michigan. She and her husband were married for seven years before they adopted Stan. During that time, Rachael struggled with "enormous feelings of loss." When drugs and surgery failed to render the promised baby, "I had a profound sense of loss of control because family is just so important to me," says Rachael. Finally she got a call one January night that the "phantom child she had longed for so long" was waiting. When Stan was eleven days old, Rachael and her husband brought him home. "I never knew two people could be so lovesick over a child," said Rachael, whose baby has brought her fulfillment and deep joy.

SURRENDERING TO MOTHER LOVE

But not all women will go to inordinate lengths to become mothers. Nor do all mothers love and protect their young. There are those rare mothers who take life. Who can forget Susan Smith, South Carolina's infamous mother, who drove her two sons, Michael, three, and Alex, fourteen months, to the John D. Long Lake outside Union and drowned her gorgeous little boys. She later claimed she could "not fathom why she killed them."[13] Smith's act destroys forever any societal illusion that all mothers inevitably love and protect their young. Her deed dramatically illustrates the vulnerability of the mother-child bond and warns us, even as we recoil inside, that it can sometimes go wrong. Biology and the act of giving birth do not a good mother make.

According to Lee Silver, Ph.D., a molecular geneticist at Princeton University, "Women are hardwired to be maternal." But "the genetic component is just a framework. On top of that you've got environment, culture, and whatever else someone runs into."[14] Good mothering, then, involves far more than simply giving birth or providing a child with adequate physical care, quality clothes, a safe family car, the right stuff. It sometimes means standing against cultural pressures that devalue children. It may mean coming to terms with our own nurturing history.

As a psychologist I have worked with numerous women over the years who have complained to me that their own mothers, while able to provide good physical care, could not do the more subtle work of mothering. They were unable to establish a warm, loving emotional bond with their daughters, who craved that closeness. These same women later came to my office for help because, never having experienced intimacy with their own mothers, they were unable to connect on an emotional level with their daughters, husbands, or women friends.

Invariably I encouraged these clients to rework their painful relationships with their mothers, for in finding healing for their own wounds they would be in a better position to establish intimacy with those who mattered most to them. They could then learn to mother by heart.

Mothering by heart is a sophisticated act. To be a good mother, a woman must be able to tune in to her child emotionally and meet his essential needs. Child development experts agree that no matter what his mother's lifestyle, every child desperately needs sensitive, consistent, and responsive mothering.

Dr. Christine Conway, a psychotherapist in Fairfax, Virginia, believes that "women who are good mothers bestow mother love as a gift to their children; they can go beyond selfishness and are willing and able to value someone else's needs above their own. Such a mother," says Conway, "gives up her right to sleep all night. She gives up her right not to worry. She gives up her right to eat her meals on any kind of schedule. She gives up her right to go to a restaurant and eat what she wants, because she eats what the child will eat." A good mother is neither controlling nor intrusive; she allows her child to set the pace for their interactions, especially in infancy. And as he grows, she is there as a comforter, encourager, consultant—sharing his joy in discovering this brave new world.

Not only is a good mother one of life's greatest gifts, she is also a national treasure. A good mother raises children who contribute to the culture; she does this by giving her son or daughter essential tools for life: the rudiments of conscience, the capacity for intimacy, and feelings of self-worth. If a child feels loved and valued by his mother, he has a major advantage developmentally. He can face life with optimism rather than pessimism. He will be able to choose right instead of wrong, and he will have a strong sense of personal worth and not continually ask others if he has any intrinsic value.

LET'S GET REAL

Sound daunting? Well, it is. Every mother alive knows all about feeling overwhelmed by the enormity of the task. And every mother alive has her bad days when she longs to flee home for a desert island or a convent, the mall or a deserted movie theater. Writer Linda Burton describes her bad days this way:

> There is a Greyhound bus in my imagination, which I dream
> of taking on the bad days at home. On the moderately bad
> days, I plan speeches and theatrical exits. But on the awful
> days, all I want to do is quietly, in an ordinary sort of way,
> tell my family that I am going to the store for a loaf of bread,
> then walk out the door, drive carefully and purposely to the
> Greyhound bus station and never look back.
>
> Where would I go? It doesn't really matter. Maybe start
> life again in another town, under some other name. Maybe

become a waitress in a quiet little diner and have a quiet little apartment. And two or three little cotton dresses and never again have to . . . have to, what?[15]

What mother alive, if she is honest enough to admit it, has not felt like Burton on occasion? That's why we can't mother our children alone. Since we have such enormous power in our children's lives and psyches, we simply cannot do the job out of our own strength, life history, and personal wisdom. Nor will our husbands be able to give our kids all we cannot. While we need good marriages to parent our kids well, even this is not enough. God alone teaches us how to become good parents, and He pinch-hits for us when we falter or fail.

With God's help, we can become the mothers we were meant to be. If we give Him our most intimate possession—our hearts—then we and our children exist under His constant care. We have access to His vast love, wisdom, and guidance in rearing our children well. And He will plant us in a community of other believers who will care for our children. We can then shape our children's lives with a clear conscience and a full heart, knowing that He is in the process of shaping their souls. We then "train a child in the way he should go, and when he is old he will not turn from it" (Proverbs 22:6). That gives our mothering focus and direction. It also comforts us at a deep level.

In addition, we always need the wisdom, warmth, and inspiration of other mothers who laugh and cry with us across the years. Where would we be without the compassion and understanding of other women—our peers and mentors? Other women normalize our feelings when we lose it with our toddlers or worry about our teenagers' problems. Often they can top our tales of terror with ones of their own. They encourage. They renew. And they also inspire, like a woman interviewed for this book who struck me as a wonderful and human mother.

"I'll Love You Forever, Mommy"

Marian Gormley loves being a mother and understands the enormous power of mother love. Yet, when she was twenty-seven, this warm, vibrant woman thought she would never be able to have children. "I had premature ovarian failure," said Marian. "One specialist even said to me, 'You have as much chance of having children as if I threw a plant out the window and it flew.'" Devastated by this doctor's insensitive remark, Marian and her husband talked about adoption. But time passed, and Marian, who calls herself "a borderline workaholic," buried her sorrows in her work as an engineer.

One day Marian felt nauseated. She thought she was coming down with mononucleosis. After all, she had been working long hours. But when her breasts grew tender and she started vomiting, she became suspicious. Could she possibly be pregnant? A different doctor confirmed that, indeed, she was, and he said to her, "Quit your job. Take it easy. You'll never have another chance." Happily, Marian agreed to do just that. And when she was thirty-two, her twins, Jake and Tara, were born.

How have her children changed her life? "Mother love is probably the most wonderful thing I've ever experienced," said Marian. "It changed my whole perspective on life. Now I look for the true meaning of things. I look at life from a broader perspective."

Marian says she has loved her children from birth. "I remember lying on the operating table. Tara was born first. When they gave her to me to hold, I felt a passion I'd never felt before. Then suddenly they took her away. The doctor said he'd have to prep me for an emergency C-section because he couldn't detect the second baby's heartbeat. With those words I went from feeling the *best* I had felt in my whole life to feeling the *worst*. Finally, Jake was born, but the nurses whisked him away because he was having problems. At that moment I was amazed at the intensity of my emotions. I was even willing to give my life for my children. Strangely enough, my feelings have only grown stronger over the years. You think you can never love your kids any more than you do, but your love keeps growing, no matter how frustrated or angry you sometimes get or how difficult mothering is on occasion."

Because of her experience, Marian doesn't take mother love lightly. She tries to stay grounded in the moment and appreciate each day she has with her children. She tells of one such moment when she felt torn between work and Jake's needs.

I was engrossed at the computer when six-year-old Jake ran up to me.

"Mom, let's do something together. Now! C'mon!"

I was ready to reply, "Jake, we'll do something in a little bit. I want to work a little longer," but I decided work could wait; my son could not.

"What would you like to do?" I asked. I thought of the new library books we could read together.

"Let's dance," he said.

"Dance?" I replied.

"Yes, just you and me . . . pleeeeez, I'll be right back," he said as he dashed out of the room. He returned a few moments later with his hair a bit wet and combed over to the side, a shy smile, and a black Batman cape flowing over his shoulders. He pulled me off my chair and led me upstairs. The blinds were up and the descending sun was casting shadows against the night sky. Jake placed me in the middle of his braided wool rug and then turned on the radio. He said, "There, Mom. I found us some rock and roll." He took my hand, and we danced, twisted, turned, and twirled. We giggled and laughed and danced some more.

My side aching, I told him I needed a rest. He responded with great seriousness, "Mom, let me put something romantic on now." He found a beautiful slow song, bowed, and then took my hand as we began to slow dance together. His head was at my waist, but our feet kept rhythmic time.

"Mom," he said a moment later as he looked up at me, "Can you get down on your knees and dance with me so we can look at each other's face while we dance?" I almost said no to his ridiculous request. Instead, captured by the moment, I laughed, dropped down on my knees, and my little man led me in a dance I will always remember.

Jake looked deep into my eyes and said, "You're my darling Mom. I'll always love you forever and ever. . . . Mommy, we'll *always* be together. Even when one of us dies, we'll *always* be together in our hearts."

"Yes, we will, Jake. We'll always be together no matter what." As dusk quietly settled, we danced together, ever so slowly, cheek to cheek and heart to heart.

While Jake may forget this moment his mother has inscribed on her heart, I believe he will, most likely, grow up enjoying the company of women and be able to love and cherish a wife someday. Psychoanalyst Sigmund Freud understood the lasting gift mothers give their children when he wrote in his book *Outline of Psychoanalysis* that a child's relationship with his mother is "unique, without parallel, established unalterably for a whole lifetime as the first and strongest love object and as *the prototype of all later love relationships for both sexes*" (italics mine).[16]

As we mother by heart, we not only teach our children lessons about love and trust, we prepare them for all later intimate relationships. That's pretty heady stuff. So when you feel mired in the present—with dirty diapers or endless carpools—it pays to remember that future years depend on moments like these. As a mother, you carry the standard for the next generation.

WHAT CAN THIS BOOK DO FOR YOU?

Books can change lives. They have changed mine across the years—providing needed input at crucial moments—and it is my hope that this book may help focus or validate your motherhood journey. As you read, I hope you will understand your role in your child's life and his power in yours in a deeper, richer way.

From my vantage point as a midlife woman and therapist who has raised two daughters and made child development her life's work, I have written a book that will help you:

- Surrender to the power of mother love
- Simplify your life and learn to live in the moment
- Understand the cultural context of your mothering and, when necessary, stand against society's pressures
- Create a secure emotional bond with your child
- Shape your child's sense of empathy, his brain, and his capacity for intimacy
- Create a deeper, richer bond with other mothers to help change society and launch a new kind of women's movement—one that stresses relationships above all else

It is my hope that this book will deepen your understanding of, and commitment to, mother love. And that it will give you courage. I have great concern for mothers who tell me they feel under fire as never before as they make unrecognized sacrifices daily in rearing their children.

You are one of the unsung heroines of your generation. You need to know that you are not alone in your attempts to rear loving, moral, compassionate sons and daughters. I've been where you are. And so have millions of other women. The women I have interviewed—the voices in this book—have slogged through the trenches, too, finding real joy and fulfillment. May *The Power of Mother Love*, with its gentle instruction, help you become the mother you wish to be.

The Power
to Transform a Life

Wynonna Judd, country music singer, believes that children change a woman forever. "I don't know if I ever would have gotten off the road for a man," says Wynonna. "Everything I ever said or did or felt was about music. It's almost like this little spirit named Elijah had to come into my life to get my attention."[1]

What has toddler Elijah taught his mother about life? "I think Elijah gave me that incredible perspective of what life is really about: learning to love," observes Wynonna. "No matter if he's a nightmare and acting up, I have to learn to love him in spite of that."[2]

Elijah, along with his baby sister, Pauline, has also anchored his mother to life in a radically new way. "The way you live your life isn't about being talented or how much money you make," says Wynonna. "To me, success can be equally as devastating as failure. *It takes you away from yourself* [italics mine]. You can forget you're just a real human being like everyone else. Now, after having two kids, I've learned that life is about balance and accepting the fact that I'm not perfect and accepting the fact that I don't have all the answers."[3]

Self-acceptance. Balance. Humility. What powerful gifts mother love has bestowed on country music's reigning queen.

Is Wynonna's experience unique to her, or is it universal? It's both. While her children have worked their alchemy on their mother's life and heart out of their unique personalities, countless other women around the globe fall in love with their own children. Like Wynonna, these mothers have discovered that their priorities, their values, and their sense of self have been changed by that love.

I have found that children will transform a woman's life if she permits it. Babies are so fresh and green, so dependent and vulnerable, that most women feel fiercely protective of their young, even before other maternal feelings kick in. Once a baby becomes responsive— somewhere between eight weeks and three months—few can resist his smile. Said one beleaguered new mom of her ten-week-old son, "I'd do anything for my baby's smiles."

Sophocles said it first, "Children are the anchors that hold a mother to life." Through his vulnerability, his small, soft body, and his adoring gaze, a baby lures his mother into loving him. In so doing, he anchors her to life in a way that work or talent or even marriage cannot.

THE MAKING OF A MOTHER

Of course, some mothers refuse to allow Prince Baby to capture their hearts. I'll never forget one woman I came across while conducting my doctoral research. As she recuperated from having given birth the day before, she lay in her bed at a Washington, D.C., hospital, talking in a loud, commanding voice while I stood just outside her hospital room. "I told you that report has to be finished for next week," she said angrily. I peered into her room and saw that this new mother was talking on the phone while her baby slept peacefully in the isolette. "Look," she continued, raising her voice to a shriek. "It's Friday. I'll be back in the office next Tuesday, and I *expect* you to have that report on my desk." Needless to say, I wasn't eager to walk into the room and deal with this woman's pulsating anger and anxiety. But I felt sad that she couldn't shift gears, let down her guard, and take time to make room in her heart and life for her beautiful new baby. This new mother illustrates a poignant reality: Becoming a mother involves much more than merely giving birth.

Recently I did a radio interview about a California case in which a husband and wife paid a surrogate to carry and bear a child. The couple divorced shortly after the baby was born, and both marital partners decided they didn't wish to care for the child they had purchased. Sadly, the surrogate mother also felt no bond with the baby she had carried in her womb. So the judge ruled that this little girl has no parents. She is an orphan because of whim and lack of commitment, as well as cultural and ethical misuse of medical technology. We've come to the place in our culture where housing a baby in the womb for nine months is a service some women are willing to provide to infertile couples if the price is right. But who owns the baby? Who is invested in the well-being of the child?

Becoming a mother is all about loving and caring for a child, whether that child is born to a woman naturally or is adopted. Becoming a sensitive, nurturing, "good enough" mother is a complicated process that occurs over time. For most mothers, it begins during early childhood, gathers momentum during a pregnancy, and peaks during labor and delivery. It continues as children enter adolescence and beyond. A mother never stops growing and becoming; her kids see to that. But for most of us it's only during our pregnancies that we begin to think of what it means to be a mother. Shortly after a pregnancy is confirmed we begin to see ourselves as mothers. This transformation is subtle yet very real to every woman who experiences it.

NINE MONTHS OF PREPARATION

First Comes Joy

A pregnancy generates nine months of significant psychological and physiological upheaval. While it's wonderful, it's nothing short of cataclysmic. Most women are awash with euphoria when they first learn from their doctor or pregnancy kit that they're carrying a child. "I jumped up and down when I got the call from my obstetrician's office confirming that I was pregnant," said Ginger, twenty-nine. "Then I speed-dialed my husband, and that night we called our parents, friends, and just about everybody in the free world."

If a woman feels safe in her marriage, the news that she is pregnant can be immensely reassuring. She may have wondered if she could even conceive a baby, especially since some of her thirtysomething friends are struggling with infertility. Finding out that she has conceived allays a woman's fears and makes her feel whole like nothing else can. While a man may strut and preen before his friends when he learns that he has impregnated his wife ("I'm a stud," one man I know said jokingly), a woman is more likely to bask quietly in the glory of fulfilling a lifelong dream that began as she played dolls as a little girl and culminated in fruitful sex with her husband.

Laurie Combs, thirty-six, of Sterling, Virginia, is a woman who's grateful to be a mother. When she was thirty, she wasn't even sure she'd ever meet and marry the right man, much less have a baby. Fortunately, she met and married Roger when she was thirty-four and conceived shortly thereafter. The day she learned that she and Roger, forty-four, were about to become parents, she called him to share her news. This woman, who had fasted and prayed for a family years earlier, told me with laughter, "I was only seventeen days pregnant, but Roger told everyone in the office."

Then Comes Terror

Sometimes, however, a woman's short-lived joy gives way to longer-lived terror as it hits home that she is indeed pregnant. In a humorous piece entitled "Mortal Terrors and Motherhood," writer Amy Herrick chronicled the rise of her obsessive maternal anxiety. When she first discovered she was pregnant, Herrick felt both "absurd pride" and "a cold shadow of fear" that was "silent and sharklike."[4] Although her husband tried to console her, Herrick's worry escalated.

> Then, one afternoon, I went into the kitchen to have some tea and I happened to pick up one of my *Everything You Need to Know about Being Pregnant* handbooks and my eye just happened to fall on the section about toxoplasmosis.
>
> Toxoplasmosis is a disease you can get from handling cat poop and it's very sinister because the mother often has no symptoms or she thinks she's just got a cold, but meanwhile it slips across the placenta and causes the baby to go blind and deaf. When you're pregnant, the book said, it is wise to wear gloves when gardening in case you inadvertently brush up against any leavings of any stray cats.
>
> Just an hour before, I had been gardening and I had not been wearing gloves.[5]

Two days later Herrick confessed "when my husband finally threatened to put his head in the oven if I didn't tell him what was wrong."[6] Not surprisingly, her husband urged her to get a blood test, which turned out negative. The test results bought them both a few moments of peace. Until the dinner party, that is, when Herrick learned that her good friend Kate, who had just fed her dinner, cleaned her oven that very afternoon.

> I stared at her in horror. Oven cleaners were one of the toxic substances pregnant people were supposed to avoid. How

could she have done this to me? How could she have been so stupid?

I spent the rest of the evening in preoccupied silence, imagining in detail all the possible cellular mistakes that even now could be repeating themselves over and over in my little one's tiny defenseless body because of the food I had just eaten that had come out of Kate's just-cleaned oven.

When it was time to get in the car and head for home, with a great sense of courage and self-sacrifice, I decided not to say anything to my spouse because I didn't want to have him spend the next few months worrying and tossing sleeplessly, as I was going to do. However, we were not halfway home before he pulled the car over to the curb and turned and looked at me resignedly.

"Okay. Out with it," he said.

"Out with what?" I said nervously.

"Out with whatever it is that's making you look like you've been taken hostage in a bank holdup."[7]

Hubby points out that dinner was pasta, cooked on the top of the stove. This granted Herrick "an ecstasy of reprieve,"[8] which was temporary, of course. She then worried about hot dogs, followed by amniocentesis, and even "whether my worrying hadn't already blighted the spirit of my baby."[9] Finally, her baby's delivery brought Herrick a momentary calm: "All was right with the world. I was home free. He was slimy and squish-faced, but he was perfect."[10] No more anxiety. At least for a while.

Adjusting to All Those Physiological Changes
Both joy and "mortal terror" are normal emotional responses to the reality of impending, first-time motherhood. After all, you have never carried a baby in your womb before.

Thank heavens our bodies propel us into motherhood, or some of us would get stuck in the early months of pregnancy, anxious and obsessive about *everything*. But once our breasts enlarge and our bellies swell, we can no longer deny that something amazing and magical is happening to us. While some women bemoan the loss of their figure and their changing body image, others revel in the freedom to eat for two and gain twenty to thirty extra pounds.

Supermodel Niki Taylor, mother of two-year-old twins, Hunter and Jake, gained seventy pounds when she was pregnant. Was she concerned about her ballooning body? Hardly. "When I found out I was pregnant, I was like 'I don't have to worry anymore.' I craved meat. I ate meat and potatoes every night. If someone had leftovers on their plate, it was like, 'Give it to Nick.'" Although Taylor later lost the weight by jogging, she is unfazed by stretch marks and able to glory in her woman's body. "I have hips now," said Taylor, "but it makes me more sexy."[11]

While it's obviously unwise for any mother-to-be to gain too much weight during her pregnancy, I'm always concerned when a rail-thin woman tries to fight her pregnant state by refusing to gain any or sufficient weight. One woman told me with pride that she was five months pregnant and no one could tell. Preoccupied with the maintenance of her twiglike figure, this mother of one was unable to relax and enjoy her changing body or the prospect that she was growing a baby in her womb.

Sometimes a woman will be concerned about weight gain because of early internalized messages to stay thin, or she may be ambivalent about her pregnancy, seeking to deny its existence. Or, because of early woundedness or abuse, she may be unable to embrace this evidence of her sexuality. In any event, I always feel sad when a woman can't enjoy her transformed, fertile body.

I remember reveling in my pregnant body. In my third trimester, my belly was so huge I could hardly tie my sneakers or even see my feet. But I marveled at this transformation. Granted, I could no longer sleep on my stomach, and I moved through life slowly, but my body was housing and growing a baby. I thought it was wonderful. It didn't matter that I looked Rubenesque; I was a fertile woman and I wanted the whole world to know it.

Adjusting to Psychological Changes

While a woman experiences radical physiological changes during the months before birth, every mother-to-be also undergoes profound psychological changes. Becoming a mother for the first time is a major milestone in any woman's development.[12] It's a time when a woman revisits her own childhood and her early relationship with her mother as she considers whom she will emulate. In my interviews with eighty-nine women for my doctoral research, many said they thought more about their mothers during the latter part of their pregnancy than they had in years.

Pregnancy and new motherhood take a woman *home*. Home to her first intimate relationship. Home to her parents' marriage. Home to her earliest feelings of vulnerability and dependency. Each of us was once a vulnerable baby and small child, and we carry those earliest feelings inscribed in our brains.

If you had a warm, nurturing relationship with your mother and grew up in a stable family, you will find it much easier to transition into motherhood. After all, you know what it feels like to be loved and feel secure. When you've experienced the comfort and joy of a positive relationship with your mother, you bring emotional supplies and commitment to the task of mothering that the woman who has a painful, bitter, detached, or unresolved relationship with her mother cannot possibly possess. If you were loved, you can embrace motherhood because you wholeheartedly remember what it felt like to be held in the loving arms and gaze of your mother. You long to pass this rich legacy on.

If, on the other hand, you had a mother who was rejecting or neglectful, or your parents were divorced or wretched together, you may feel conflicted and vulnerable once you become pregnant. Those feelings of vulnerability and dependency will only increase as your baby grows. I've worked with women over the years who became extremely anxious the more vulnerable they felt. They had learned as small children that it was risky business to depend on someone else to take care of them. So they became compulsively self-reliant and attempted to deny their feelings of vulnerability. Having a baby meant they couldn't do that any longer. Hence, their heightened anxiety.

It helps if a woman has a good marriage and a nurturing husband. An expectant mother may wonder: *Can I trust my husband to take care of me? Can he handle my increased sense of dependency and vulnerability? Will he be there for me during the delivery and help me when the baby comes? Is he as invested in becoming a parent as I am? Will he be faithful when sex is nonexistent for a few weeks before and after delivery?* These are key questions that every pregnant wife needs to discuss with her husband, since these issues can generate a lot of anxiety.

Dr. Christine Conway told me, "I remember having a conversation with my husband before I got pregnant with our first child. It's remarkable to me that I had enough sense to be as scared as I was. I remember saying to him, 'You know, this is really going to be a life-changing event for me.' I wasn't entirely sure he was buying into it as much as I was. What I was really asking him was, 'Is this going to be my baby or our baby?' I had a sense even then that we were talking about a person who would be totally dependent on us for its survival." Conway laughed and said, "I thought I had signed on for twelve to twenty years; now I know I've signed on until the end of time."

A woman's past matters as she faces impending motherhood. It matters greatly whether she had a positive or negative nurturing history, for this is part of the well she will draw from to nurture her baby. This doesn't mean the die is cast if beginnings were painful. It's always possible for a determined, thoughtful mother to find healing for her wounds and pass on more love and security to her children than she experienced during a childhood of privation or suffering. (In a subsequent chapter we'll go into greater depth on reworking the past.)

Nine months of pregnancy can be a rich time as a woman reflects on becoming a mother and addresses any past wounds. If you are overwhelmed by the feelings that going *home* surfaces, then pregnancy is a good time to get your internal house in order. Seek counseling if necessary. I urge my clients to view this period of time as a gift—a time of preparation for the road ahead. A time to begin dealing with the past in earnest. A time to stretch and grow. The fact that a baby is coming is powerful motivation for *any* prospective mother.

The more you are able to identify with the baby in your womb, the more likely mother love will transform you into a nurturing, loving mother. Even though you carry a baby you can't see and can only begin to feel around your fourth month, it's important that you begin to feel some degree of ownership. *There's a baby growing inside, and he or she belongs to my husband and me.*

While women of my generation began to feel attached to their babies with the advent of the "quickening," modern medical technology allows my daughter's generation a different kind of gratification with the sonogram. I shall always remember the day Kristen arrived at my home carrying an oversized white envelope. "Want to see our baby?" she asked, waving it in front of me. Soon we were standing by a window, poring over the soft, fuzzy photographs of a four-month-old fetus. It was amazing for me to realize that those black-and-white images were pictures of my first grandbaby! We gazed raptly at the baby's rounded head and gently curved spine as he lounged on the floor of Kristen's womb-house, one arm nonchalantly cradling his head.

As Kristen, clearly excited, recounted her experience, I could tell she was also immensely relieved. "I was anxious during the exam," she said, describing the undignified process of lying on a table while an ultrasound technician slathered her abdomen with a thick, gooey cream. "Greg was fascinated by the pictures of our baby on the monitor, but I was pretty tense until the doctor finally said, 'Everything looks fine.' Then I could relax." As we chatted, I realized that Kristen had edged further along in her journey toward mother love and that my son-in-law was quietly joining her on a parallel path to fatherhood.

THE WONDER OF BIRTH

Finally the long-awaited moment arrives. As a woman pushes her child out into the world, her body courses with oxytocin, the same hormone that produces orgasms during lovemaking. In addition, her body is flooded by morphinelike hormones called endorphins that help her relax and feel close to her baby after birth.[13] This is the beginning of the emotional bond a mother forges with her baby. This process is also aided by high levels of adrenaline that flood both a mother's and her baby's bodies at the time of delivery. These wonderful adrenal hormones not only help a mother to push and strain, they also cause her baby to be wide awake and alert at birth.[14]

Why is this critical? According to French obstetrician Michel Odent, "Mothers are fascinated by the gaze of their newborn babies. It seems this eye-to-eye contact is an important feature of the beginning of the mother-baby relationship, which probably helps the release of the love hormone, oxytocin."[15]

I get excited whenever I am around newborns; not only are they gorgeous, but they also give testimony to the very existence of God. Who can ever doubt the presence of a loving Father when holding a new baby, stroking his silky-soft skin and seeing his tiny but perfect fingers and toes? The Mastermind of the universe has orchestrated all of this. Birth is a beautiful experience.

Recently I visited a young friend in the hospital just two hours after she had given birth to her first baby and witnessed all of those hormones in action. After fourteen hours of labor, this new mother was holding court to family and friends and proudly displaying her gorgeous new son. Expecting her to be exhausted, I saw that Leyla's eyes were bright and alive. She never took her eyes off her baby. When others held him, Leyla was a she-bear of protectiveness, commanding family members to wash their hands and sit down before they could touch *her* baby. I knew that she would soon collapse, but for those few marvelous hours Leyla was queen of all she surveyed. She was awash with strange and powerful feelings she could not possibly have antici-pated. While important psychological work and physical exhaustion lay just ahead for Leyla, for the moment all was new and glorious. She had become a mother.

ADJUSTING TO A NEW IDENTITY

All too soon, however, every mother finds herself home alone with her baby. Then a whole new life begins. In *Discovering Motherhood*, Heidi Brennan, mother of five and director of public policy for Mothers at Home, says she had no idea how she would feel once she brought her first child home from the hospital.

> I wasn't able to adequately anticipate how I would *feel* about my new baby, as well as about myself and our new life as a family. As I left the hospital, I was overwhelmed by unfamiliar feelings of protectiveness and even fear. I did not want to let my new son out of my sight. At the same time, I did not know how I would possibly take care of him.[16]

Although her mother came to stay with her for several weeks, and her husband worked shorter hours to provide her with physical and emotional support, eventually they went back to their professional lives, and this new mother was left home alone in a too quiet house with her son, forcing her to answer the question, "Who was I now that I was a mother?"

> While I knew I was the same person, I also felt myself to be different. My bonds with my son had grown stronger. I had begun to change my expectations about motherhood. Having a child had transformed me, and now I wasn't sure what my new life meant and how I was going to live it. I had become an adult in a culture that said, "Don't base your identity on motherhood." Yet how was I to explain my intense desire to give my time to our new baby? I felt that society was asking me

to ignore my feelings and to believe that it was wrong to make child rearing the central focus of my life. I was not prepared for this internal conflict, and I felt alone as I struggled with it.[17]

Heidi captures the dilemma many new mothers face in this culture. While they have a professional identity, they haven't yet forged an identity as a mother. So when they come home from the hospital with engorged breasts that incessantly drip milk and they can only fit into maternity clothes and rise every hour or two to answer the call of the wild, life can be depressing. And isolating.

Heidi told me, "That's why I call those early months of mothering the boot camp of motherhood. A woman loses her identity as a worker and is home alone, asking, What is a mother? What's my mission? Do people still value me? How do I feel when my baby cries? What can I do when I feel helpless?"

It doesn't help in those early days of struggle when coworkers and friends call from the office and ask, "When are you coming back?" The struggle to care for their babies and deal with loneliness may be more than some women can handle. Some women cut their maternity leave short because the house is just too quiet, the neighborhood too empty, life too lonely, the baby too demanding. Heidi admits that she felt a decided sense of loss after her baby was born.

Home alone, my adjustment to motherhood was a time of stress and confusion. It was not that I couldn't ever "get out." But trips to the market and walks in my neighborhood did not replace what I needed most—the frequent and spontaneous contact with people who knew me, cared about me, respected me, and included me in their daily activities. I had enjoyed this type of support at my former workplace, and now I missed it.[18]

Heidi was comforted by the realization that the transition to at-home motherhood was somewhat similar to making a job change.

31

In taking on the new career of motherhood, she knew she would need to learn new skills, handle new responsibilities, and find supportive new relationships. She allowed herself to feel sad at the loss of her work identity. "As I started to accept the loss, I was able to get to know the 'mother within me.'"[19] For Heidi Brennan, that meant drawing on the positive relationship she had always had with her own mother and forging a mothering identity that was uniquely her own.

A TIME OF INTERNAL CHAOS

I Feel Tired and Overwhelmed!

This is what new mothers invariably tell me. And rightly so, for the first several months after the birth of a first child are a time of internal, and sometimes external, chaos. Although the media portrays this time as idyllic, most new moms would probably say they feel disorganized, tired, helpless, lonely. Moreover, they are sleep deprived. Said one weary mother, with dark circles under her eyes, about her seven-week-old daughter, "My baby's pretty unresponsive right now. All she does is sleep, suck, poop, and pee. And I have yet to get more than a few hours of sleep at a stretch during any given night."

When I interviewed Kirsten Phalen, twenty-eight, she had been a mother for just thirteen days. As she spoke to me by telephone from her apartment overlooking Baltimore's Inner Harbor, I could hear her baby crying. Kirsten, who had been excited during her pregnancy, was unprepared for the sheer exhaustion that was part of new motherhood. "I feel overwhelmed just now," she said. "When Mike and I brought Kelsey home from the hospital, she started to cry. And I cried, too. Poor Mike. He just stood there, not knowing what to do."

Should I Go Back to Work?

Some of the new mothers I interviewed for this chapter had been employed right up to their delivery date. They told me that work looked extremely appealing during those first eight weeks postdelivery. "I know now why mothers go back to the work force," said one new recruit. "You don't get much return for all your work when your baby doesn't smile and doesn't seem to know who you are." Besides, life at home can be lonely and boring.

If you are grappling with the dilemma of staying home or returning to work, give yourself at least six months at home with your baby—long enough to make the initial transition to motherhood and to get to know your child. Carlie Dixon, a former law partner, did just that. When we were on the *Jenny Jones Show* together, she told the audience that she had six months of maternity leave—just long enough to fall in love with her first son, Peter. After that, Dixon decided she couldn't bear to return to work and leave baby Peter with someone else.

Be sure to allow yourself enough time to ease into motherhood if you're facing the work-family crisis—and enough time to begin to fall in love with your new baby. I have never felt that three months of maternity leave were all that helpful to a mother or her child. Too many adjustments are going on in that period for any new mother to make sound decisions about childcare for her baby's critical first year. If a mother returns to the work force during that time, she will miss the on-site, moment-by-moment enchantment of her baby's growing attachment—something that occurs between six and twelve months. That's when her baby falls in love with her and she falls in love with her baby. And as we shall see in later chapters, it's a crucial time for the development of conscience, intimacy, and self-esteem. So every new mother needs *time* with her baby to forge a secure emotional bond and to learn about child development. But time is not all she needs to embrace her new and sometimes confusing role as mother.

WHAT EVERY NEW MOM REQUIRES

A Husband's Support

A husband's love, presence, and support make all the difference as a woman experiences the transition to motherhood. During those difficult, early postdelivery months, a supportive husband is every wife's ace in the hole. Studies show he's her number-one support player during pregnancy, birth, and new motherhood. For a woman to wholeheartedly embrace motherhood, she needs to know that her husband is as committed to their baby as she is. His kindness and practical help keep her going during difficult times. "My husband used to get up with me at night when I'd throw up," says Grace, thirty-seven, "and often at 3:00 A.M. he'd send me back to bed and clean up the bathroom." Both worked, and Grace admits she would have felt resentful if Tom had slept through her middle-of-the-night sickness.

But what about labor and delivery? What's a husband's role then? During her pregnancy, Antoinette Clyde of Amityville, New York, says she sometimes wondered if her husband was really "with" her in the momentous transformation to parenthood. Would he be emotionally available during the hard work of birth? She writes:

> As it turned out, my husband was a wonderful coach throughout the twenty-four hours of hard labor. Immediately after giving birth, I watched as my husband cradled our beautiful son in his arms, welcoming him into the world as only a father can. I witnessed the love shared by these two most important men in my life and thought to myself, "He really did understand what I was trying to say after all."[20]

So, a wife watches carefully as her husband welcomes their new baby into his heart and life. As he steps up to the challenge of fatherhood, diapering and bathing their baby, a husband underscores the importance of his wife's role as mother. It's critical, during those early months after the baby's birth, that a husband is tender, nurturing, and faithful. A woman needs to feel that she can count on her man as she makes possibly the most demanding transition of her life.

In reality, both spouses are stretched as they experience huge role changes to incorporate the baby into their lives. Psychologists who love to create graphs showing marital satisfaction have discovered that a big drop occurs following the first child's birth. This is a time of radical role changes for both parents.

I spoke with the mother of a six-week-old son who was struggling with her role as first-time mother. "My marriage has changed drastically," she said. "No longer are my husband and I just lovers, friends, and partners who can go out for dinner on a whim, but now we are the parents of this little baby. While we both had careers, now he goes to work and I stay home. Although he tries to be supportive at the end of the day, he can't possibly understand all I am experiencing. Nor do I understand all he is feeling."

What this mother and her husband need to do is talk about the cataclysmic role changes in their lives. This is a time for frank, open conversations. Both need to tell each other how it feels to be a struggling new parent. In addition, I urge couples to find a baby-sitter and go out for dinner or dessert every week. The marital relationship needs to be nurtured, even if a woman is grappling with the constraints of breast-feeding. It's important for every new mother to be alone with her husband weekly, however briefly, so that she can feel like her old self again.

Sadly, not all women have warm, supportive husbands when they have babies. Sometimes a couple is estranged or the mother is unmarried. I read a poignant account of a mother who abandoned her three-day-old baby in the lobby of a building in New York City. She had placed her daughter in a Warner Brothers shopping bag along with two handwritten pages. The baby was dressed in a T-shirt, diaper, and jumpsuit. Here is the mother's letter:

My sweet angel baby Sarah,

I am so sorry to give you such a bad start in your life. You must never for a moment think I don't love you. I love you more than I dreamed possible. If I knew for a way for us not to be apart, that's what I would do. Please know that I never meant to harm you. All I can think about is the things I would like to give you. I don't think anybody would love you as attenfully (sic) as me. Take care. May the angels watch over you and may God forgive me. I'm already missing you. I can't stop crying. *I don't know where your Daddy is.* (italics mine)[21]

Poor sweet angel, baby Sarah. In having no loving, responsible, on-site father, she lost her mother as well. For without a loving husband, a mother has a rough, demanding course. She can feel quite alone with her baby and overwhelmed by life, whether she's an unmarried mother or a mother lost in a painful, unhappy marriage.

A dad—a tender, loving, faithful father—is absolutely essential in undergirding and supporting a wife's capacity to mother their children well.

Some thirty years ago I read a quote from a boy in Harlem, the source long forgotten. In speaking about the fallout from divorce, he said that a home without a father is "a tree without roots." I have never forgotten that image. A father, with his strength and support, shelters and protects his growing family. And without that security, a mother and her child will feel unprotected, vulnerable to all the slings and arrows dealt by life.

I know. I've been there. While my first husband was "with" me during Holly's birth, he had found a new love by the time Kristen was born. I then spent five long years as a single mother, and though I tried to be a stable, nurturing mother, I know the girls suffered. Perhaps that's why I want to toss a bouquet to my second husband, Don, who has always supported my desire to be a good mother. When he learned that I, a latchkey child, wanted to be physically and emotionally available to Holly and Kriss after school, he encouraged me to pursue an at-home writing career. He even typed the manuscript for my first book on his college typewriter after working all day. And he has negotiated every literary contract I've ever signed—nine to date.

Along the way, Don attended the girls' track meets, awards ceremonies, PTA meetings, and conferences with teachers. At night he tutored them in math and history. And when I enrolled in a Ph.D. program, he helped me with statistics. He has edited essays for college applications and pages of books. The man who never made company president paid for his wife's doctoral degree and cheered each stepdaughter into publication. Now in his later years, Don is dusting off deferred dreams. He wants to write a book, improve his golf game, and own his own business.

What has been my husband's best gift to me? Not his substantial support of my writing career, nor his encouragement that I get a midlife Ph.D. when the girls were attending college and we needed the extra money. Don's best and truest gift has been the freedom to become the kind of mother I always wanted to be. And I will always be grateful for that. For all of us, Don is president and CEO of our family company, a first-rate kind of guy.

A Mothering Community

In addition to her husband's love and support, every new mother needs to be mothered. She needs a nurturing mothering community that consists of her own mother, as well as peers and mentors who will help her negotiate the rapids of early motherhood. Usually it's only as a woman finds her mothering community that she is finally able to transition into her new role as mother.

"By the time my son was four months old," said Heidi Brennan, "I was in four mothers' groups: Gymboree, a church support group, a baby-sitting co-op, and a neighborhood support group." In addition, she hung out with three neighbors who had older children. "I didn't care what they talked about. I just needed to be with them. They were so at ease with themselves. I thought that if I was just around them, some of that laid-back attitude would rub off on me."

While Heidi found her mothering community among mothers at home, Dr. Jenny Noll, a thirty-one-year-old developmental psychologist who shares the care of her baby with her husband, found hers among the support staff at work. Ironically, the other developmental psychologists, who are predominantly female and childless, have not been particularly supportive. Instead, Noll has found support from the technicians, receptionists, and secretaries she works with. Since Jenny's mother lives in another state, she's grateful for this daily mothering support.

Toni Townes, mother of five-and-a-half-year-old Preston and sixteen-month-old Salina, found her first mothering community in a unique place—Gabon, Africa—where she worked as a Peace Corps volunteer in her early twenties. A vibrant thirty-year-old African American, Toni says she learned a lot from these village mamas. "As I watched the mamas in my village carrying their children on their backs, I learned that a mother's proximity to her child is key to emotional security," says Toni, who would later carry her own children on her back. "Those children were so tied to their mothers' bodies that it almost looked like they were one. It was only when a mother took her baby off her back that you saw separation anxiety."

Back in my own suburban village, I watch Kristen prepare to enter this larger community of mothers. As she begins her third trimester, she has joined a Titus 2 group at her church and cherishes these meetings with older, experienced moms. (She's the only young woman in the group!) When we chat, I encourage my daughter to have two to three anchors in her week—get-togethers with other mothers of all ages. This is exactly what I urged my clients to do when they came to me struggling with new motherhood. I encourage you to do the same.

As I've worked with new mothers over the years, I've been struck by the longing they have for nurturing relationships with other women. Most would say if they were honest, "Mother me." Sadly, some cannot count on their own mothers to nurture them. Either their mothers live far away or they're on a career track. Sometimes they and their mothers are estranged. When this is the case, a new mother may feel bereft indeed once she has her baby. Who will mother her so she can nurture her child? Where are the wise women in her village who will teach her the art of mothering?

Years ago I heard the late British psychiatrist John Bowlby, father of attachment theory, speak at an American Psychiatric Convention. That day he told the audience that all mothers of young children need to be mothered themselves, especially those who are wounded. He called this "mothering mom," indicating that the more support a mother has the better mother she will be.[22]

I have enjoyed nurturing younger mothers, both as a friend and as a therapist, over the years. And, oh, how they need it. As I've walked my younger friends and clients through the birth of their babies, the early years of child rearing, the healing of parental relationships, peri-menopausal angst, and marital woes, we've laughed and cried together over coffee and during countless lunches. While I'm not sure what my friendship has meant to them, I do know what these younger women have given to me. They've added fun, zest, and challenge to my life. I would encourage any older woman to adopt a new recruit and nurture her. I promise any woman that she will receive much more in return than she could ever imagine from her grateful younger friend.

FINAL THOUGHTS

While the transition to mother love is seldom easy, it becomes wonderful over time. All of the women I interviewed said that while the early months of motherhood were challenging and involved a kind of "psychic earthquake," once they fell in love with their babies and found their mothering community, life got better. Richer. Happier.

They felt more competent in caring for their children, and they changed in their self-perceptions.

And what's more, these mothers said they continued to be transformed across the years. For once they had fallen captive to their children, they never wanted to be released from their spell.

CHAPTER 3

The Power
of Surrender

"Whose life is this anyway?" writes Iris Krasnow, referring to her new identity as "the keeper of four small sons, ages four and under, and a very wild house."[1] The former United Press International feature writer says that at forty, she finally has it all.

Before Iris married, she interviewed personalities like evangelist Billy Graham; Elie Wiesel, holocaust survivor and writer; Queen Noor of Jordan; Senator Ted Kennedy; and Yoko Ono, John Lennon's widow. "UPI was my identity. It filled me with purpose and direction. . . . People thought I was important; often so did I." Iris said that she was "always hungry for the story, starving for the story," but at the core of her success was a feeling of emptiness. Her career, her success, and all the hours she spent with important people simply did not fill her up or give her any lasting joy. Like Willy Loman in *Death of a Salesman*, Iris said she felt "kind of temporary about myself."[2]

Now Iris Krasnow *is* living a vastly different life. When she became pregnant with her first child, she quit her job at UPI. Instead of interviewing celebrities, she now spends her days with her four young sons:

days of "bloodshed and stitches," which Iris says come with the territory when one is the mother of sons.[3]

Here's how she describes a typical day:

> 5:30 A.M. Fetch yowling twins, Jack and Zane, haul 54 pounds of babies downstairs, juggle them on hips while mashing banana into their oatmeal.
>
> 6:30 A.M. Make cheese omelet for two-year-old Isaac, wash 20 baby bottles.
>
> 7:00 A.M. Get four sticky boys cleaned and dressed.
>
> 8:00 A.M. Sit on the kitchen floor entertaining twins with cookie monster puppet while waiting for the coffee to drip.
>
> 8:15 A.M. Change three diapers.
>
> 8:30 A.M. Stop at grocery store to spend $139, mostly on baby food, diapers, and formula, then drop off older boys at nursery school.
>
> 9:30 A.M. Collapse on couch while babies are napping.
>
> 10:30 A.M. Fetch yowling twins, pump them full of Isomil, then crawl around the house after them until it's time to pick up their brothers at school. By noon I feel like most people feel at midnight.[4]

What a consuming schedule! Yet no matter how frenetic her life, Iris writes that it is "hopeful and sweet." She no longer obsesses about her identity. "I'm no longer concerned with who people think I am, because I'm certainly not that person they have in mind. I know this because I am no longer even the person who I thought I was. I have no idea who I am. I just am."[5] Iris Krasnow has finally found her "true self" at home with her sons. "My kids have captured me and I have surrendered," she reports. "I am no longer mine; I am theirs."[6] The result? Iris testifies that she's so fulfilled and happy she's "bursting."

How does a mother get to the place where she's "bursting" with a sense of deep and profound fulfillment? What does it mean to be "captured" by our children? Just what is this business of "surrendering" to mother love? Is it some kind of process or a one-time event? These were some of the questions I asked the women I interviewed. Looking for consensus, I discovered that each woman's experience was unique.

For Ann Marie McMichael, forty-three, of Hampton, Virginia, motherhood did not involve a conscious surrender but was instead a "coming into fullness." Ann Marie, whose children range in age from fourteen to twenty, said, "When I had Aaron, my first child, I told myself, 'This is what I've always wanted.'" Ann Marie, married to Scott, a retired lieutenant colonel, stayed home with her three children while her husband pursued a career in the army. For a number of years she homeschooled Aaron, Patrick, and Sarah. Now she works part-time at a local bank. She still manages to be home when her children return from school. Why? She wants to be emotionally available to them, just as her mother was to her.

While some mothers may embrace motherhood with the ease Ann Marie describes, most of the women I interviewed felt that surrendering to motherhood involved some radical identity changes. Women who had spent years in the work force, forging a professional persona and earning high paychecks, often had some difficulty making the transition from the world of accomplishments, business lunches, and conversations with coworkers to a realm of drooling babies, stacks of unwashed dishes, and long-delayed showers.

Judy Dungan, a forty-three-year-old mother of three children ages seven to ten, who lives in St. Louis, Missouri, remembers her early months of motherhood as a time of great inner struggle. "I was a legislative director on Capitol Hill and had been married for eleven years before I had our first child," said Judy. "I had entrenched, ingrained lifestyle habits and personality traits that had to change radically when I became a mother."

Before her first child's birth, Judy worried only about herself. "Mark, my husband, was self-sufficient. If I wanted to go golfing on a Friday night after work, I could do that. I had the financial ability and the time. When I got up on Saturday morning and wanted to go shopping, I went. My time was my own. But from the moment Madeleine was born, that was no longer true."

How did this new mother deal with the loss of freedom her baby brought? She got angry. "Mark didn't take on the responsibility for Madeleine the way I did. He didn't think about her schedule or about what she needed at a certain time or on a certain day. He left all of that up to me. It caused a lot of stress between us for a while. I resented the fact that he didn't lose his freedom the way I did."

Judy admits she handled this dilemma with great difficulty. At first she fantasized about giving her baby away and resuming her old life. "I remember one day when I was still on maternity leave. I needed to go to the drugstore and get some toothpaste before I picked Mark up at the metro. I pulled into the drugstore parking lot. Madeleine started raging as I tried to get her out of the car seat and into the Snugli. Frustrated, I finally put her back in her car seat. I went on to the metro and let her scream at me there instead of in front of all those people at the drugstore. Madeleine was twelve weeks old at the time. All I knew was that I wanted to give her back—to anybody who would take her."

By her own admission, it took Judy Dungan years to surrender to motherhood.

THE STRUGGLE TO SURRENDER

Many new mothers can identify with Judy Dungan's plight. To become a good mother, a woman has to give up far more of herself than she ever dreamt. One mother of a ten-week-old daughter told me, "I knew I would have to give up a lot when Karen was born, but I didn't realize how much of myself would be required." Cornelia Odom writes that when she was a brand-new mother there were moments when she found it "almost unbearably irritating" to put aside her own agenda to take care of a crying baby. "I found it unbelievable that my day could be interrupted so many times and in so many ways by such a young child!"[7]

In recent years I've spent a lot of time with new mothers. Most mothers struggle in the early months with the constant demands their babies and young children place on them. Sometimes they feel angry and frustrated by their children's unending neediness. Sometimes they feel terribly alone until they establish a network of other mother friends. They definitely feel depleted and exhausted. If you're a new mother, it's important for you to know that the difficult months will eventually pass. As you get to know your baby, you will become more confident as a mother, and demands will become easier to handle as you fall deeply in love with your child.

I recently had tea with a mother of a three-month-old son who has finally been able to sleep through the night. When I saw her earlier, she had dark circles under her eyes and was somewhat depressed. At this meeting I told her, "I know you've really had a hard time these past several weeks, but there's a light in your eyes I've never seen before. No man put that light there." My young friend smiled, hugged her baby, and replied, "I love my little guy. He's mine."

As a major life transition, new motherhood shakes most women to the core. Why? *Because this is a strategic time for surrender to mother love.* Though every child will ask his mother to surrender to mother love again and again as he matures, those first months of mothering are critically important, for that's when every woman consciously or unconsciously decides if she will pay the price and invest herself wholeheartedly in her child.

What I'm addressing here is a sophisticated, subtle, and profound decision. A woman can go through the motions of caring for her child while her heart and mind are elsewhere. Or she can let someone else— her mother, husband, or a baby-sitter—do the hard work of mothering for her. It's no easy thing to struggle through the early months and years of motherhood until you reach a place of joy. But it's necessary if you are to give yourself unreservedly to your children.

WHAT DOES SURRENDER LOOK LIKE?

By the term *surrender* I am not advocating total self-denial or abnegation or suggesting that you lose yourself in the care of your child. Nor am I suggesting that you form an enmeshed relationship with your child that allows neither of you to have a separate sense of self. That would be psychologically unhealthy. What I am encouraging you to do is give yourself wholeheartedly to your child and to the task of mothering.

Surrender always involves some degree of yielding and letting go. In fact, *Webster's* defines *surrender* as yielding to "the power, control, possession of another upon compulsion or demand." Surrendering to mother love, then, means giving your child your love, your time, and your attention when he needs it. It means choosing to live your life in such a way that you are physically present and emotionally available to your child for large chunks of "quantity" time, even when it's inconvenient. It means making difficult choices—professional, financial, and personal choices—so you can be *with* your child in body, heart, mind, and soul. It may mean postponing your dreams. It will definitely mean making sacrifices. But if you persevere through the diaper days, the years of runny noses and sassy adolescent back talk, you will discover the glory of being the first love in your child's heart, of finding the sweetness, hope, and fulfillment that Iris Krasnow has experienced.

To surrender requires a measure of ego strength. Dr. Jeff Berryhill, a Northern Virginia clinical psychologist, says, "It requires a certain amount of personal security to give yourself to anything or anyone intentionally." He believes that some women do possess such a strong maternal instinct that there's no intentional surrender involved when a child is born: "These are women who have wanted to be mothers since they were little girls playing with their dolls." But for those women whose surrender is a conscious choice, some degree of emotional security is necessary.

Other Mothers Speak Out

How do any of us surrender to mother love? Is it a one-time act, a process, or a daily event?

Heidi Brennan remembers the moment she understood what surrendering to mother love was all about. She was out walking with Charlie, her first child, and became aware that she needed to relax and give up some of her need for control or else meeting her baby's demands would become too difficult. Before that day, Heidi had been so immersed in Charlie's care that she could not see beyond the present. But that morning she had an epiphany, a new way of "seeing," that control was an illusion anyway and she needed to "let go." "That was my breakthrough moment," says Heidi. "After that I felt more confident and enthusiastic about each new day of motherhood. I also felt new power in not worrying about control. My newfound freedom was profound."

Like Heidi, Dr. Melissa Hoagland remembers a particular time when she surrendered to mother love. "I'd had a bad couple of days," she says, "and was thinking that my kids would be better off if I weren't at home. I went back and forth over this issue of career versus the kids over and over again. And then I was offered the perfect job for me. I thought about what to do, and I turned it down." From that point on Melissa has devoted her considerable energies to simplifying her life and taking care of her family. In the process, she has come to believe she's having a far greater impact at home than she would ever have had in medicine. "I am deeply influencing the lives of five people, including my husband."

As a result of her surrender, Melissa says, "I have a much more cohesive and all-inclusive sense of why I'm doing things. I'm more self-aware." This surrender allows her to live in the moment with her sons. "I'm not a patient person. But if you can't stop what you're doing, if you can't set it aside and sit down with your kids, you're going to miss it. *They live in the present moment* [italics mine], and if you're not in that present moment with them, they're going on to the next one."

SURRENDER AS A PROCESS

But not every mother remembers a moment in time when she consciously surrendered to mother love. For some, surrender is a process. Judy Dungan remembers her surrender this way: "I didn't wake up one day and say, 'I'm reconciled to this.'" This mother, whose dining room ceiling had to be repaired after daughter Hillary tried to flush whole rolls of toilet paper down the upstairs toilet, said, "I don't know when the awareness dawned on me that I was accepting my new role and not fighting it anymore. I can't point to a day on the calendar when I said, 'Oh, the battle is over.' It took years."

Carlie Dixon, who left a partnership in a law firm in her midthirties when her first son, Peter, was born, found it "very hard to surrender to mother love. It was quite contrary to the way I was living. I had to redefine accomplishment. I had to learn that when you're with a child, accomplishing is *being*, not *doing*. Just *being* has required a fundamental shift for me, and it didn't happen overnight."

What helped in her struggle to *be* and not just *do*? "Children's needs are rooted in the basics of life," says Carlie. "'Mommy, wipe me off. Mommy, I need a drink.' And as I live life through the eyes of a child, it changes my perspective. With kids, it's very easy to cut through it all and prioritize. It keeps the important things very clear, all the time."

For Cindy Heaney, mother of two young children, surrender has meant accepting the fact that the house isn't always clean, that she can't entertain as often as she used to, and that she and her husband haven't had a night away from their kids in two years. Cindy said, "It helps when my husband reminds me to stop fighting letting go and remember that our kids are young for a really short season."

Charmaine Yoest, mother of three and coauthor of *Mother in the*

Middle, a book about the struggle to balance work and motherhood, views surrendering to mother love as a daily exercise. She admits, "Surrender is a daily thing for me. Just this morning I was having a pleasant time with John, my two-year-old, and the baby. John rode his bike around the kitchen while I chopped vegetables. I thought to myself, *I wish I could always be this happy and not sometimes feel this inner compulsion to do too much, creating stress for myself and the children.*

"I believe that surrender is a core issue, both in the life of a mother and in the life of the Christian," says Charmaine. "Motherhood is all about self-sacrifice, something that drives feminists crazy. But that's what Christianity is about too—loving God and giving ourselves to others."

THE ULTIMATE SURRENDER

Charmaine Yoest raises a critical point. It's easier to surrender to mother love if we have already surrendered our hearts and lives to God. Once we give the control of our lives to Him, we can then follow His direction in the dailiness of our mothering. His priorities become our priorities. We know that He will carry us as we carry our children through life. I love that verse in Isaiah which says, "He gently leads those that have young" (Isaiah 40:11). I discovered this fact when I was a single mother carrying a baby, a diaper bag, and a purse, and struggling to hold little Holly's hand. It comforted me to know that God was leading me through that difficult time.

Dr. Jeff Berryhill says it's easier for a mother to surrender if she can say, "'God will take care of me so I can take care of you.' The woman who feels that she has a safety net—she has God's support and is in a supportive environment—will find it easier to surrender to mother love when need requires it." Berryhill adds, "This safety net is crucial. It's a lot easier to give yourself over to nurturing a child if you have someone to look after you." And to find that someone, a woman needs to go deeply into her spiritual self and surrender to God. This ultimate surrender informs all other surrendering.

Recently as I was reading the biblical account of Jesus' birth, I was struck by Mary's response when she was asked to surrender to God in a radical way. Imagine her predicament. The angel Gabriel had just told her she had been chosen to bear the Son of God. "Do not be afraid, Mary; you have found favor with God. You will be with child and give birth to a son, and you are to give him the name Jesus." Betrothed but unmarried, Mary was deeply troubled and asked, "How can this be, since I am a virgin?" The angel replied: "The Holy Spirit will come upon you, and the power of the Most High will overshadow you. So the holy one to be born will be called the Son of God."

What did Mary do? Did she panic or run away? Did she avoid and deny her situation? No. She surrendered. Quietly, beautifully, she said, "I am the Lord's servant. May it be to me as you have said."

Ah, the power of surrender. Because Mary had given her soul to her Lord, she was able to surrender her body, her reputation, her future. The result? Not only did her womb house the Savior of the world, but Mary realized that future generations would call her "the happiest of women." And from Mary's surrender comes one of the loveliest passages in all of literature, the Magnificat. In this song Mary thanks God for noticing her, His faithful servant, and expresses gratitude for all of the great things He has done for her. (See Luke 1:26-56.)

What a wonderful example Mary is to us who are still earthbound. She shows us that once we surrender our hearts to God, then all other surrenders become easier. Why? Because then we have His love and help in confronting the pressures, both internal and external, that would take us away from our children—pressures such as the cultural messages that devalue children, our pressing financial needs, and those personal ambitions that make it hard to be wholehearted about a choice that requires sacrifice and personal denial.

BARRIERS TO SURRENDER

The Cultural Mandate: Put Children Last

The thought of surrendering to mother love is anathema to many to-day. This is true to such a degree that any mother looking for reinforcement for her decision to put her children first won't find much help from most child development experts or media personalities. In an article in *Commentary,* Mary Eberstadt said that American middle-class parents have dramatically changed their attitudes toward child rearing during the past two decades.[8] At the same time we have been cutting back on welfare programs and admonishing the poor to make responsible sacrifices for their children, childcare experts have urged middle- and upper-middle-class parents to focus on self-fulfillment at the expense of their children.

We don't need to look far to find the proof of a massive sea change in cultural attitudes toward child rearing. Several experts who rose to fame proclaiming a child's need for on-site mothering have since changed their message to suit the spirit of nineties parenting. While T. Berry Brazelton, America's leading pediatrician, voiced his concern in the sixties about mothers who left their babies and young children to go back to work, he has now changed his mind.[9] In his 1969 book, *Infants and Mothers,* Brazelton wrote: "Two mothers are not as good as one,"[10] and he urged mothers to avoid leaving their babies at all costs. When he updated this book under his daughter Christine's watchful eye, Brazelton shifted his focus from the baby's needs to the mother's guilt. In the book's latest edition, Brazelton wrote: "Inadvertently I may have added to mothers' feelings of guilt when they were not able to stay at home throughout the first year. This has not been my intent, for I have seen how critical it was to many young women to include a job in their daily lives."[11]

According to Mary Eberstadt, such authorities as Brazelton, Benjamin Spock, and even Britain's famous Penelope Leach in their most recent books have all changed their focus from *what children need* to *what parents want.* Leach has even come to believe that full-time exclusive mothering is a myth of the postwar West. No longer should we expect parents to meet their children's needs because "everything parents can do is clearly not enough." If we can't expect parents to rear their kids, then who will do the job? According to Leach, "the top of society," "the public and private elite," should handle this monumental and significant task.[12]

Eberstadt states that the experts have reached the illogical conclusion that if employment makes a mother a happier person, it must therefore make her a better mother. She writes, "If Benjamin Spock's famous dictum to parents—'You know more than you think you do'—were adopted to the mood of today, it would probably read: You are freer than you think you are."[13]

How are modern moms to preserve their vaunted freedom? In her review of national magazines, Eberstadt culled suggestions for ways that absent parents could show their children they loved them: They could read favorite stories into a tape recorder, leave a prized possession behind when they go on business trips, or send messages to their kids by fax rather than spend billable hours with them. The cultural message that modern parents repeatedly hear, writes Eberstadt, is that they cannot adequately take care of their children unless they first take care of themselves: Parents must, at any cost, stay happy and content. The end result of these messages? We are, says Eberstadt, "putting children last."[14]

THOSE UNENDING BILLS

In addition to the cultural mandate to put children last, many mothers and fathers struggle with very real economic pressures. You may long to surrender to your child but feel that you simply can't live on your husband's paycheck alone. Even more difficult, you may be a single mother, as I was, who must work to put food on the table. So instead of knowing the joy and fulfillment of surrender, you are torn and conflicted, like the mother who wrote the following in a New Jersey newspaper, the *Record*.

My son is approaching the two-year mark, and, on many levels I seem to be plagued by more fears and worries now about his well-being when I am at work than I did when he was an infant. He is the light of my life, and I realize how little insight I had into my maternal potential before his birth. I was used to doing exactly what I wanted, when I wanted, with my husband. I liked to have time to myself. But then he arrived, and changed our lives and attitudes radically, none more so than mine.

Hence the guilt, the discomfort with the way I am leading my life. And the feelings refuse to go away. . . .

Throughout the day, even when I have a fulfilling day, with lots of positive interaction with my peers, I know that I am waiting for that moment. The moment when I turn the key in the lock and hear the pitter-patter of tiny feet come running to greet me from the den, hear the squeals of greeting . . . Mama, mama, allo. For me, it's more than the literal coming home. *It is an emotional and mental coming home* [italics mine]. The separation anxiety that he feels when I leave the house is probably not as keen as the one I experience each day I leave him with the baby sitter.

This reality of having to cope with working far from home and being a caring mother is unbearably heavy for me. The financial realities of the late nineties in this country prevent me from walking into my boss's office, and saying, "It was nice being here. I like the work a lot, but I love my son more, and I want to be with him while he is still small and exceedingly vulnerable." . . . While I adore my husband, I am not yet fully convinced that we could manage on his salary alone for very long. What a generation to be living in, one in which financial practicality frequently conflicts with some mothers' deep emotional needs.[15]

What poignant longing this mother expresses. Based on my own experience as a psychologist, I would urge her to follow her heart rather than her head. Why do I say this? This sensitive woman is mothering from a divided heart, and it's tearing her apart. Eventually, her internal dis-ease will affect her mothering, her emotional health, and her marriage. Because she is torn and conflicted, she will probably become angry and resentful that she cannot count on her husband to provide for her and allow her the luxury of caring for their child at home.

This woman's plight—which is that of millions of American mothers—is a perfect setup for depression. And no depressed mother can give her child the sense of wonder and joy he needs to grow well into himself. In fact, when a mother is depressed, her child is also likely to be depressed, as we will see in the chapter on attachment.

It would be far better for a woman to follow her heart and find creative solutions to make ends meet than to be torn asunder. Usually it's possible to live on less and, if we are Christians, to expect God to provide the rest.

I learned this lesson well as a single parent when I chose to work from home to be available to my girls. I needed to work but elected to work part-time because I wanted to put my daughters first. When I added child support to my paycheck, the three of us lived on seven hundred dollars a month in the seventies, a modest income even then. Yet we always had what we needed, if not what we wanted. Later, when I married Don, we had one small car, no savings account, and a bit of equity in my little yellow house in a slightly run-down neighborhood. Even when Don lost his job after our first year together, I continued to work part-time. He always supported my desire to commit myself fully to mother love, and when I would falter, he would say,

"Be wholehearted, or the girls will suffer. No work you will ever do is more important than taking care of Holly and Kristen." He was right. And today we have no regrets about our commitment to put the children first. Along the way God has blessed us financially, more than we ever dreamed possible.

WHY SURRENDER TO MOTHER LOVE?

You Are Irreplaceable

If you are struggling with this area of surrender to mother love, let me encourage you by sharing what I've learned, first as a mother and later as a psychologist: No one can ever replace you in your children's lives. For them, you are the sun, the moon, the whole universe. You are your children's only mother, and if you are too often absent, harried, or preoccupied, they may yearn for you all of their lives. If, on the other hand, you do your job well, they will grow up believing they are loved and worthy.

Although she's near the beginning of her motherhood journey, Toni Townes understands that she's irreplaceable in her children's lives, and that knowledge informs her choice to surrender to mother love. How did she come to this awareness? "I kept reading Dr. Seuss's *Horton Hatches the Egg*—a wonderful story about Horton the Elephant, who's asked by Mazie the Bird to help her out by sitting on Mazie's egg. While Horton does egg duty, Mazie flies off and comes back at the end of the story. Finally the egg hatches, and guess what? The baby is half-elephant and half-bird. I thought about the fact that you basically have to sit on the egg, since the egg is going to look like whoever sits on it. I have a strong desire for my children to 'look like' our family, to reflect our values. That's why I know I'm irreplaceable in their lives."

We have to sit on the egg. And if we choose to do otherwise? Then we, and our children, are the losers.

You Lose Out

Not only are you irreplaceable in your children's lives, but they are irreplaceable in yours. And the moments you miss together can never be recaptured. You will never be able to summon up two-year-old Dora for halting steps in the kitchen, five-year-old James for kickball in the park, eight-year-old Ben for a roll in the grass with the family dog, ten-year-old Sarah for pillaging mommy's makeup, twelve-year-old Sam for a discussion on cheating in math class, and fourteen-year-old Ruthie for advice on boys. That time is gone. If you were present for those moments, you have many wonderful memories when the kids are grown and gone—golden hours you can evoke to relive much happiness. But the converse is also true.

Iris Krasnow recounts a conversation she had with the founder of the Arena Stage in Washington, D.C. When Krasnow asked Zelda Fichandler if she had any regrets, Fichandler answered: "If I had a perfect life to live over again, I would spend the first five years of my children's lives at home. But at the time, I never felt guilty about leaving the kids. I kept feeling, 'This is worth it.' Now I give advice to young women embarked on missions to be very careful whether it's worth it. I'm not absolutely positive now that it's been worth it. Because of life not lived, books not read, art not seen, vacations not taken, conversations not held, flowers not smelled." Then Fichandler added, *"I never had enough of my kids* [italics mine]. I do feel I was always there when they needed me. But I don't think I was always there when I needed them."[16]

Looking back after years in a successful career and a lifetime of child rearing, Fichandler speaks with real regret. All those golden hours with her children are gone. She can't turn back the clock and relive her children's childhood. She may have honors and awards, but she never had enough of her kids, and we don't know how her children feel about the maternal absence they experienced growing up.

We, and our kids, lose if we can't surrender to mother love. In my work as a therapist I have seen many adult men and women who, failing to experience enough maternal warmth and affection, told me that no honor or award would ever fill their inner emptiness or what one client called the "hole in my soul." As I've worked with them to process their pain, in time I've often seen God provide a drawstring for the hole in their souls. But they did their work at great cost and told me that while they had experienced some measure of healing, they knew the hole—though smaller—would always be there.

How much better it is to do it right the first time. Said one mother of a twelve-year-old son, "It's easier to love a boy than to mend a man."

"My Children Are My Greatest Gifts"

Unlike Zelda Fichandler, Ann Gadanyi is making sure that each day she "has enough of her kids." A forty-five-year-old former art therapist and mother of two daughters ages thirteen and sixteen, Ann waited twelve long years for her first child, Emily, to be born. She speaks of those years of infertility and her several miscarriages as a time when she often despaired over her inability to conceive.

"I felt desperate," Ann said. "I come from a family of eight children; I was the third oldest in my family. And I just couldn't imagine going through life without children." Yet, by the time Emily was conceived, Ann had begun to accept the fact that childlessness might be part of her life. Said Ann, "Ironically, when she did come, I was finally trying to come to terms that this might be God's will for me, that maybe this would be what He might ask of me. That I might really have to let go of that and not make myself sick about it." Since she worked with children in her role as an art therapist, she wondered if God wanted her to care for children only in that capacity. While she was doing the internal work of surrendering to God her desire for children, she learned that she was pregnant. "I was thrilled; the joy was so overwhelming that I was ready to give up just about everything to have the experience of motherhood."

Now Ann, who homeschools Emily and Juliana, is working on another level of surrender. A deeper one. A year ago she learned that she had an aggressive tumor growing in her left breast. Ann had a mastectomy followed by six months of chemotherapy, during which she lost her hair and had some bleak days. As she deals with her life-threatening illness, once again she is learning to let go. Grappling with her mortality, this attractive, gracious woman said, "I think a lot about surrender these days. Going through this illness has been a process of letting go." Then Ann commented reflectively, "I think we're carried through many places in our lives—motherhood, suffering—where we learn to shift our priorities. These experiences lead us into unconditional love—to a deeper place inside us. But it doesn't come naturally. It takes a lot of practice, a lot of looking inward."

Ann feels that her ability to be home with her children and home-school them is a great gift. "When I started homeschooling, I thought that for the first time I would see the fruit of my labors, and that gave me hope. I am shaping the souls of my children. I think it was Cardinal Vincent who said that motherhood is one of the noblest professions. He said that though mothers can't claim the honor of having built the Notre Dame Cathedral, they have built something far more magnificent: a dwelling for an immortal soul."

How has Ann's bout with breast cancer affected her children? "Obviously my girls were frightened. As for me, when I faced the possibility that I might lose my life when my children were still young, I saw what a vital role I played in their lives. It caused me to question how their lives would go on without me. I remember raising that question with someone, and the response was such a consolation. She helped me to see that our Lord loves our children far more deeply than we do. As great as our love is, it can't compare to His love for them. If something were to happen to me, my children would have what they need. I really believe that. In the beginning of my illness I wasn't so sure, and I was very frightened for them. But I have grown spiritually through this illness. I have come to trust God more and more."

Ann believes that if we can just give up some of the control we fight to hang on to, "a way will be made for us and needs will be met. But we can't calculate how the help will come."

What does Ann want her legacy to her children to be? "I want them to know how precious their lives are and hope they understand that no matter how difficult life may be at points, no matter what their weaknesses or faults or how many times they fail in life, they are loved, not only by me and their father but by their heavenly Father also. Then they can always pick themselves up and move more deeply into their relationship with our Lord because it's an eternal relationship."

Ann Gadanyi is a woman who understands the power of surrender, both to mother love and to God. How does she feel after her harrowing year—a time when she has reflected on the fragility of life? "I am happy," said Ann. "I understand that the future is uncertain, but I love every day with my girls."

Then Ann added, "My children are my life's greatest gifts."

And so they are to any mother who has discovered the beauty, power, and joy of surrendering to mother love.

The Power
of Simplicity

If you yearn for a simpler life, you're not alone. Whether we work in the marketplace or from home, too many women—especially mothers—feel driven to live overscheduled lives. We squeeze in activities every moment of the day only to fall into bed at night exhausted, wondering when life will slow down and we'll have sufficient time for our children, the housework, the correspondence piled high on untidy desks, and ourselves.

Books about simplifying one's life, slowing down, and caring for the soul have topped the bestseller lists in recent years, books such as Elaine St. John's *Simplify Your Life*, Sara Ban Breathnach's *Simple Abundance*, and Thomas Moore's *Care of the Soul*. Why are these books so popular? They address the longing many of us feel to have a life less harried, less driven, less soulless. A life that gives us hours of peaceful sleep and mental tranquillity. A life ripe with time to squander on our children, doing simple things like sharing an ice cream cone, taking a walk in the park, or having a deep and meaningful conversation.

One of the books on the simpler life that I have enjoyed this year is *Simple Abundance.* In the introduction the author admits that the book grew out of the unrest in her own soul. She was "hurtling through life, miserable and unfulfilled." Ban Breathnach describes her experience:

Several years ago, after I'd written two books celebrating nineteenth-century domestic life, I was about to begin writing one on Victorian decorative details. But the thought of ruminating on ruffles and flourishes for a year brought dread to my heart. What I wanted to write was a book that would show me how to reconcile my deepest spiritual, authentic, and creative longings with often-overwhelming and conflicting commitments—to my husband and daughter, invalid mother, work at home, work in the world, siblings, friends, and community. I knew I wasn't the only woman hurtling through real life as if it were an out-of-body experience. I knew I wasn't the only woman frazzled, depressed, worn to a raveling. But I also knew I certainly wasn't the woman with the answers. I didn't even know the questions.

I wanted so much—money, success, recognition, genuine creative expression—but had absolutely no clue as to what I truly needed. At times my passionate hungers were so voracious I could deal with them only through denial. I was a workaholic, careaholic, and perfectionist. I couldn't remember the last time I was kind to myself. Was I ever? More often than it feels comfortable to admit, I was an angry, envious woman, constantly comparing myself to others only to become resentful because of what seemed to be missing from my life, although I couldn't have told you what it was. The secret sense of longing contributed to a perpetual state of guilt because I share my life with a marvelous man and our smart, sweet, witty, beautiful child, whom I adore. I had so much. I felt as if I didn't have the right to want more.

Money was an enormous, emotionally charged issue that controlled my ability to be happy because I let it; money was the only way I could measure my success and self-worth. If I couldn't write a check on my accomplishments, they didn't exist. Frustrated and unable to fathom why some women appeared to lead much more fulfilling lives—even though I was conscientiously connecting all the dots—I careened between feeling that I was frittering my life away to feeling that I was sacrificing it on the altar of my own ambitions.[1]

So begins a book that has topped the *New York Times* bestseller list for nearly two years. Harried and unhappy, Ban Breathnach began a personal pilgrimage that has led her ultimately to contentment and joy.

WHERE DID THE SIMPLE LIFE GO?

Why are so many of us living crazy lives, rushing pell-mell through our days, whether we work inside or outside our homes? And what about the quality of mothering we are able to do between the dry cleaners and soccer practice? Are we, like Ban Breathnach, torn between feeling that we're "frittering our life away" or sacrificing it on the altar of ambition?

Part of our unrest and our inability to live simpler lives stems from the fact that we've been told during the past three decades that our work is our worth. Never mind that "worker" is only one of our many roles. It's the *only* role as far as many feminists are concerned; all other roles—wife, and especially mother—are subservient to it. According to Anne Roiphe, author of *Fruitful*, the message of the contemporary feminist movement has been "that you didn't have to, you didn't need to, you had other choices; whether this was a turn against marriage, a turn against cooking, a turn against babies as destiny it was all about not having to, not being coerced into, about not polishing the furniture till it shone, *about searching for meaning outside the home*" (italics mine).[2] Unfortunately, this frenetic search for meaning outside our homes has not delivered promised joy. Instead, many of us feel that our lives are spinning out of control, or to use the New England philosopher Henry David Thoreau's words, we are living "lives of quiet desperation." Yearning to be centered and less driven, we may desire to spend more time with our children but are unable to do so because of our unrelenting commitments.

While mothers who stay home may also live helter-skelter lives if they choose to be overcommitted, it's usually the mother who works outside her home full-time who feels trapped in a stressful life. In fact, a "women and work" reader's poll in *Parents* magazine found that only 4 percent of 18,000 mothers surveyed would choose to work full-time if they did not feel compelled to earn money and achieve.[3] Also, 83 percent of working moms said they didn't have enough time for themselves, and 74 percent said they were tired all the time. Forty-three percent even said they'd like to turn back the clock and live in the 1950s.[4] Imagine! So, contrary to what the media contends, many of us who swell the ranks of full-time workers would rather be home with our children, at least part-time, savoring the moment.

When our bodies are one place and our hearts are elsewhere, we are living high-stress lives. Writer Danielle Crittenden says the dilemma many employed mothers face is not a lack of state-subsidized, high-quality day care but a real internal conflict that will not go away. "Despite three decades of reassurances on the contrary, the woman who kisses her child's forehead each morning before walking out the door to her office still harbors the agonizing suspicion that what her child needs most is her. And this denial is contributing to a kind of madness in the lives of working mothers."[5]

To illustrate her point, Crittenden describes a young business woman who "has it all." This unnamed bank executive, who started out as a local bank manager and worked her way up the ranks, struggles to balance her children's needs, the demands of marriage, the care of a house with a "new kitchen the size of a small urban park," and her own needs.[6] A mother of two sons, a four-year-old and an infant, she reluctantly admits she's unhappy. She told Crittenden:

> I'm efficient. I can juggle a lot of balls in the air. But it feels now like there are so many demands on me. Everyone wants a piece of you—your children, your husband, your boss, your staff. There is no *time* for anything else.[7]

No time to kick back; no time to hang out with the kids; no time to have a two-hour lunch with a best friend, take a walk, go shopping, purchase some daisies, read a book, be creative. No time to find quiet in your mind—to nourish a marriage, care for yourself, care for your soul. No time to pursue a simpler life. And it's exactly this kind of tension and strain that tears some mothers apart.

Sarah Ban Breathnach says that women today "know how to start successful mail order companies, launch banks and news magazines, walk in space, trade secrets on Wall Street, anchor nightly news, write Supreme Court decisions, and win Nobel prizes."[8] But they also run to the grocery store with tired children in tow and live in "overwhelming pandemonium"—in other words, many women can run their businesses, but they are clueless when it comes to running their households competently.[9]

I remember a client I saw for a single session. This attractive thirty-five-year-old, clad in a designer suit, breezed in and sat down. When I asked what had brought her in to see me, she began to rattle off a host of problems. She had a high-powered job that required travel, three young children under the age of five, a baby-sitter who had just resigned, a new home under construction, and she was physically ill a lot of the time. She believed her immune system wasn't functioning up to par since she had come down with the flu several times in recent months and innumerable colds to boot. Last but not least, she struggled with depression.

If she had elected to come for further sessions, I would have worked with her on her choices, since they were obviously hurting her. I would also have worked with her on simplifying her life, on self-care, and on what kind of mother she wanted to be to her small children. Her depression wasn't surprising, given her health problems and her feelings of helplessness and hopelessness. She felt like she was in a cage, yet *she had the capacity to make new choices . . .* we all do. We don't have to run on empty or feel that everyone is cannibalizing a little piece of us.

How can you change and begin to discover the power of simplicity? Start by acknowledging that you're a finite creature who doesn't have limitless energy, boundless juggling skills, and endless patience— even though everyone around you expects you to have these qualities. Just like everyone else, mothers get tired and need fallow time, and you're no exception. You, too, need rest and fun and quiet. Besides, it's only when you're collected and quiet that you can hear the rhythm of the universe in your children's voices.

LISTENING WITH THE HEART

My doctor, a general practitioner in his early forties, told me he practices medicine only four days a week because working longer hours makes him less able to "hear" what his patients are telling him when they describe their physical ills. As he listens to their heart and lungs, this affable man also "listens" to their body language, facial expressions, and all those things they're not saying, except in snippets—references to broken marriages, hurts, disowned dreams. This doctor, a philosopher as well as a physician, struggles to be true to himself within the current American medical paradigm that emphasizes profit rather than empathy. Instead of rushing his patients through the office in fifteen minutes or less, he spends an hour with each one. His nurse tells me he's done this for years. When I praised him to a friend, also a general practitioner, my friend's response was, "Well, I make a lot more money." Because my doctor wishes to "hear" his patients and stay emotionally connected to his own three children, he and his wife have chosen to live on less.

What can you do to hear the people who are most important to you? How can you breathe simplicity into their lives? The answer is around you every day. While you can read books on the simple life and yearn for a slower pace, your children will slow you down naturally and teach you how to tap into the rhythm of the world around you if you let them. You have built-in help sitting at your kitchen table, eating a peanut butter sandwich and dripping bread crumbs on the floor or practicing the piano in the next room. You have coaches in the form of your adolescent sons and daughters who just want to hang out in the kitchen with you after school. As your children inspire you to be "at home" with them and with yourself, they will also anchor you in the moment, slowing you down and teaching you how to simplify your life. You will begin to see life through their eyes.

LIFE THROUGH A CHILD'S EYES

Living in the Moment

Diane Fisher, a clinical psychologist and mother of three, is well aware that she's curtailing her achievement needs to nurture herself and her family and to live a simpler life. In *New Beginnings* magazine, Fisher wrote, "There is a powerful, continual and appealing cultural pressure to use my education, stay in the fast lane, be 'all' the woman I can be. There is great internal pressure as well. For me, professional success and acclaim is a siren song. It is painful to walk away from the mainstream, full-tilt work world. Sometimes, I am afraid I have lost myself, my professional edge, and my connection with colleagues."[10]

So why did Fisher cut back from full-time employment to part-time? When she realized she spent most of her emotional energy at work and felt distant and detached from her kids, she decided to use her time for what mattered most: being emotionally available to her family. The result? She describes what it feels like to have *time* to focus on her children:

> On a good morning, I stand in my robe at the door and
> watch with a feeling of pride and accomplishment as they
> [her two sons] walk down the street. I am grateful for the
> moments when my rhythm matches theirs, when I am happy
> to contain and nurture this burgeoning, squiggly mass of
> male energy. . . . My infant daughter awaits, blowing bubbles
> and teething wetly on whatever toy has miraculously
> remained in front of her. Primary-colored plastic objects
> mark my path as I pick my way through to that last cup of
> coffee. If I had my choice it would always be like this. I
> would not forget the preciousness of my children in the rush
> of the day.[11]

Fisher, who admits she fights ambivalence about her decision to cut back on her career, came to see the irony of sitting in her office listening to her adult patients talk for hours about the power of their unmet emotional needs from childhood while her own children waited at home for her. When she and her husband made a conscious decision that she would focus primarily on home and family, Fisher discovered her own simple abundance: blossoming children and "a home where life is celebrated together from morning until night."[12] She also found *time*—time for music, time to read inspiring books, time to care for her soul. Best of all, Fisher has experienced that heightened awareness and simple joy that comes from living in the moment:

> When I center myself, I can cradle my baby and feel in every
> pore the preciousness of this time. I inhale her sweet smell,
> feel her tiny feet in the palm of my hand, and I get it, I really

get it. This is the reward I have given myself through all of the struggle. I flop on the floor and play a silly board game with my younger son when he returns from school—supper is waiting on the stove and I am not exhausted. I look up into his blue eyes and see contentment. My older son dances and plays his keyboard, happy within the periphery of the family circle, watched but not watched, held by us even as he grows away from us. In large part, *I have created or orchestrated this harmony of home, this sense of well-being and calm.*[13] [italics mine]

Living in the moment. What a powerful experience this is. Notice that Fisher's senses were alive. She *inhaled* her baby's sweet smell, *felt* her tiny feet, and *cradled* her body. When was the last time you were aware of touching your child's soft skin or inhaling his scent? Plus, Fisher says that she is "centered," and since she's the hub of the family wheel, her home exudes a sense of harmony and calm. And supper is waiting. That means no waiting in line for greasy fast food at McDonald's or dealing with everybody's low blood sugar and bad moods as you throw prepared food in the microwave.

Recently I had an experience that paralleled Fisher's. I often play with the four-month-old baby of a young friend who drops by for coffee and a chat. I hold her squirmy son, a gorgeous blue-eyed darling, who this day sports a soft gold-and-blue jumpsuit. He lies in my lap, kicking and cooing, exuding a clean baby smell. He's in the phase of development where he will soon discover his hands, the joys of reaching and grabbing, and how to dazzle audiences with his smile. I'm captivated as he grabs my finger and sticks it into his rosebud mouth, his laboratory for learning about the world.

I stroke his dimpled cheek, stand him up, and nuzzle his soft neck. How I love to hold this cuddly, squirmy baby! And in these months following my diagnosis of breast cancer, little gives me more simple pleasure than holding my new little friend and playing with him. Then I am a psychologist enjoying a refresher course in infancy, and I get to experience the wonder of touching his silky-soft skin.

I am not alone in feeling joy as I watch a baby experience his world. When Dr. Melissa Hoagland took her nine-month-old son, Tyler, to the beach for the first time, she experienced the magic of seeing life through her child's eyes. It was an alive, vital moment. "When Tyler saw the ocean for the first time, I remember holding him as he got so still. He just looked at the waves and listened." As her baby listened to the sounds of nature with his whole being, his mother learned what it was like to sense ocean, wind, and birds—all for the first time.

What pleasure and calm await us when we live in the moment. We are kept from anxiously focusing on the future or being morbidly preoccupied with the past. We're fully alive in the *now*. And since our children always live in the present moment, we're more attuned to them emotionally as we turn down the background noise and focus on the now. Children are keenly aware when we're there in the moment with them. We can't fool them. And when they sense that we're "there but not there," then their incessant demands, their crying, and their whining are artless attempts to call us back to be *with* them.

Children, then, can anchor us in the moment and teach us how to enjoy life's simple pleasures, such as watching a sunset or stroking a kitten or reading a book. They can help us learn what recovering alcoholics and cancer patients alike discover as a result of their duress—that when we live in the now, the whole texture of our lives becomes different. We feel more alive. We're in tune with our surroundings. We're happier. We're focused. We are centered in the only day we've been given to live for sure: today.

In my recent attempts to live in the moments that make up today, I've been comforted by Christ's words at the end of the sixth chapter of Matthew. I call it the "do not worry" segment:

Therefore I tell you, do not worry about your life, what you will eat or drink; or about your body, what you will wear. Is not life more important than food, and the body more important than clothes? Look at the birds of the air; they do not sow or reap or store away in barns, and yet your heavenly Father feeds them. Are you not much more valuable than they? Who of you by worrying can add a single hour to his life? (Matthew 6:25-27)

Since I tend to worry, these words call me back to what's important and remind me that my worries are useless. If I can't even add an hour to my life by worrying, then how foolish to worry. God in His kindness has given us children to distract us and engage us and teach us how to see our beautiful world from a child's perspective. But to do this, we must not only cease to worry, we must stop hurtling through space, having, in Ban Breathnach's words, "an out-of-body experience."[14]

Slowing Down

Toni Townes says that her children have captured her in the now, slowed her down, and taught her a new way of seeing. She remembers the day her son Preston taught her to see a reindeer's antlers in a tree limb outside her living room window and to "listen" to Play-Doh. "At three," she told me, "my son would take a lump of Play-Doh and then sit and look at it. I kept wondering, *Uh-oh, do we need to see a specialist, or what?* But that child heard something, and to this day I'm not sure what. Preston would simply make an animal and then meditate. *And it slowed my whole day down* because I was just dying to hear what he heard" (italics mine).

Entering her children's world and slowing down to see and hear what they see and hear has been the source of great joy for Toni. "What this means," she says, "is that you have no background noise.

You just slowly peel off all of that, and you simply watch your kids. I've been at this game for five or six years. I can go to the playground, or I can sit in my living room and just watch them. And I don't feel like I have to justify my time. I don't worry about what other people think. I don't know what piece of the puzzle this is for who I should be, but I don't think I had that capacity before I had children."

Imagine what your day would be like without any background noise. What would it do to your blood pressure if you could sit quietly with your children, whether toddler or teenager, and attempt to enter into their world without letting your mind wander down your "to do" list? What would it do to your overcrowded schedule? To your pleasure quotient? To your senses?

"I've experienced a growing appreciation for life as my children have helped slow me down," said Dr. Melissa Hoagland, an admitted overachiever who gave up her medical practice to rear her children. "I am a completely different person than I used to be. Doctors are all overachievers. It's always the great grades. We define our worth by the externals—our salary, our position, whether or not we get tenure. But my kids have changed me."

In addition to slowing her down, Melissa's children fueled her desire to live a simpler life. She and her husband, also a physician, are members of the Religious Society of Friends. According to Melissa, one of the deeply held convictions of Quakers is the power of simplicity. Before she and her husband moved to Florida, they lived in Pennsylvania, where she grew much of their own food. Although she's had to struggle to recapture the simple life in Florida, Melissa has cut back the family's budget, limited Christmas spending, and buys only durable wooden toys she can pass on from one child to another, reducing the amount of time she spends toy shopping.

ENJOYING THE POWER OF SIMPLICITY

If you live in the moment and match your children's pace, they will become your teachers, and you will be the richer for it. Marian Gormley says that her children have taught her rich lessons about simplicity. "Not only am I sharing my perspective on the world with them, but they're sharing theirs with me. They've taught me simple things, like having picnics in bed, making wishes on dandelions, screaming as you go down a slide. Once I had gone down the slide, I had to admit that I'd done it for me. But I would never have done it if I didn't have children."

Marian Gormley recounts a tradition that evolved without conscious effort. One rainy day a few years ago, her children woke up excited about the weather. "What's so great about rain?" she asked them. The twins responded, "Remember? We get to have a picnic in bed with you. We do that every time it rains." Says Marian, "I hadn't realized we'd started this tradition of having hot chocolate, cheese, crackers, and fruit on a tray on my bed, but apparently we had." So that day, as on other rainy days, Marian, Jake, and Tara had their picnic in Marian's bed, and afterwards they whiled away happy hours reading.

This process can span a child's life. Our teenagers need us to be with them in the moment just as much as our toddlers and young children do. Sometimes being emotionally available to our adolescent children means we have to slow down, unplug the phone, play a board game, and just observe and listen. Other times it means we need to take radical measures to become more available to them.

When my girls were young, I was conscious that I had a choice: I could either force them to keep pace with me (hurry, hurry, hurry), or I could elect to slow down and match their pace. Slowing down and simplifying meant working no more than half-time hours. Every afternoon I was able to pick up Krissy from the neighborhood daycare center at two o'clock, and we would then amble over to Holly's neighborhood school just three blocks away. Fall, winter, and spring we three walked along, holding hands and chatting, while we reconnected after hours apart. After a snack we'd go exploring or shopping, drive to see friends, or go to the dentist or to lessons. Or we'd go out to our favorite tea shop, Olive's East, where the girls had juice and split a pastry.

Years later, Holly wrote me a letter when she was a freshman at Columbia University in New York City. She remembered our tea times and said, "I thought I was in heaven." When I look back over the terrain of my life, those afternoons are among my happiest.

After I remarried, I took summers off to spend time with Holly and Kristen. We had lazy, halcyon days, driving to the local swimming pool, reading good books, going to the library, visiting their friends and mine, and taking excursions to the local beach. I tried to live a simple, balanced life because I wanted to give my daughters the gift of a childhood where they could while away hours simply playing or being creative. Play is, after all, the work of childhood.

The French writer Montaigne observed that children at play are engaged in serious business. Yet few children have the luxury of whiling away hours in their own homes, engaged in creative play. In a comment I agree with, Britain's famous child psychologist Penelope Leach said, "For many 'privileged' children life is packed full of activities intended to be fun, perhaps even to improve the child. That is very different from play where children generate their own ideas and rules and are free to explore fantasies and let their imaginations run. In this kind of play, children solve problems, work through things which worry and puzzle them and experience real enjoyment."[15]

I often listened outside the closed bedroom door while Holly and Kristen played "family," using Sunshine Family dolls and working through the maze of their parents' divorce. Kristen, in particular, voiced her anger through a little girl doll, while Holly played the role of the wicked stepmother, sometimes getting her doll-holding hand whacked in the process. Their play sounded pretty raucous, but I didn't intervene or sermonize because I knew intuitively that my girls were working through some confusing and painful family experiences as they played. My job? To be the consultant on duty, protecting their right to play for hours. I was there if they needed me.

I've tried to be my children's companion across the years, just as my granddaddy, Charlie Knox Morrison, was mine. At fifty-six, I have no regrets for all those hours spent in the company of my daughters. In fact, some days I wish I could do it all over again. I guess that's what grandparenting is all about.

TIME FOR OUR SOULS

As we simplify our lives, we will have more time to care for our souls. Sarah Ban Breathnach says that she spends an hour at the beginning of each day just meditating, praying, and getting in touch with her personal dreams. This is the optimal way to start the day. I believe reading the Bible gives a sense of calm, realigns priorities, and allows God to speak to our hearts about the concerns of the day.

At our house, Don and I arise at six o'clock (a welcome relief after all those years at half past five), and he puts on the coffeepot. Then he heads for the family room to read the Bible, and I gather my journal, pen, and Bible to sit in the colorful living room. For up to an hour I read and then write a letter to God. I write about the concerns of the moment—difficulties with a friend, anxiety, needs, dreams, a child's concerns. And then I search Scripture for His answers to my dilemma. At breakfast Don and I share what wealth we have just discovered, and then we pray. By eight o'clock I'm ready to live the day—centered, peaceful, energized.

Of course, we're a middle-aged couple, but even if you have a small child, you could find time to develop your spiritual life while your baby naps. Forget the dishes. Forget the laundry. Forget cleaning house. If you make time for God in your day, you'll find that time magically expands, and you'll feel a lot more peaceful.

SOME PRACTICAL WAYS TO SIMPLIFY YOUR LIFE

Decide today to simplify your life. It's always possible to throttle back, re-examine your priorities, and, if necessary, move to a cheaper apartment or buy a cheaper house as did best-selling author Elaine St. John, who wrote *Simplify Your Life*. She and her husband, Tony Gibbs, sold their big, expensive house for a condo. Perhaps you can also cut back on hours at work or choose to work from home and avoid commuting time. And you can relearn how to soak in a bathtub until your whole body relaxes, take a slow walk to the park with a three-year-old, or sit at the kitchen table in the afternoon sun, just listening to your teenager talk.

Here are some additional ideas to help you enjoy the power of simplicity:

Control the outside intrusion into your home:
- Cancel the daily newspaper and opt for Sunday-only service.
- Sell your television or establish rigorous guidelines for viewing hours (the fewer the better).
- Control the negative input in family life—don't watch the evening news.
- Don't answer the phone during dinner to avoid being the prey of telemarketers.
- Have family members refuse to participate in sports, lessons, or meetings that require Sunday attendance.

Enhance family togetherness:
- Insist that all family members gather for a nightly dinner.
- Limit children's involvement in outside sports and activities that disrupt family time and require constant chauffeuring. (Kids need fallow time, and so do you.)
- Make Sunday family day. After church, decree that there will be no homework, no television, and no lengthy phone calls (at least until

nightfall). Then allow a different person to select an outing or activity that everybody participates in.
- Establish a reading night, and take your young children to the local library.
- Unplug the phone on days when you need a quiet house.

Streamline the family budget:
- Develop clothing swaps with relatives, neighbors, and friends to cut down on the cost of school and sports clothing.
- Plant a family garden and have each child be responsible for a plot.
- Cut down on outside labor by using Saturday mornings as the time when kids perform chores and learn manual tasks—how to fix a leaky faucet, change the oil in the car, mow the lawn, or paint siding.
- Make meals from scratch—prepared food is expensive and lacks the nutrients your growing children need. Since raw food is easier to digest, eat as many salads and fresh fruits as possible (at least five servings a day). And don't buy the cookies, chips, and sodas that depress immune systems, increase weight, and decay teeth.

You may find these suggestions too radical for your family. You may even be thinking, *I bet Brenda Hunter never lived like this.* Well, I did. In fact, our family lived without a television for sixteen years, until Kris had taken the SAT exam and passed with flying colors. We also took a weekly newspaper and discouraged sports on Sundays. And we ate dinner together as a family until the girls left home for college. They even learned to change the oil in a car, dismantle walls with a crowbar, and take care of a lawn. So I have walked my talk.

What's important is that you carefully evaluate the way you spend your time, energy, and money. If you conclude that you're in a cage, open the door and bask in the sunshine. If you're working full-time, you may want to choose to work fewer hours. Scale down until you find the optimum mix—enough stimulation to keep you happy, but enough fallow time to have peace of mind and enjoy sweet sleep. Your children will rejoice when you stop running pell-mell through life, because they love spending time with you, and your husband will be glad to have a wife with something in her emotional tank when he walks through the door at night. He will also be pleased when you have some time and energy to do some of the tasks you both have traditionally done together on evenings or too-short weekends, like grocery shopping or cleaning the house.

No mother is at her best when she's overworked or overscheduled. One woman said to me, "I get so angry at the kids all the time. It seems that when I come through the door at night, I start barking orders. I'm afraid I'll hurt them emotionally if I don't find out why I'm so angry." Sometimes we get angry because we're always overwhelmed and overextended. And yes, we will hurt our kids if we're always driven, ever pressing, never quiet and at peace.

YOUR HOME, A REFUGE

As you live in the moment—as you slow down and care for your soul—you will discover that you're living a qualitatively different kind of life. You will live a *quality life*, nurturing relationships with those who matter most. Instead of trying to "squeeze twenty-eight-hour lives into twenty-four-hour days," you'll come to the end of your day with some energy left, supper waiting, and contented happy kids in harmony with themselves and each other. Like psychologist Diane Fisher, you will be able to say, I have "orchestrated this harmony of home, this sense of well-being and calm." And when that happens, your home will cease to be an address and will become instead a place where life is lived calmly, richly, deeply—a refuge in a frantic world.

CHAPTER 5

The Power *to* Heal

According to the late psychoanalyst Selma Fraiberg, who was famous in her era for her work with severely distressed mothers and babies, our parental past may sometimes intrude and cause us to reenact a disturbing scene from our childhood, even if we had families where love and stability reigned.

> In every nursery there are ghosts. They are visitors from the unremembered past of the parents; the uninvited guests at the christening. Under all favorable circumstances the unfriendly and unbidden spirits are banished from the nursery and returned to their subterranean dwelling place. The baby makes his own imperative claim upon parental love and, in strict analogy with the fairy tales, the bonds of love protect the child and his parents against the intruders, the malevolent ghosts.[1]

Fortunately for most of us, these brief intrusions from a relatively stable past are inconsequential. For others, the ghosts from the past haunt us and influence our parenting. Either way, once we become mothers we soon discover we are reliving the past.

COMING HOME

Heidi Brennan, whose parents separated when she was seven, said, "I don't think there's any question that I'm reliving my childhood since I had my children. The hardest part of motherhood is revisiting the negative part of your past; the greatest joy is in reliving the happiness of your early life. Either way, it's a great opportunity."

Heidi's right. Mother love takes us "home," whether we're ready or not. Why is this so? What is so magical about becoming a mother that it causes a woman to revisit her past? I believe that once a woman gives birth she "remembers" at an emotional level what it felt like to be a baby and a young child. She "remembers" all those primitive feelings of vulnerability and dependency. And if she was fortunate enough to have been well nurtured, she will want to pass this positive parental legacy on. But if she was abused, criticized, rejected, and abandoned—some of the mothers I've worked with were—then she will want to create a new legacy for her children and give them more love, more tenderness, more empathy than she ever received.

To do this a woman must rework her past, otherwise she will do to her children what was done to her. After I spoke at a women's gathering, a mother of three came up to me and said, "I find myself treating my children as my mother treated me. She came down so *hard* on me. All the time." This woman told me she was often angry at her children—especially her eldest daughter. (She was herself the eldest daughter in her family of origin.)

Daughters have the power to take us "home" to our relationship with our own mothers in a way that sons never do. "I see myself in my daughter," says a mother about her baby, a fourth child who is eight months old. At forty-two, this woman is just beginning to sort out how her mother influenced her feelings about being a mother. "Since my daughter and I are both female, I feel tied to her; and I wonder if my mother ever felt that way with me. I'm identifying with my mother more these days. She, too, had four children and a husband who was often gone, struggling to build a medical practice. She probably did the best she could with the resources she had."

Whenever we decide we need to look at our nurturing legacy (whether we're in our twenties or forties), we embark on an important journey. Possibly the most meaningful work I've done as a therapist has been with mothers who found themselves repeating painful scenes from their childhood with their children. These women often came for therapy when they had their first child and experienced irrational feelings of anger or rage—feelings that signaled that something was radically wrong. Sometimes these women had enough self-awareness to understand that their memories and feelings were "ghosts" from the past. Other times they were depressed or anxious, troubled in the present, but unsure why.

Because I believe it is possible to rework the past, I tried to help these clients increase their awareness about how their childhood was encroaching on the present. In the process, they owned long-repressed feelings, grieved their losses, and learned healthier ways of parenting their children. One lovely part of my job has been to watch my clients' babies grow into toddlers as I've coached their mothers on building strong emotional bonds with their babies and implementing basic discipline later on.

JESSICA'S STORY

One woman came for help when her daughter was four months old. "I'm afraid I will hurt my daughter because I get so angry at times," Jessica confessed. As I worked with Jessica, her sad story spilled out. She had been the target of her father's unreasoning rage as she grew up. At different times—and for no obvious reason—her father, who had been abused by his own father, would physically attack her. With tears,

Jessica told me about a significant memory: She was lying on the sofa in the family room as a fourteen-year-old, watching TV, when her father flew into the room and began hitting her. "After he stopped, my lip was swollen; my face was bruised, and I guess it rattled my dad because he told me he would never hit me again. And he didn't."

In addition to a rageful father, Jessica was still grieving the loss of her mother to death four years earlier. Oh, how she missed her mother. While Jessica's mother had not been able to protect her daughter from her husband's wrath (she, too, was hit), she was physically present and loving to Jessica, her brother, and four sisters.

I could see our work was cut out for us: In addition to processing her anger at her father and experiencing deep grief for his lack of love and protection, Jessica needed to learn ways to manage her anger so she wouldn't hurt her baby daughter. It would take time for me to forge a bond with Jessica and help her process old hurts. Meanwhile, her baby needed immediate protection from Jessica's anger. So we worked on increasing her awareness of what made her angry (stress, anxiety, hurt) and developed her coping skills. We talked about ways to cool down, either by going outside momentarily or by walking into another room when she felt her anger rising. Since Jessica remembered what it felt like to be a vulnerable, defenseless child, she was adamant that she wouldn't do to her daughter what had been done to her. And she hasn't.

As Rachel became a cherubic six-month-old, Jessica began to forge a strong attachment relationship with her. As I heard the mother's cries, she listened to and attended to her baby's cries. From time to time I offered Jessica parenting education. I realized that in addition to acting as a therapist, I was a surrogate mother to Jessica, who had no wise older woman to turn to.

Part of our work centered around the loss of Jessica's mother. Jessica felt her mother's absence keenly when Rachel was born, and she needed help transitioning into motherhood. She was sad that her mother hadn't been there during the early weeks and months of motherhood to comfort, nurture, and instruct. Jessica said she missed her mom daily. I worked with her to reclaim some of the positive gifts her mother had given her. She wrote a letter to her mother, thanking her for her encouragement and love, naming the good memories she and her mom had shared. I tried to bring to her conscious awareness all the positives in the midst of a sea of suffering. "What would your mother have told you to do in this situation?" I asked. "How did your mother comfort you as a small child? Can you do this for Rachel?"

We also worked on finding nurturing women to play a part in Jessica's life. Since she lived in an isolated, rural area, miles from town and her church, this proved difficult. But she did reach out to a neighbor and other women she knew. In addition, we worked on strengthening the ties with her four sisters who lived nearby. Those key relationships were estranged, and this left Jessica with lots of pain and limited family support. Over time, Jessica improved her relationship with each sister, and this has given her much joy.

I even met with the sisters together for one session to strengthen their bonds and allow them to talk about their mother. We also talked about carrying on some of the rituals they had learned at their mother's knee, particularly those around the holidays. The sisters left my office, agreeing to see each other more often, to talk more openly about their mother, and to support each other in ways she had taught them.

How did all of this affect Rachel? As Jessica mourned her losses and strengthened her family ties, she became less depressed. Hence, little Rachel had a happier mother. Also, Jessica came to understand that she could evoke a loving grandmother for her daughter through the power of stories. As she told her daughter tales about her mother, she could, in a sense, introduce Rachel to her grandmother, albeit an absent and somewhat idealized one.

In addition to mourning for her mother, Jessica wept over her father's physical abuse. She talked about the feelings of shame, hurt, anger, and terror that accompanied each attack. As she began to heal,

Jessica expressed a longing for a better relationship with this man. She and I worked on improving her relationship with her father, who has mellowed in his later years. She chose to visit him more often and to invite him into her home. As they started to find common ground, Jessica experienced some degree of comfort and healing for her battered self-image.

While work remains to be done, in our most recent session we talked about the many changes in Jessica's life: the fact that old angers are diminishing; that she has a tentative but improved relationship with her father; that she has learned techniques for managing her current anger—which means becoming angry at the person who's hurting her rather than acting out her anger and pain in front of Rachel. And when she feels strong enough, perhaps she will choose to talk with her father about the physical abuse and the pain it caused her.

Today, Jessica is proud of the strong, loving bond she has with Rachel. While she realizes she needs ongoing help with parenting, especially as she tries to shape her daughter's strong will, she believes she has become a sensitive, responsive mother. And she has. The proof? Her toddler adores her. As she has grown in expressing mother love, Jessica has found that her self-esteem has increased. Her child's love and her own conviction that she is a good mother have helped heal her. How beautiful this is.

ANN'S STORY

Several years ago I met Ann, a forty-seven-year-old psychologist, who was never a patient of mine but was instead a colleague and friend. And while she, like Jessica, felt rage toward her first child, I've included both accounts, since Ann suffered greatly at the hands of her mother rather than her father. "There were plenty of times I felt rage toward my children," admitted Ann, an attractive, beautifully dressed woman.

"Nothing happened, but it scared me. I would feel this huge rage over silly little things. So I said to myself, *You'd better get help, and you'd better get it fast.*"

As I listened to Ann's story, I soon understood the reasons for her toxic rage. She told me, "It's very hard to look back and think of things that felt like love from my mother. I really don't know if I can think of one single incident when I felt loved by her." Ann went on to describe life in what she called a "very rigid, legalistic, fundamentalist home" ruled by a violent mother who dominated her meek minister father. Ann described her mother as "manipulative, vindictive, and very physical."

But it was Ann's older sister who became the target of her mother's rage. "She would get beaten to a pulp when my father was at church," said Ann. Because Ann's sister was strong-willed and defiant, the physical abuse she experienced was severe. "One time she was beaten so badly that my younger brother ran to the garage to get a golf club because he was so sure my mother was going to kill my sister."

Although Ann kept out of her mother's way, she paid a high price for the violence in her home. By watching the battles, she was also victimized. How could she ever trust a mother like that? What was particularly painful for Ann were those times her mother offered to make her clothes, an act that could be interpreted as loving, only to hurt Ann in the end. She insisted that Ann wear the matronly dresses she made, no matter how much Ann pleaded otherwise. "I always felt ugly in those clothes. I would beg her for something else." But her mother, because of her own impoverished nurturing history, did not hear Ann's pleas for understanding and empathy.

Sometimes Ann's mother took the dressmaking ritual to a new level of pain. If her daughter had a special event at school, she would offer to make Ann a new outfit. So Ann would obligingly choose the material, but inevitably, the night before the event her mother would fly into a rage. "I don't like the look on your face," she'd tell Ann, "so

I won't finish this." "Sometimes," said Ann, "all that remained to be done was to hem the dress or sew on buttons."

When Ann, who has two serene children, sat in my office remembering her relationship with her mother, she began to cry. "Isn't it funny? Here I am, forty-seven years old, and just thinking about this makes me cry. That particular memory brings back the feelings of humiliation I felt the next day when the teacher said to me, 'Didn't you know it was a special day?'"

What does a woman do with such pain? How does she keep from inflicting that same abuse, rejection, and emotional detachment on her children?

WHY DO SOME PARENTS REPEAT THE PAST WHILE OTHERS DON'T?

Psychoanalyst Selma Fraiberg asked the same question, acknowledging that "morbidity in the parental history will not in itself predict the repetition of the past in the present."[2] So why do some parents repeat the past while others do not? Fraiberg found in her clinical work that those parents who remembered the pain at an emotional level and could re-experience the suffering, like Jessica and Ann, were those who said, "I will never let my child go through what I went through."[3] For these parents, the pain and suffering did not go the way of total repression. "In remembering, they are saved the blind repetition of that morbid past," wrote Fraiberg.[4]

Why is remembering so healing? As we remember our past and become aware of old feelings, we identify with the injured child (our childhood self) rather than the brutal or rejecting parent. This helps us become more compassionate and nurturing toward ourselves—and thus toward others, especially our children. But what about the parent who refuses to remember? At an unconscious level, this parent has already identified with the "aggressor" (the wounding parent) and will, even unconsciously, feel compelled to perpetuate the pain.[5] Of course, it's always possible to say, "Enough of this. I'm not going to continue this pattern. I will get help. I will change."

ANN'S GREEN PEOPLE

What helped Ann rework her painful past? While she says she's never had professional counseling, Ann admits that in her training she learned a lot about family dynamics, and through reading and reflection she has been able to apply what she's learned to her own family of origin. Also, she has colleagues, particularly other therapists, who have listened over the years and shared their wisdom with her.

In addition, Ann has come to see that throughout her childhood she had helpful people enter her life and extend warmth and compassion. "I was happy by nature," says Ann, "and lots of people reached out to me. I call them green people because they helped me grow. Sometimes I'd spend the weekend with people who didn't have any children. I remember going to different friends' homes, even when I was three years old. Later I had a close friend and spent lots of time with her family. She had a grandmother who sat and talked to me for hours. And when I became a teenager, a number of people offered me jobs. Those jobs were a far greater gift to me than they could have ever imagined."

What about Ann's ability to mother her own children? "When my son was born, I felt very detached for about the first six months," said Ann. "This little person lived in my house, but I didn't really feel attached. Then, at six months, it was as if something clicked, and I felt like I was falling in love. A romantic kind of love. Nothing erotic. From that point on I adored this little boy. It was harder for me to connect with my daughter initially, but not now. She's a charmer."

Fortunately for Ann and her children, she was able to connect with them on an emotional level by the time each was six months old. That's the time babies begin to forge that all-important emotional bond that determines self-esteem, the capacity for empathy, and conscience. The fact that Ann fell in love with her son tells me she was ready to create a secure attachment with him. It's not surprising that this task was harder with her daughter, since her relationship with her mother was central here. Although forging a bond with her daughter proved more difficult, Ann believes she got the job done and that her little girl feels secure in her mother's love.

Ann admits she's worked hard on her own psychological growth. A workaholic before her children were born, she now works part-time so she can be physically and emotionally available to her children most of the time. She does, however, feel that her half-time job may have "saved" both her and her children. "I wonder about whether I would have been more like my mother if I'd had the same desperate life situation—feeling dried up with nothing to give. Then a quiet rage developed, and her rage came out at us."

"I also think that if I hadn't worked through my feelings, hadn't grieved, if I hadn't gotten the poison out, I wouldn't have anything to give" (italics mine). In the process of reworking her past, Ann had to acknowledge that her minister father, whom she adored, had colluded with her mother and that her mother, scary as she was and still is, needs her compassion.

What's the payoff for Ann's hard work? "When I look at my family [of origin], there's chaos all around. But my life is an aberration," said Ann, who admits that she's been serious about her relationship with Jesus Christ since she was a preteen. She believes Christ sent all those "green people" who reached out to her and made a difference in her life, as well as the heady career she had prior to marriage, the good man she married at thirty-five, the loving extended family that marriage added to her life, and the children who bring her daily joy.

When I met her towheaded children, I was struck by their faces. Ann's children are peaceful and happy and experiencing a far different childhood than did their mother. Ann's four-year-old daughter, who spent most of the evening cuddled up in her daddy's lap, was quite taken by Don and gave him radiant smiles all evening. When she and her parents walked us to the door that summer night, she flashed a million-dollar smile at my sixty-three-year-old husband and said, "Bye, other Daddy." Quite a charmer indeed.

This little girl's healthy sense of self and inner joy are evidence enough that Ann has done good internal work and that the female legacy of brutality and pain stopped with her mother. Ann has chosen to be the generation that cried out, "Enough of this craziness and pain. Let there be something better than mothers taking out their rage and frustration on their children. Let there be healing and compassion and, ultimately, joy."

MOTHERS OF OLDER CHILDREN

While I believe it's best if a mother confronts past "ghosts" when her child is an infant—less damage may be done, and the chance of forming a strong emotional bond is greater—I have seen improvement in relationships between mothers and their older children. These women recognized their need for healing of old wounds later in their lives yet were motivated by their desire to deepen their attachments to their children, to discipline with greater effectiveness, and to communicate with greater honesty and integrity. Even middle-aged mothers with enmeshed or detached adult daughters can, in time, reframe those relationships and come to enjoy a more satisfying and healthy connection.

One mother came to me complaining about her adult daughter's freewheeling lifestyle but soon began talking about her own rejecting, critical mother. She wept when she told me, "Nothing pleases my mother." My client was, in her forties, still trying to earn her mother's love. One day I told her, "The only thing worse than a rejecting mother is trying to win her love and approval." As we worked on this significant relationship and my client grieved over her estranged bond with her mother, her relationship with her own daughter began to improve. When my client finally saw her mother as she was, not as she wished her to be, then she could allow her adult daughter to have a separate self. She recognized that while she didn't always approve of her daughter's choices, she loved her and wanted to reach out to her. So my client focused on finding common ground and refraining from exhortation and criticism. In time, both mother and daughter moved toward each other and became friends.

My years as a therapist have convinced me that God has provided parenting not only as a way to reproduce the species but also as a way to rework—and redeem—the painful parts of our childhood. No matter what your age or how painful your past, if you have the honesty, courage, and tenacity to do the hard work, you can achieve a greater degree of emotional freedom and psychological health. As one client said several months after we ended our sessions together, "The fruits of therapy just keep rolling in." On the other hand, if you refuse to confront your painful parental past, as well as the emptiness in your soul, your children will suffer as you have suffered. And the generational pain will roll on.

DO I NEED TO REWORK MY PAST?

At this point, you may be asking, "How do I know if I need to rework my past?" Maybe your ghosts are transient visitors and not permanent residents. You may feel that you have little if any of the parental past to deal with. My work as a therapist has shown me that if and when it's time to rework your past, you'll know it. You will no longer be able to ignore the signs, and your desire to have better relationships with your children and others will motivate you to seek help. Here's my advice: Begin by looking for emotional barriers or irrational feelings. Are you able to give your baby consistent, loving care? Can you connect emotionally with your seven-year-old? Your teenager? Or are you detached, enmeshed, angry, rejecting? Your answers will give you the clues you need.

Dr. Melissa Hoagland told me she had worked through her anger at her mother several years ago but is now realizing she may have more work to do. "My mother was not a very motherly person," she said reflectively. "I probably got more mothering from siblings than I got from her. Since I was the youngest, she was really burned out by the time she had me. So she sent me off to school a year early. My parents said it was because I was really bright and this was being wasted at home, but I was miserable at school and wanted nothing more than to come home. I can remember being sick and going to the nurse's office every day and having my mother pick me up. She was never happy to take me home. Finally it dawned on me—I was staying; I was stuck. I think my mother needed me out of the house."

Melissa told me she had never wanted to have kids. "My husband wanted four children before we ever married, and I didn't want any. So we were married eight years before we had children. My family thinks it's hysterical that out of the four children in my family of origin, I'm going to have four children. I hated kids growing up. I was the youngest, and I was so uncomfortable around kids that it was a standing joke that every time I'd get on an airplane, I'd end up sitting in front of the kid kicking my seat or next to a screaming baby."

Melissa admits her transition to motherhood hasn't been easy. "I really floundered. I got depressed." She felt, however, that she had no choice but to persevere through some unpleasant moments, what she calls "her baptism by fire." What helped? Time. Writing in a journal. "The other night I was reading through my old journals and realized I had chronicled lots of my painful feelings. And during the time I was floundering, someone sent me a copy of *Welcome Home* magazine written by other mothers in the trenches." She also found a number of books helpful: *Whole Child, Whole Parent* by Polly Berriens Berends; *Managing Motherhood* by Mary Ann Seidensticker; *Sequencing* by Arlene Cardoga; and *The Heart Has Its Reasons* by Mary Ann Cahill.

In addition, some good friends reached out to Melissa when she was depressed. As time passed, this mother got in touch with some nurturing feelings that had been buried under her drivenness. "Nurturing was not something anyone got kudos for in my family. But now, after four children, I can say that I've become a nurturing person. I feel connected with my children in a way I never felt connected with my mother."

I hope you can see at this point that I believe so strongly that if you've been wounded in childhood, you need to exorcise the "ghosts" from the nursery and find solace and healing for your soul. That way you can become the mother you always wanted to have. And that will give you lasting joy and deep fulfillment.

A PERSONAL ACCOUNT

Like many of the women in this chapter, I, too, was motivated to re-work my past when I became a mother. When Holly was born, I had no idea I had just embarked on a psychological journey that would last well into my fifties. All I knew was that I was temporarily unemployed, and motherhood was overwhelming. I tried to be a sensitive mother, but even as I busied myself with Holly's care, I sensed that something long repressed was demanding to come out into the light.

My early life had been punctuated with major losses: the loss of my young father to death when I was a toddler, the loss of my mother a year later when she moved to a nearby town to work, and the loss of my granddaddy when I left the farm to go live with my mother as a five-year-old. And though I spent three happy years on a dairy farm with my beloved grandparents in early childhood, when I became a mother, it was my erratic, depressed mother who occupied my thoughts.

My mother, a telephone operator, struggled with single parent-hood and managing her emotions. She, too, had a string of early and profound losses. Her own mother died when she was four, and she was twenty when she watched two Cherokee Indian girls in Bryson City, North Carolina, bring her drowning husband's body to the surface, only to inexplicably release it. So sometimes mother was in a reasonable mood. Most often, she brooded. And with her chronic depression, she proved to be an angry, unpredictable presence.

I learned to give her a wide berth. How could a child trust an unpredictable mother who might be okay one day and meanspirited the next? I learned to read my mother's moods as the weatherman tracks the winds and rain. Life together made me wary and anxious. I'm sure that anxiety influenced my early mothering just as did my tendency toward depression—my genetic and environmental legacy.

In attachment research, adults are classified as *autonomous* (the adult equivalent of the securely attached infant) if they value close bonds, are generally thoughtful and reflective, and can examine the effects of past experiences. Even those who have been rejected, abused, or neglected may be able to create secure bonds with their children if they have "convincingly forgiven their parent(s) for the maltreatment."[6] While I was hardly autonomous at this point in my life, I was definitely on the road to greater wholeness.

When I was twenty-nine, and my first marriage ended, I took the girls to London to live for two years in a Christian community. It was then that I forgave my mother for being who she is, a wounded woman with limited inner resources. It was an antidote to toxic, draining emotions.

Forgiveness ushered in some good and happy years in my thirties, when I remarried and the girls were in elementary school and junior high. Those were the years when they absolutely adored me, and I loved it. But it wasn't until my forties that I began my inner work in earnest. Then, with the help of a six-foot-two burly therapist from the Bronx, I finally opened the door of my maternal closet and swept it clean.

Something wonderful happened at this time. Painful memories—no longer repressed but felt and expressed—began to fade. I was forced to look at my relationship with my mother as it really was, not as I had always longed for it to be. During this time, I had a particularly negative visit with her, and afterward I told my husband, "It doesn't matter. She didn't devastate me this time." But when we finally arrived home after that visit, I cried off and on for several days. My therapist said simply, "You're grieving for what you never got and will never get from your mother." How true. How devastatingly profound.

And so I grieved. I also relinquished my right to good-enough mothering. In the process, I began to see my mother in a whole new way. I could now see that she was a separate person with her own particular nurturing legacy. She was different from me. I understood that I'd had advantages she had never known: helpful people who reached out to me, nurturing grandparents, college and graduate school education. From my twelfth year, when I became a Christian, I have felt that God, the father to the fatherless, watched over me. As I understood that my mother and I were two separate, different women who shared parts of a personal and genetic history, I became more compassionate toward her. She has had a tragic life. And this sense of concern and compassion has fueled my interactions with her ever since. Now I can say along with writer Victoria Secunda, "The difference between my mother and me is that where she was trapped by her emotional demons, I could face mine and banish them."[7] And having done that, I find that I have no lasting, painful regrets when I think about my mother who has, in recent years, become a positive part of my life.

MEMORIES OF TWO WHITE-HAIRED WOMEN

Three years ago, Mother's internist called from another state and said, "Your mother is dying. She hasn't eaten for twelve days. She's lost much of her power of speech. She may have had a stroke—she's going to have an MRI. But you and your sister need to begin to think about funeral arrangements." When I got off the phone, I prayed, "God, I'm not ready for Mother to die yet; neither is Sandy" (my sister). I asked

God for more time. But more time for what? I wasn't sure, but I knew that with all the work I'd done on our relationship, something vital was still missing.

What was missing were simply warm, happy, relaxed times together without past baggage—and I have had that with my mother this past year. Because her depression was finally treated medically, she and I have been able to have a closer relationship. No longer angry or critical, she has become a sociable, cheerful, engaging woman.

When she began to recover, Don and I took her to Seabrook, South Carolina, for her seventy-fifth birthday, though she could hardly walk. She told us she longed to see the sea before she died. So we hoisted her in and out of the car, carefully helped her up and down the stairs to the beach, and together enjoyed the sight of porpoises and fishes literally leaping out of the ocean in the hot noonday sun. We took her to our favorite Charlestonian haunts and ate she-crab soup at 82 Queen. Slowly we wandered through the old slave market, admiring the straw baskets women sold on the street corners, and in the evenings we watched old movies.

Last Thanksgiving my husband made two round trips to the nursing home hundreds of miles away to bring Mother to our farmhouse for a family gathering. I have memories of simple evenings in front of the fire, cracking nuts and watching movies—two white-haired women with brown eyes sitting on the sofa chatting and laughing. I even had the experience of having a pregnant daughter and a semi-handicapped mother in a J. C. Penney's dressing room while I tried to find clothes to fit both. Exhausting! Stressful!

Simple things. Warm family times. Some good, tension-free conversations. Of course, we've had earlier family gatherings, but none without stress and anxiety. I know some fortunate women who have always had good times with their mothers, but others of us can't say the same. And during those times when I was caring for my mother, brushing her hair, helping her dress, fixing her meals, taking her to the hairdresser, I was also in some way—which I do not fully under-stand—nurturing myself.

So whether my mother dies this year or in twenty years, she and I have had our good times together. And for that I will be eternally grateful to God who cares about such things and carefully orchestrated it all.

I don't for a moment believe that Mother and I would be able to enjoy her twilight years if I hadn't long ago dealt with my own toxic emotions. I know too many daughters who deeply resent having to care for frail, white-haired mothers whom they feel neglected or re-jected them in childhood. Even as they visit their mothers in houses or in nursing homes, these women are prisoners held in thrall, not by their frightened, fragile, or critical elderly mothers but by their own anger, pain, and resentment at the mothers they once knew.

Fortunately, any of us can go beyond the suffering of the past and choose to live in a peaceful present. Said one newly liberated woman, "I finally came to see the problem was not my mother. It was me. And I understood that if I was ever to have a better relationship with her, I would first have to go into my own heart and deal with my old anger and wounds."

Once we finally rework the past and exorcise the parental ghosts, our whole life is different. We're freer, happier, lighter. And our rela-tionships are better. Not only do our relationships with our husbands improve, but we become better mothers. Surely these are reasons enough to turn and face our childhood pain in the company of God and others.

A HOPEFUL LETTER

I have on my desk a letter from a mother of two little girls who lives in Charlotte, North Carolina. Nancy wrote, "Mom and I have always acted like best friends without really having the depth of a relationship to back up the facade of closeness. I had too much resentment to let her in." But then a friend sent Nancy a copy of my book *In the Company of Women*. After she read the book, Nancy asked her mother to do the same so they could discuss their relationship. "I knew if I could trust her with this, I could trust her with deeper things," wrote Nancy.

One morning both women headed off to a coffee shop with their books, a timer, pens, and notebooks. They set the timer for five minutes, and each wrote down her assessment of their mother-daughter relationship. Then they shared their perceptions. "Was I shocked at my mother's insight!" wrote Nancy. "Her assessment was so accurate. (I had expected to be misunderstood.) And she accepted my analysis, even the parts I thought I couldn't tell her."

Nancy ended her letter with these hopeful words. "I cannot even begin to write here all the healing that took place in those two hours! But I can say that our intimate and *real* friendship was born that day, forever changing the way I relate to my mother and my two little girls."

The ghosts quietly left the nursery as another daughter made peace with her mother. A new day had begun.

PART TWO

THE POWER OF MOTHER LOVE

IN A CHILD'S LIFE

Child of mine—

Do you know you carry my dreams?
  Do you understand that you have taught me lessons about love, laughter, sacrifice, and truth that I never knew and could never have learned from anyone else?

As I have watched you grow from infancy to adolescence—from absolute dependency and vulnerability to fledgling independence—I have been grateful that I've been your mother. You shaped my personality and life in ways I never dreamed possible. You made me more womanly and less selfish. With your neediness, you taught me patience. With your vulnerability, you opened my eyes to the needs of others. With your passionate, primal love, you satisfied my need to be loved unconditionally.

In return, I have watched you develop the conviction that you are loved, you are worthy. I have tried to teach you all I know about living life to the full: I have encouraged you to be empathic to those in pain, to love with intimacy, to choose the high road wherever possible. And I've urged you to preserve your integrity and self-respect at all costs because yours is the face in the mirror you will see the morning after.

When you fell, I picked you up. When you cried, I reached out to comfort you. When your friends hurt or betrayed you, I was there to listen and put my arms around you. I wanted you to know that I would always comfort you, so that you could comfort others. Out of my frailty and sin I've shared with you all I know about God and encouraged you to knock on heaven's door daily with your questions, pleas, and praise. God is an infinitely lovely being, and He loves you just as you sit, walk, and stand.

I've tried to tell you all of this, child of mine.

And while your father has carried you from birth and has taught you how to excel academically and negotiate life's challenges, I like to think I've taught you how to love. How to be human.

I love you dearly.
I will love you always.
Dream bearer.
Child of mine.

CHAPTER 6

The Power
of Attachment

T he limo is here," shouted Don as the girls and I hurried to grab
our purses and coats. Soon our family was en route to the
CNN studios in downtown Washington, D.C., where I was
to be a guest on *Larry King Live*. The year was 1991, and I was near-
ing the end of a number of live television debates on the subject of attachment and childcare as a result of the publication of my book
Home by Choice.

I was scared and nervous, but I also loved the nerve-racking excitement of television with its intense lights and rolling cameras. I was
thrilled to be able to talk about mother love to a worldwide audience.

My family settled in the "greenroom" to watch the show while I
was hurried off to the makeup artist. Soon I was seated at a long, narrow table alongside my opposite number, a British woman who owned
a nanny care agency. Across from us sat our famous host, Larry King,
clad in a blue shirt and gray pants held up by his trademark sus-
penders. Larry King is a short, slight man with a large personality. He
rapidly took charge of the interview. Our topic: nanny care. At the end

of the first segment, he asked me the perfect question: "Brenda, do the arms that hold the baby really matter?"

"Yes, Larry," I replied. "Babies are born programmed to fall in love with their mothers, not nannies or baby-sitters."

And so they are. Babies are fortunate indeed if they have mothers who are psychologically able to return all that love and adoration. Sadly, because of their own attachment histories, some mothers cannot—like the one I observed while shopping at a department store.

A little girl about three years old wandered several paces behind her mother. The child sobbed as the two walked through the store.

"Stop crying," commanded the mother, a petite brunette with short hair. "Stop it. No tears. I don't want to see any tears." The child cried harder. Whisking her behind a mannequin, the mother proceeded to hit her in front of other customers who watched surreptitiously.

"Take my hand, Mommy," pleaded the crying child, trying to reach out and connect with her angry mother.

"No, you're being a very bad girl," said her mother as she pushed her daughter's hand away. Then the irate mother stalked off, leaving her child to follow and continue to sob helplessly.

My ire was up, and my heart was pounding. It was obvious to me that this little girl was miles away from her mother's heart, and their attachment relationship was insecure at best.

ATTACHMENT

Why is attachment so important? And what do I mean by attachment anyway? Babies forge an attachment relationship, or emotional bond, with their mothers and fathers in early infancy that will significantly influence all later personality development.[1] From this emotional bond, a baby develops a conscience, the capacity for intimacy, and a sense of his own worthiness. How does this occur? British psychiatrist John Bowlby believed that a baby is programmed to fall in love with his mother from birth. A baby is wired to establish an intimate emotional connection with the mother that will influence all later intimate ties, as well as his or her mental health. Bowlby said, "What is believed to be essential for mental health is that the infant and young child should experience a warm, intimate, and continuous bond with his mother or permanent mother substitute in which both find satisfaction and enjoyment.[2]

How does this intimate emotional bond evolve? During the critical first year of life, a baby is learning his first lessons about love and trust. When he cries and his mother comes, he begins to learn that he can count on her. His world feels like a safe, happy, secure place. A baby's mother becomes his "secure base," or "touchstone," allowing him to explore his world with confidence.[3] But what happens when his mother ignores his cries or is insensitive to his needs? Then a baby is likely to internalize the feeling that the world is a bleak, comfortless place where he cannot get even his basic needs met.

As he matures, a child will assume that others will treat him just as his father and mother have done. Prince Baby will carry the lessons he learns about love, trust, and his mother's emotional availability into the whole of his life. When he falls in love and marries, that capacity for intimacy he developed—or failed to develop—in his mother's arms and beyond will affect his ability to be emotionally close to his wife and children. To echo a greeting card I picked up in a Seattle bookstore years ago, "Our lives are shaped by those who love us and those who refuse to love us."

MOM AT THE APEX OF THE PYRAMID

Though assailed by critics, Bowlby never let mothers off the hook. A critical tenet of his attachment theory, which has been supported by more than two decades of research, is something called *monotrophy*. What did Bowlby mean by this term? He believed that every baby has a hierarchy of attachment figures he comes to love and trust, and in the early months of life he comes to love one the best. That person is usually his mother. She resides at the apex of the baby's relational pyramid. And when he's tired, ill, or distressed, a baby will make a beeline to his mom during his first two years, even if both parents are present.[4]

One new mother told me her husband was distressed that she could comfort their six-month-old baby better than he. I smiled. The baby was right on target in forging his first love relationship with his mother. "Tell your husband to keep loving the baby. Soon your son will toddle after him and ape his every gesture. But right now you're his primary caretaker, so you're the one he needs when life overwhelms him."

A mother's love is critical. But what does this mean for mothers who join the work force, leaving their babies for long hours in the care of dad, a baby-sitter, or nanny? When dad is a warm, affectionate Mr. Mom who cares for the baby for long days while mom is away at work, he may become the nurturing mother substitute who sits at the top of the pyramid. That's okay as long as the mother doesn't mind that dad's the one her baby may cry for. Even a sensitive baby-sitter or caregiver can win an infant's primary devotion if she is more attuned to his needs than his mother and spends most of his waking hours with him.[5] The key for every baby's optimal development is a consistent mothering figure who comes to know, love, and enjoy him—who responds to his coos, who shares his joy that he is alive, who spends most of his waking hours with him and stays in his life, not moving to another job in a month or a year.

Bowlby wasn't particularly sympathetic toward professional women who wanted to pursue their careers while rearing their babies. I heard him speak at the 1986 American Psychiatric Association meeting where he was asked how early mothers could leave their babies to return to work. He said that what was important was what was "optimal for the child, not what a mother could get away with."[6] Fighting words for some women! He added that every child needed consistency of care, and nannies and baby-sitters rarely provided consistent care-giving. He looked out across the room of physicians and stated tersely, "If you want a job done well, do it yourself."[7]

What I've just said may be troubling to those of you who feel you must work, spending long days away from your baby, especially if you'd rather stay home with your child and become queen of his heart. If this describes you, I would advise you to move heaven and earth to spend as much time as you can with your baby during his critical first year, like the mother I met who works flextime and does tag-team parenting with her husband. Even though she has to work full-time, she said she didn't want to miss out on her daughter's developmental milestones. So sometimes she goes to work very early; some days she spends mornings at home and works late at night. But she's home during some of her baby's waking hours.

Since your baby's first year is so important developmentally, you need to be there as much as you can. Remember: The attachment relationship he forges with you and his father that first year will affect the whole of his life. Besides, you don't want to miss this exciting and joyous experience by having someone else do most of your mothering for you.

HOW A BABY'S BOND WITH EACH PARENT DIFFERS

Whether a mother works outside the home or not, she will most likely carry the psychological burden for her baby's physical and emotional well-being. This is the way we women are wired. In *Good Morning, Merry Sunshine*, journalist Bob Greene contrasted his role as a fairly typical father to his wife's role as mother of their baby, Amanda. He wrote:

> "We're not very happy today," Susan said to Amanda this
> morning. "You only slept from eleven to five." I think Susan
> means exactly that: "We're not very happy today." She uses
> the first person plural so much it can be a slip of the tongue;

when she thinks of Amanda, she thinks of herself; when she thinks of herself, she thinks of Amanda. As much as I love Amanda, the relationship is not the same; in my mind we are still separate people. In this era of new attitudes on the part of men, I wonder if other fathers are different? Somehow I don't think so. I think there's a built-in distance there that, if you're a man, you can never quite close. You can try all you want, but it won't happen.[8]

Greene is right. While both parents forge an attachment relationship with each child, fathers and mothers differ in the way they create that special emotional bond. In the first year and beyond, mothers establish an attachment relationship with their babies through acts of caretaking, while fathers do so through play.[9] Of course, mothers also play with their babies, but the type of play is different. For example, mothers engage in visual games, such as peekaboo or pat-a-cake, while fathers engage in games that involve bodily movement.[10] Babies come to recognize the difference early on. Who hasn't noticed that a baby "turns on" when Daddy comes through the door? His eyes light up, and his whole body shakes. Why? His playmate and buddy has arrived!

I remember the first time I became acutely aware of male/female differences in relating to babies. One weekend when Holly was about eight months old, her exuberant and lively Uncle Elliott came to visit. David, Elliott, and I went to the park. To my horror, Elliott took Holly and started up the steps of a slide. "Catch her," he yelled to David. Then he and David laughed exuberantly as Elliott sent Holly careening down the slide on her back to her father who waited below. While both brothers thought this was great fun, I was horrified. My baby! Grabbing Holly, who was surprised rather than upset, I held her close and patted her. Fortunately, both she and I survived.

Not only do parents relate in distinctly different ways to their child, but their emotional bonds with their baby are also independent.

of each other. It's possible for a baby to have a loving, secure emotional bond with his father and an insecure one with his mother. Or vice versa. Obviously, it's best for a baby if he has two sensitive, responsive parents. That way he will have an optimal start in life and develop a sense of his own worth based on both parents' loving regard. One study of sixty infants found that children with a secure relationship with both parents were the most confident and competent; those who had a secure relationship with neither were the least; and those with a secure bond with one parent were somewhere in the middle.[11]

This need for a secure emotional bond with each parent extends far beyond infancy. Even our teenagers need us to be their secure base, especially as they leave home to enter the larger world. In his book *A Secure Base*, Bowlby wrote about the support parents provide their children well into adolescence.

> This brings me to a central feature of my concept of
> parenting. The provision by which both parents are a secure
> base from which a child or an adolescent can make sorties
> into the outside world and to which he can return knowing
> for sure that he will be well cared for when he gets there,
> nourished physically and emotionally, comforted if distressed,
> reassured if frightened. In essence, this role is one of being
> available, ready to respond when called upon to encourage
> and perhaps assist, but to intervene actively only when clearly
> necessary.[12]

How true this was for Holly and Kristen. Not only did we have our daily chats when they were in high school, we spoke on the phone one to three times a week when they were in college. When they spent one summer in Europe, sometimes traveling together, sometimes alone, each asked to call home weekly. Initially I was worried about the cost, but as it turned out, each girl had hair-raising experiences and needed to talk them through.

I believe this need for a secure base exists throughout life, especially when our children lose a job, a baby gets sick, or life becomes overwhelming.

MOTHERING STYLES

At this point you may wonder how psychologists know what kind of attachment relationship a baby has with each parent. Is this only supposition? Although Bowlby created the theory of attachment, it took the work of psychologist Mary Ainsworth, the famous professor emeritus at the University of Virginia, to measure the attachment relationship a baby has with his parents. To do this, Ainsworth created a scientific procedure in the late seventies that proved the veracity of Bowlby's attachment theory. A colleague of Bowlby's, Ainsworth began her work by studying how mothers in Uganda cared for their babies. When she returned to the States years later to teach at Johns Hopkins, she developed a brief laboratory experiment called the Strange Situation, which has provided a scientific method to study the mother-child bond.[13]

This procedure examines children's behavior during brief separations from, and reunions with, their mothers. As a result of her work, Ainsworth discovered that children exhibited three different and distinct behavioral patterns during the reunion episodes of the Strange Situation.

The securely attached: The securely attached baby made a beeline for his mother when distressed, knowing he could trust her, and eagerly greeted her after brief separations. He was easily comforted by his mother's presence.

The anxious-avoidant (or avoidant): This baby avoided his mother after brief separations, and he sometimes hit her in the lab. Seemingly independent, he was more interested in toys than people. He also avoided looking at mom and sometimes crawled past her when she returned.

The anxious-resistant (or ambivalent): This ambivalently attached baby was the most anxious of all. Clinging and demanding, he proved inconsolable when his mother returned after a brief separation. Angry or passive, he could not be soothed.[14]

Later, a fourth category, called the *disorganized-disoriented,* was added to describe those babies who exhibited "confused, conflictual, or fearful" behavior in the Strange Situation. Babies with this attachment classification were found primarily in families where the parents were poor, alcoholic, or abusive.[15]

Why did these babies behave in such markedly different ways? Ainsworth discovered that their mothers had quite different caretaking styles. For instance, the mothers of secure babies were sensitive to their cries and were apt to pick them up more promptly, to hold them longer and "with more apparent pleasure" than were the mothers of emotionally insecure babies.[16] These warm, engaging mothers were also more emotionally available to their babies.

What about the mothers of the insecurely attached? Ainsworth and her colleagues discovered that the mothers of babies classified as anxious-avoidant were rejecting. Not only were these moms less affectionate and emotionally expressive, but they also tended to be gruff and rough with their babies. When they held or touched their babies, tenderness was not part of their repertoire.[17] For whatever reason, these mothers didn't like physical contact, and they discouraged their babies from coming to them for comfort and holding.

As for the mothers of the anxious-resistant, they were sometimes meanspirited and detached, sometimes pleasant. Although they loved their babies, "what they all had in common was difficulty responding to the baby's attachment needs in a loving, attuned, and consistent way."[18] These mothers could be hostile and rejecting; they could also be kind. They were as unpredictable as the weather. So these confused

little babies never knew just how their mothers would respond, and
this made them quite angry.

WHAT ABOUT YOU?

If you're like me, you're probably analyzing your attachment relationship with each child at this very moment. Let me encourage you by
saying that the majority of mothers and babies forge a secure attachment relationship. In fact, in cross-cultural attachment research, using
the Strange Situation, about 65 percent of the babies were securely attached to their mothers.[19] And the participants in these studies were
just normal moms.

As we shall see in the next chapter, the rate of attachment insecurity
rises when babies enter day care in their first year. So it's important for
a mother to think carefully about putting her baby in full-time care, especially during that critical first year of life when her baby is falling in
love with her and forging an emotional bond that will last a lifetime.

Since you're reading this book, I assume you want to engage in
conscious, thoughtful mothering—whatever your attachment history.
For that to happen you need to understand your own mothering style.
To help you assess this, I've included four key dimensions delineated
by Ainsworth and her colleagues:

- *Sensitive* mothers are aware of their babies' needs and respond
  to their schedules consistently. On the other hand, "*insensitive*
  mothers interact primarily on their own schedules and
  according to their own needs."[20]
- *Accepting* mothers are able to deal with their babies' moods,
  whether positive or negative. *Rejecting* mothers take their babies'
  negative moods personally and become angry and resentful.
- *Cooperative* mothers allow their babies some degree of
  autonomy and don't intrude into their activities. If they must
  take control, they do so in a "congenial" way.[21] *Interfering*

mothers force their babies to do what they want them to do and on their schedules.

- *Accessible* mothers pay attention to their babies' signals; *ignoring* mothers fail to notice or do so only at scheduled moments.

Not surprisingly, researchers found that mothers of securely attached babies had high scores on all four dimensions: These moms were sensitive, accepting, cooperative, and emotionally accessible. But what about mothers of avoidant babies? They were rejecting and insensitive. And mothers of babies classified as anxious-resistant or anxious-ambivalent were sometimes rejecting, and either interfering or ignoring.[22]

LET'S TALK, AMERICA

Recently I was on my favorite radio talk show, *Janet Parshall's America*. About once a month, Janet graciously invites me on the air to discuss a topic of my choice. The topic that day was my book *What Every Mother Needs to Know about Babies*. After Janet and I had chatted for a few minutes, all the phone lines lit up. Boy, had we hit a hot topic! The primary question of both male and female callers was, "Do I pick up my baby when he cries, or do I let him cry it out?"

Now, no one likes to hear a baby cry. In fact, most of us probably feel our blood pressure rising and our hearts beating faster when we hear crying babies. Psychologists have a term for a baby's cry: *aversive*. Whether we hear a baby cry on an airplane, in church, or at the grocery store, most of us are probably uneasy until the baby's mother or caretaker can soothe the unhappy child.

Yet there's growing support in evangelical churches for a Christian parenting curriculum called "Growing Kids God's Way" created by a husband-wife team, Gary and Anne Marie Ezzo. The Ezzos—he's a pastor and she's a pediatric nurse—claim they have taught their child-rearing principles to over 400,000 parents.[23] Their program is designed to be used in churches to instruct parents on how to deal with children from infancy to adolescence. The most controversial aspect of the Ezzo program (and the one I'm most concerned about) is their manual *Preparation for Parenting*, which advocates an inflexible feeding and sleeping schedule for babies. What concerns me is the adversarial nature of the relationship that the Ezzos' program subtly creates between parent and baby. With a strong emphasis on control and taking charge of the baby, the Ezzos state early on that babies are sinful creatures who must not be allowed to disrupt a family. In *Preparation for Parenting*, the Ezzos wrote: "When we say that an infant is born with a sin nature, we are not referring to his ability to make right and wrong moral choices. Newborns do not make such cognitive decisions, but they are subject to the base elements of depravity. Depravity is not a barren state of corruption; it actively affects mankind biologically and spiritually."[24] As an evangelical Christian I would agree with this theological concept, but I question this particular application to parenting. After all, a newborn is a needy creature.

Stressing the concept of original sin, the Ezzos:

> . . . teach new parents to schedule their baby's sleep time,
> play time, and meal time. Instead of feeding babies when
> they are hungry (on demand), the Ezzos advocate feeding
> newborns every three hours. Although they cite some Bible
> verses to support their program, they base their teaching
> primarily on the idea that since God is a God of order, the
> concept of "demand" feeding is wrong and unhealthy, leading
> to "metabolic chaos," while "parent directed feeding" leads to
> healthier babies and happier moms.[25]

Although the Ezzos acknowledge that "the Bible is silent" on such topics as feeding, they nevertheless warn anxious new parents, "What you believe about feeding a baby will usually be representative of your overall parenting philosophy."[26] They then advocate taking charge of the baby and feeding him every three hours "because he is not as emotionally fragile as attachment theorists believe."[27]

When it comes to the question of whether to respond to a baby's cries, the Ezzos are definitely proponents of a delayed response to any crying. According to the Ezzos, parents should be "sober-minded" and assess their baby's cry. And if parents always pick up the baby when he cries? The Ezzos believe this reactive, nonthinking behavior raises "serious theological and practical concerns."[28] To rush in and pick up the baby leads to "emotional mothering," which can "set the stage for child abuse."[29] Instead, parents need to stop, listen, and think before responding to a baby's cries, and if he cries for fifteen minutes, so be it.[30] The Ezzos stress that couples should create a parent-centered rather than a child-centered marriage and force their baby to accept life on their terms.

While the Ezzos have popularized what they feel is a new and rational approach to nurturing, part of this is an old trend in child rearing. For years parents have been urged not to respond sensitively to their babies' cries but instead to "let them cry it out."[31] The Ezzos have attempted to add theological clout to their admonitions. But is picking up a crying baby really setting the stage for future bad behavior?

CRYING AND COMMUNICATION

Studies show that crying is the primary way a newborn communicates with his mother, usually to signal a desire to be close to her or to have needs met. Granted, babies do cry for reasons psychologists can't always explain. According to child psychologist Evelyn Thoman, a classic study at the Mayo Clinic found that when babies cried, 36 percent of the time they were hungry, 29 percent of the time they needed their diapers changed, and the other 35 percent of the time they cried for unknown reasons.[32] But are we to let our babies cry it out simply because we can't figure out why they're crying? Perhaps those "unknown reasons" have to do with a need to be held, soothed, and comforted. Perhaps the baby just feels scared or lonely. All babies need lots of touch and affection to become peaceful, happy toddlers.

Psychological research shows that you actually make life harder for yourself and your baby if you don't attend to his cries early on. Researchers Silvia Bell and Mary Ainsworth found that when a mother promptly responded to her baby's cries in the first three months of life, her baby seldom cried when he was a year old.[33] By then he had learned happier ways of communicating his needs, such as cooing and babbling. So a mother may work against herself (and her new baby) by ignoring his cries.

Many mothers and fathers worry that they will "spoil" their babies if they respond quickly to their cries. Is this what happens? Not at all. For this to be true, a baby would have to possess the cognitive ability to figure out how he can manipulate his unwary parents. In the early months, babies simply can't do this. The neocortex, or the thinking part of the brain, is only partially developed at birth.[34] Your crying baby is not thinking, *Gee, I'm going to manipulate Mom and control her and Dad.* He simply doesn't have the sophisticated brain power to do that. What is well developed at birth is his limbic system—the seat of his emotions and feelings. That's why psychologists say that babies feel before they think.[35] When your baby cries in those early months, he's probably feeling lonely, tired, uncomfortable, overstimulated, or maybe even a little queasy.

In referring to the fear of spoiling a baby by responding to his cries, Ainsworth was adamant: "It doesn't spoil them. It doesn't make them clingy. It doesn't make them addicted to being held."[36] In fact, in their seminal study on infant crying, Ainsworth and Bell had this to say: "Those infants who are conspicuous for fussing and crying after the first few months of life and who fit the stereotype of the 'spoiled child' are those whose mothers have ignored their cries or have delayed long in responding to them."[37]

Bell and Ainsworth found that a mother's responsiveness to her baby's crying was directly related to her level of sensitivity. In other words, sensitive mothers responded to their babies' cries quickly, while insensitive moms did not. And the latter had babies who became more insistent in their crying over time. They cried harder and longer.

Let's get specific. How long should you wait in those early weeks and months when your baby cries? Should you wait ten to fifteen minutes to see if he will stop? Or should you ignore his cries altogether, especially if it doesn't fit into your schedule? Evelyn Thoman, who studies babies and their mothers, says it's okay to allow a baby to fuss "a little" so that he begins to learn to soothe himself.[38] This minor time lag also helps him acquire the sense that he has some small control over his world: He cries and his mother comes. But in her research Thoman found that when a mother picked up her baby after ninety seconds, he "soothed more readily." And when she waited longer? Then it was harder to calm her baby.

What can you do when your baby cries? Thoman suggests six things:[39]

- Pick up your baby promptly.
- Carry or rock your baby (rocking up and down makes him drowsy, while rocking him side to side makes him more alert).
- Sing a lullaby or play soothing music if your baby likes it.
- Try a pacifier (if you choose to use one).
- Try wrapping or swaddling your baby in a blanket.
- Try a gentle baby massage (this works best to prevent, rather than stop, crying).

Keep in mind that your baby needs you to be a sensitive, consistent, and responsive mother because he's learning his first lessons about love and trust from you—lessons that will last a lifetime. The way you and your husband treat him will determine, to a great degree, whether your baby becomes emotionally secure or insecure. In the early months he's also learning about his ability to make an impact on his world, and *you* are his world. So it matters what you and your husband do when your baby cries.

While some may dismiss attachment theory and research as irrelevant, let me say that an enormous body of research exists in this particular area. Currently, attachment theory is the most well-researched theory of a child's social and emotional development.[40]

I have seen significant attachment deficiencies in adults diagnosed with depression and anxiety. These clients complained of chronic sadness, rage, feelings of helplessness, and clinging dependency, all symptoms that something went awry in their early attachment relationships. I have also counseled couples who, never having been emotionally close to anyone, did not know how to love. They came to me, accusing each other of withholding the love they had never experienced and so desperately needed. While I believe that certain skills, such as communication, can be taught, the capacity for intimacy and the ability to trust are difficult to acquire in adulthood without a lot of emotional work and healing.

That's why I believe babies need to be handled with great sensitivity during the early months of life. Then, as they grow, they will become sunny, happy children who feel emotionally secure and will mature into adults who can love and trust.

Carol Smaldino wrote an article for *Mothering* magazine, stating that she "tossed and turned" over the issue of letting her baby cry without trying to soothe him. When her son was ten months old and her pediatrician suggested that she and her husband let Paul cry it out, Smaldino said, "My insides rebelled."[41] Finally, she and her husband consulted well-known psychologist Lee Salk, who urged them not to allow their baby to cry it out. Salk told them their baby was developing a sense of trust and was using the only resource he had—crying— to get his parents to come, because he needed them. "Crying was, in fact, . . . a means of making an impact, of knowing that he mattered."

This mother learned from Dr. Salk what she sensed intuitively—that babies need comfort and they "build their resources gradually."[42]

HOW NOT TO SPOIL YOUR BABY

It is possible to spoil your child but *not* in the first six months of life. In his book *The First Three Years*, Burton White suggests that while babies up to six months old need to be promptly comforted when distressed, babies begin to cry with intentionality between six and eleven months. Then, when baby cries in the middle of the night, White suggests a parent go into the nursery, pat the baby, speak soothingly, and depart.[43] This is a useful technique to help a baby sleep through the night at five or six months of age—when he should be able to give up his nighttime feedings, unless he's ill or teething.

It's important that parents investigate and find out why their baby is crying and, even when the baby is older, decide how to respond. Maybe he needs to be patted and talked to soothingly; maybe he's bored or needs a change of scenery. Maybe he needs to play. Attuned parents will always try to understand why their older baby cries.

CONCERNS ABOUT THE EZZOS' PHILOSOPHY

As one who has reared two daughters and studied child development extensively, I have deep concerns about the Ezzos' child-rearing philosophy, particularly when it comes to babies. I am not alone in my concerns. Even Focus on the Family has commented:

> We do have concerns and reservations about the Ezzos' work, including the updated edition of *Preparation for Parenting*. We are aware that some of the authors' proposals—notably those having to do with controlled feeding schedules for infants— are controversial. Some critics have suggested that they might

possibly result in child abuse if applied legalistically, inflexibly, and without regard for circumstance and the special needs of individual children, though we believe such misuse would be contrary to the authors' intent. For these reasons we do not recommend this material to our constituents. Further, we would suggest that, if and when it is used, its principles be implemented only in conjunction with generous measures of common sense, intuition, and natural parental affection.

To be fair, we must acknowledge that some parents do very well with the Ezzos' approach, and appear to be raising healthy, contented children. As with any other systems, so much depends on the mother and father who implement it. The question of whether to use or not to use the Ezzos' material remains, in the final analysis, a judgment call.[44]

I'm concerned about any child-rearing philosophy that might encourage some parents to be insensitive to their babies' needs. Insensitivity, remember, is linked to insecure attachment. While most couples want order and control over their lives once they become parents, they need to give their helpless baby some time to adjust to his or her new environment. A baby's emotional security needs to be a top priority in that critical first year. Yes, that means that you and your husband will be inconvenienced and will probably lose a little sleep for several months. Is that too great a price to pay to help your child get well launched in life? Besides, a baby will naturally begin to develop a feeding and sleeping schedule around three to four months of age.

The way you as a mother handle your baby's feeding and crying schedules will have powerful and long-lasting repercussions. For your baby, it's all about comfort and trust and feeling some small sense of power. And some feeling of power is essential to our mental health— to feel ever powerless is to be prone to depression. Besides, long after your child has learned to walk or drive a car, long after sleepless nights have been forgotten, your child's feelings of emotional security or insecurity will endure. Believe me, over the long haul, parents will have a lot more pain and discomfort if they rear needy, insecure kids than if they have kids who feel loved and worthy.

At the 1997 White House Conference on Day Care I had the privilege of interviewing Dr. Robert E. Hannemann, then the national president of the American Academy of Pediatrics. When I asked him to address the needs of babies, he said, "The Academy has always supported attending to the child's needs and adapting to the characteristics of the baby. We have always been strong on breast-feeding and believe in flexible feeding schedules. We feel very strongly about responding to a baby's cries and needs." He went on to say that if a baby cries and no one comes, he may come to view the world as "unresponsive." He may think, *I don't trust the outside world to help me.* "You don't have to be a scientist to know you may create an insecure attachment if you fail to respond to your baby's signals." Dr. Hannemann stated that he's impressed by "tolerant, flexible mothers whose babies are happy and smile a lot."[45]

GET YOUR OWN NEEDS MET

To be the responsive mother you wish to be, you obviously need to be in good emotional health. What can you do, then, if you struggle with feelings of depression? First, let me say that fleeting depressed feelings are normal and no great cause for concern. What concerns clinicians is a negative, depressed mood that lingers on, week by week or month by month, fueled by feelings of hopelessness and helplessness.

If you're depressed, you will tend to push your baby away or may even respond to his needs and cries with anger. You probably feel depleted—helpless, hopeless, and unable to cope with your own needs, much less those of a demanding baby. You may be so caught up in your internal noise that you can't hear your baby's cries or mirror his feelings of pleasure and joy.

Be aware that if your depression is severe and lingers, your baby is likely to be insecurely attached.[46] When Douglas Teti and his colleagues conducted a study of fifty mother and baby pairs and fifty-four mother and preschooler pairs, they found high rates of insecure attachment among the children of depressed mothers. Eighty percent of the babies and 87 percent of the preschoolers were insecurely attached when their mothers suffered from depression.[47] Because I have struggled with depression in my own life, especially after my first husband left and the girls were very young, I know just how hard it is to nurture babies when one feels depleted and used up. That's why I urge you to seek professional help if you need it. I did, and it helped tremendously.

An empathic therapist (and I recommend an older woman) can help you work through your sad and hostile feelings. Yes, there's a great deal of hostility in depression and some bitterness and resentment too. I used to tell my clients that there were three Hs involved in depression: feelings of helplessness, hopelessness, and hostility. It's important to process these feelings with a trained professional who can help you reframe your negative thinking. Since cognitive therapy has proved to be as successful as drug therapy in treating depression, it may help you to learn to talk back logically to your negative ideas. I also suggest you read *Feeling Good* by Dr. David Burns.

Those of us who are prone to depression are often passive in our relationships, so it's important to become more assertive; and when someone hurts you, it's important to tell the person calmly and logically and to work things out. As my clients monitored their negative thoughts, reworked the past, and became more assertive in their relationships, their moods improved.

It's also important to get regular exercise (at least thirty minutes a day) since this releases endorphins, or mood elevators, in the brain. And last but not least, we women always need the presence of other women in our lives. Show me a woman—any woman—who denies her own needs for friendships and sociability, and I'll show you a depressed woman. So plan those coffees and lunches out. You'll not only feel better, you'll be a better wife and mother.

THE GOD OF ALL COMFORT

Our children's attachment relationship with us as parents will ultimately affect their attachment relationship with God. Why do I say
that? Because the way we treat our children has a lot to do with their expectations about God. Early on, they either acquire the belief that God
hears them when they call or that God is unresponsive to their heartfelt
needs. Said one woman who grew up with parents who were neglectful
and rejecting: "I have struggled all of my adult life believing that no one
cares for my soul. I know intellectually that God loves me, but I've had
great trouble feeling that He cares on an emotional level. It took me
well into midlife and the experience of a significant crisis before I came
to believe in my deepest heart that my God really loves me."

In truth, God is a comforting, responsive parent. I love the first
chapter of 2 Corinthians where He is described as "the source of all
mercy and comfort," a Father who gives us comfort in our trials so that
we can pass on His empathy and comfort to others. It comforts me
when I'm hurting to know that the word *comfort* is used nine times in
this particular chapter. And when I feel needy, I race to all the marked-
up verses in my Bible, particularly in Isaiah and Psalms, that assure me
I have a sensitive, loving, responsive heavenly Father who can hear my
inconvenient middle-of-the-night longings as well as my convenient
noonday cries. Here are some of my favorite Scriptures:

He tends his flock like a shepherd:
    He gathers the lambs in his arms
and carries them close to his heart.
Isaiah 40:11

Listen to me, O House of Jacob,
    all you who remain of the house of Israel,
you whom I have upheld since you were conceived
    and have carried since your birth.
Even to your old age and gray hairs

I am he, I am he who will sustain you.
I have made you and I will carry you.

Isaiah 46:3-4

As a mother comforts her child,
    so will I comfort you;
    and you will be comforted over Jerusalem.

Isaiah 66:13

I love the LORD, for he heard my voice;
    he heard my cry for mercy.
Because he turned his ear to me,
    I will call on him as long as I live.

Psalm 116:1

Notice that God "carries" us from birth to old age. He comforts us in a motherly and fatherly way and hears our cries. Should we not do the same for our children? Should we not nurture our babies in a tender way and carry them when they are distressed? I think so.

HOW TO REAR A SECURELY ATTACHED CHILD

What can you do to create a loving, secure emotional bond? You can become a CSR mother. Child development experts agree that children need consistent, sensitive, and responsive mothering to grow up feeling loved and worthy. Since this is the case, I believe a CSR mother will:

• Respond promptly to her baby's cries and, as he grows, answer when he calls. That way her child will learn that he can count on his mother to hear him, whatever his distress and wherever life takes him.

• Establish an early feeding schedule that is flexible and meets her newborn's needs for nourishment, knowing that as she responds to her baby he is more likely to be securely attached and have fewer behavioral problems later on.[48]

- Enjoy holding and cuddling her baby and, as he matures, continue to be a warm, affectionate mother.
- Establish good communication patterns, listening and responding to her child's coos and babbles and later to his words.
- Stay tuned in emotionally across the years and refuse to allow outside pressures to keep her from mothering by heart.
- Communicate her joy that her baby exists and belongs to her and her husband. Because of her joy in him, her child will grow up feeling that life is a "gift to be enjoyed" rather than a "burden to be borne."[49]

TAKING THE LONG-RANGE VIEW

Why have I placed such a heavy emphasis on the quality of a child's attachment relationship? Because our earliest feelings about ourselves and others do not evaporate. Studies show that the insecurely attached baby often becomes the insecure preschooler who will either bully others or play the victim on the playground. In middle school, the insecurely attached child has difficulty making and sustaining the friendships he so desperately needs.[50] Conversely, the securely attached child is popular and possesses high self-esteem even as a preschooler. By the time he enters middle childhood, he has lots of friends and is comfortable in groups.[51] The formation of a secure attachment relationship in the first year is critical, and studies show that attachment patterns tend to be stable across the generations.

LOVE YOU FOREVER

I want to end this chapter with a bit of whimsy. I believe simple stories capture truths that psychologists work hard to communicate in their dry and sometimes boring studies. One of my favorite children's books, *Love You Forever* by award-winning Canadian writer Robert Munsch, captures the cross-generational aspect of attachment security beautifully. In this profound and simple little book about a secure mother-son attachment, a mother holds her new baby, rocking him slowly back and forth while she sings:

> I'll love you forever,
> I'll like you for always,
> As long as I'm living,
> My baby you'll be.[52]

The baby, of course, becomes a toddler, driving his mother crazy as he flushes the toilet or pulls food out of the refrigerator. But at nighttime when her son sleeps, his mother picks him up and sings their lullaby: "I'll love you forever." And we are asked to believe the improbable: that this ritual continues across the years—when the boy is nine, when he's a teenager, and as an adult. Even then the mother drives across town and picks up her sleeping giant, rocks him, and sings their song. Time passes. The mother grows old and frail. One day she calls her son to say, "You'd better come to see me because I'm very old and sick." Her son comes, and when he enters his mother's house, she tries to sing their song but can't. She is simply too old.

So what does this much-loved son do? He picks up his small, frail old mother and rocks her. Now it is his turn to sing their song. Later that night, when he goes home, the man climbs the stairs and enters the nursery where his baby daughter sleeps. Picking her up, he rocks her and sings the song his mother has inscribed in his heart over many years:

> I'll love you forever,
> I'll like you for always,
> As long as I'm living,
> My baby you'll be.

And that, folks, is what secure attachment is all about—loving our children deeply and wisely so they can pass that golden legacy from one generation to the next. Of course, insecure attachment also rolls on across the generations. What makes the difference? Basically, the choice is ours.

CHAPTER 7

The Power
of Separation

If a mother wants her children to feel emotionally secure, how does she deal with the issue of separation? How much time apart from mother can a baby or young child tolerate without feeling that his or her world has been upended?

In June of 1992 I had the privilege of testifying to the Presidential Commission on the Assignment of Women in the Armed Forces. The topic? The high cost of separation. On my right sat Penn State developmental psychologist Jay Belsky. I was intrigued by what Belsky said that day about the price children pay when separated from their mothers due to combat. Acknowledging that "from the child's point of view, all parents are not created equal,"[1] he went on to add: "Uncontrolled separations are tremendously painful and can have long-term and potentially devastating effects on the developing child."[2]

While Belsky was addressing "uncontrolled separations" such as those caused by military deployment, our children are confronting other instances where we leave them for extensive periods of time. Yet the evidence shows that prolonged separation from mother is hard for a child of any age to bear but particularly for the youngest.

> We begin life with loss. We are cast from the womb without an apartment, a charge plate, a job or car. We are swelling, sobbing, clinging, helpless babies. Our mother interposes herself between us and the world, protecting us from overwhelming anxiety. We shall have no greater need than this need for our mother.[3]

So writes Judith Viorst in her account of "the loves, illusions, dependencies, and impossible expectations that all of us have to give up in order to grow."[4] Yet the truth is, millions of babies and young children give up their mothers' comforting presence for days or even weeks when careers demand it.

I spoke to a newly separated mother who is readying herself to reenter the work force. In an interview with a large accounting firm, this mother of a two-year-old was asked, "Will you travel?" "Sure," she responded, thinking she would be asked to go out of town for a day or two. To her consternation she learned that the firm would expect her to travel a week at a time.

This mother is distressed and worried about what her absence will mean to her daughter. And well she might. A toddler lacks the cognitive ability to say to herself, "It's okay. Mom will be back soon." Very young children don't have a sense of "object permanence"; they simply don't have the cognitive capacity to understand that separations from us are temporary. For the very young child, separations are a serious threat: When mother is gone, she's gone forever.

Psychologist Lee Salk described separation this way:

> Most people think that it does no harm to go away and leave a very young child because they feel the baby does not know the difference. This is not true. In fact, the opposite is true.

The very young child does know vividly. Because he has very little concept of "now" and "later," a baby does not understand that if you go away you will ultimately come back. . . . If he cannot see you, you are no longer there; in fact, you don't exist.[5]

When does a child begin to understand that his mother will return? While child-development gurus have difficulty pinpointing the exact time that object permanence develops, most concur that around two years of age a child develops the cognitive capacity to know that mom will return. Yet psychologist Selma Fraiberg felt that our youngest could only tolerate short absences without anxiety. In her book *Every Child's Birthright: In Defense of Mothering,* Fraiberg wrote about a young child:

> He can tolerate brief separations at two-and-a-half more easily than he could at one year. But prolonged separations of several days will still create anxiety for him. The anxiety is a measure of his love and a measure of his incapacity, still at two-and-a-half, to grasp fully the notion that a mother, though not present, must be someplace and will certainly return. *He can hold on to this notion for a few hours, or a day or two, and then if his mother does not magically reappear . . . she is lost, he is lost.*[6] [italics mine]

That is why maternal absence in the early years can have a profound effect on the child, especially if it is prolonged.

One of my close friends has been caring for her two-year-old grandchild while the parents are on a week-long vacation. My friend and this granddaughter are particularly close, so close in fact that the little girl calls her mother "Mommy" and her grandmother "Mom-Mom." While we were having breakfast, I asked my friend how she and little Rachel were faring. She laughed and said, "She's tired of me.

I think she misses her mommy. In fact, yesterday she pushed me away and said, 'I want *my* mommy.'" My friend added, "She seems sad sometimes and retreats to be by herself."

BRIEF DAILY SEPARATIONS

Most of us would feel intuitively that a week away from mother is hard for a toddler, but what about brief daily separations? Currently, half of all working mothers leave their babies in day care, beginning at four to six months of age. And nearly half of all babies in this country who are under a year old are cared for by someone other than their mothers.[7] That's a huge number of children. Although it's politically incorrect even to suggest that daily separations from mother are tough for young children, I've found over the years that mothers want to understand the research findings to make a thoughtful, careful decision about leaving their young ones.

One study looked at very brief separations from mother to see if they produced stress in the child. Psychologist Mary Larson and her colleagues examined infants from 8.6 to 10.3 months of age to see how they were affected by a thirty-minute separation from their mothers.[8] In this particular study, mothers left their babies with a stranger. When the researchers tested the separated infants' saliva, they found a significantly elevated level of cortisol, a stress hormone released by the adrenal cortex. What do I conclude? Even very brief absences from their mothers may prove stressful for babies.

But what about ten-, twelve-, and fourteen-hour daily separations? Numerous studies in the eighties found that when a mother worked more than twenty hours a week in her child's first year, her baby was more likely to be insecurely attached to her or to the baby's father. This means that a mother's absence can even affect the baby's attachment relationship with the father. In *Zero to Three,* the publication of a Washington, D.C., clinical infants' program, Jay Belsky ignited a firestorm among female child-development experts when he wrote:

It is certainly not inconsistent with attachment theory that repeated separations in the first year of life, as routinely associated with day care usage, might affect the emerging attachment relationship, and even disturb it from the standpoint of security (or at least avoidance).[9]

In a separate piece for the publication, Belsky cited extensive research findings that indicated children who were placed in some form of day care in the first year were not only at risk for emotional insecurity but also for increased aggression, noncompliance, and social withdrawal as preschoolers and kindergartners.[10]

While early research on infant day care raised concern about full-time maternal employment among child-development experts and mothers alike, the latest long-term study of attachment and infant day care, financed by the federal government, seems at first blush to repudiate earlier findings. But does it?

THE NICHD STUDY: A DRIZZLE OR A STORM?

In April 1996, the National Institutes of Child Health and Human Development (NICHD) released initial findings of a new childcare study "and fired a shot heard round the world."[11] This long-term study plans to track the effects of childcare on children's development through age seven. The results of phase one seemingly dealt a body blow to full-time mother care. Reporters were quick to trumpet the results: the *Los Angeles Times* declared "Child Care No Risk to Infant-Mother Ties,"[12] while the *London Guardian* crowed "Child Care Report Backs Working Moms."[13]

When the NICHD study came out, a Washington, D.C., think tank, the Family Research Council, asked me to analyze it and write a report. The study, which has followed thirteen hundred families at ten different sites since 1991 found that childcare, *in and of itself,* does not harm a baby's emotional bond with his mother.[14] Indeed, the researchers stated that the type of care, the quality of care, the number of hours per week in care, and even the age the baby enters care did not create insecure attachments. This ammunition was all the media needed to conclude that early childcare does not harm the baby's attachment relationship to his mother. But are the findings really this simple? Let's take a closer look.

At first glance, the NICHD study appears to be a blanket endorsement of full-time childcare during the baby's first year of life. However, when the study is teased apart, we find a different picture emerging. For example, if a baby is unlucky enough to have an insensitive mother, then the dual risk of an insensitive mother *plus* poor quality care *or* inconsistency of care *or* more than ten hours per week in day care increases the likelihood of attachment insecurity. So babies need to be lucky in love *and* in the quality of day care *and* in the number of hours they are away from mother to maintain close emotional ties with her. As we might expect, the sensitive mothers in the study were more likely to have securely attached babies than were the insensitive moms.

The researchers also found that attachment security differed by gender. Boys were more vulnerable to separation than girls. Infant boys who spent *more* than thirty hours a week in childcare were at risk for insecure attachments, and girls who spent *less* than ten hours per week in care were "somewhat" more likely to be insecurely attached to their mothers.[15] How to explain this latter finding? Frankly, I'm not sure what to make of it. Psychologist Jay Belsky said: "Separation might prove stressful for boys, but girls who are at home with mothers extensively may become too close and enmeshed."[16] Belsky's strange interpretation prompted *Washington Times* columnist Suzanne Fields to write, "In other words, mommies who spend a lot of time with their infant daughters are dangerous to their daughters' mental health."[17]

While the unexpected finding on baby girls received much media fanfare, other important results didn't get reported in the media. For example, the NICHD study found that:

- Forty-two percent of males were insecurely attached when their mothers worked more than thirty hours a week.[18]
- Fifty-six percent of the babies were insecurely attached when their insensitive mothers placed them in day care with insensitive caregivers—an obvious double whammy.
- Forty-six to 48 percent of babies of insensitive mothers were insecurely attached if they were in day care for more than ten hours per week—proof that mom is needed even if she's relatively insensitive.

These numbers gain relevance when we are reminded that, cross-culturally, about 35 percent of all babies are insecurely attached. Yet in most analyses in the NICHD study, between 42 and 56 percent of the babies studied were insecurely attached.[19] This difference becomes significant when translated into numbers of emotionally insecure children.

In other words, the NICHD study supported the idea that mothering *is* essential for attachment security, even if a mother is relatively insensitive to her baby's cues. It also found that working more than *ten hours* per week puts the child of the insensitive mother at risk. That's a small number of hours! So how's a mother to know for sure that she's creating a secure emotional bond with her baby when she goes off to work for ten to twelve hours per day? Unless a woman is confident that she's a sensitive mother, it's wise to err on the side of *quantity* rather than *quality* time during her baby's first year of life and work less than ten hours a week.

When asked for comments about the final outcome of phase one of this study, Belsky told the media, "It's too early to tell. In my early observations, lots of childcare posed a risk factor [in developing attachment relationships]. In this study, even more than ten hours of care were important. It's the most vulnerable children who are the most adversely affected. The study shows it's drizzling now. It could be a cloud cover, or it could be the leading edge of a storm. We just don't know."[20]

PHASE TWO OF THE NICHD STUDY

While phase-one findings seemed to give the green light to infant day care, phase-two results, which were released in April 1997, without the same media hoopla, were not as positive. For example, phase two found that full-time day care *can* have a negative effect on the budding mother-child relationship, *if the child is placed in day care before age three.* Among the findings:

- No matter what the quality of day care, mothers who did not use it when their children were six months and three years old—the two test times—were more sensitive to the needs of their children than the moms who did.
- Three-year-olds who were not in day care had more positive relationships with their mothers than three-year-olds who were in day care.
- When their children were fifteen months old, mothers who had left their children in day care were more negative toward their offspring than were mothers who stayed home.[21]

According to the *Washington Times*, "the more hours the child is in day care, the less positive feedback—hugs, kisses, and praise—there was for them."[22]

My take on the NICHD findings? I believe mothers should be extremely cautious about placing their babies in full-time day care. Child development experts agree that a warm, sensitive emotional bond with his mother is essential for a child's development, and phase two of this study clearly shows that early and extensive day care may jeopardize this important relationship.

We also need to understand that the NICHD researchers have yet to examine the data on the three-year-olds in terms of attachment, as well as behavioral and social issues. Since aggression is well established by age three, I expect they may find increased aggressiveness among the little boys who were insecurely attached early on. Or they may find heightened passivity. In the meantime, countless mothers will struggle to make their decisions about leaving young children. Most will do so with great unease in their hearts.

DIVORCE AND AFTER

While day care generates daily separations, divorce can tear a child from his mother or father for weeks, months, or even years—sometimes forever. Like some of you, my children and I are quite familiar with divorce-induced separation. When Holly and Kristen were four and six years old, an Oklahoma judge mandated two-month-long visits with their father each summer. My girls were ill-equipped to handle the fear and anxiety these visits inevitably produced. Holly remembers counting the days until she could return home. While I could be summoned by letter or phone, these glimpses of me brought more tears—more evocations of a seemingly insurmountable loss. Kristen recently wrote about how these repeated separations affected her as a young child.

> Airplanes scare me. It isn't the flying I mind. For me,
> airplanes have always been agents of fear, conveyors from the
> known to the unknown, from the safe to the unsafe. A
> painful and frightening bridge. And in my case, a bridge
> between two lives. From one parent to the other.
> My father moved out when I was thirteen months old, a
> chubby baby with brown eyes, chicken-feather hair, and a
> toothless smile. Obviously, I can't remember the day he left,
> or the stillness that settled on our house in Clinton,

Connecticut, as my distraught mother drove him to a nearby hotel.

It seems strange to me that I can't picture what it was like for him to live in the same house with my mother, my sister, and me. My sister, who was three when he left, doesn't remember him either. It's as if, for better or worse, our minds were wiped clean with his departure. My memories of my father came later, when as a four-year-old I began my journeys on airplanes to spend summers with him, his new wife and family, and his baby son. I wish I could remember those times in sharp colors or vivid pictures. But my memories of those early visits are encompassed by a feeling of numbness.

I do remember my first flight across the country without any parent, leaving familiar Seattle for my father's house in unfamiliar Vermont. I was eight and my sister was ten. As I wedged my body into the airplane seat next to my frightened but brave sister, I clung to her small hand, sobbing as my mother tried to comfort me. She stood helplessly by until the stewardess said, "It's almost time for take-off." As she left, my desperate sobs overwhelmed me. I couldn't see; I couldn't breathe: I felt like I was drowning. Later, I could dimly see my mother waving from the airport terminal, her face stricken as she watched the plane taxi down the runway and climb up to the clouds, spiriting me away from the only world I knew, for a two-month, court-ordered visit.

Stewardess after stewardess approached, offering plastic wings, crayons, and other trinkets, but I pushed them all away. Terrified, unable to comfort myself, I thought my life was ending. I could not understand why my father had left, or why I had to leave the only parent I really knew, but I could sense one thing: My life had changed forever. And I

began to feel, in the core of my being, that what I loved most
could be wrenched violently from me. As I left my mother's
presence for those two-month visits, what began to take
shape in my heart and mind was the conviction that I could
not keep or control the good things in my life.

I can't read my daughter's account of this early and painful separation without feeling my stomach tighten and my heart ache. I grieved
for years because I couldn't give my daughters the security and stability they craved. Many of you have had the same experience and know
the angst of having your children leave you when they're too young
and too vulnerable, and you were powerless to protect them because
you needed the child support or you were afraid of being in contempt
of court.

What did I do? Like many of you, I did what I could. Each summer I spent several weeks preparing the girls for the frightening yet in-
evitable visit and when they returned, spent several more weeks
talking, holding, and comforting them. As I prepared for our separation, I made each girl a little bag that contained a book, candy, gum,
and illustrated letters that she could read in my absence. While Holly
internalized her feelings and was stoical, Kristen grieved openly. She
had me kiss her brown bear each night so she could cuddle and kiss it
during the long days she was away from me.

Years later, Kristen told me that when she was at her daddy's, surrounded by his wife and stepchildren, she worried that she might
never see me again. She had nightmares that I would die while we were
apart. Her anguish is not uncommon. Since one out of two marriages
today ends in divorce, many young children are shuttled between parents at an age when they are ill-equipped to deal with the feelings that
maternal separation, new surroundings, and a new lover or stepparent
evoke.

What helped me endure the separations and handle my anxiety
was my firm conviction that God would somehow see us through. I

remember being depressed and sad during the first month of separation each summer, but I prayed daily for my little girls. I can't tell you today that they have no scars. If I did, I'd be lying. As young women they continue to work on healing for their early pain. At the same time, both are wonderful young women who are deeply compassionate as a result of their suffering, and the three of us are emotionally close in spite of lengthy separations. Sadly, neither of my daughters is close to her biological father.

ADOPTION AND SEPARATION

Recently there has been a new twist in the problem of separation and loss for children. Some of you who have adopted children most likely remember reading about four-year-old Baby Richard, who was taken from his adoptive mother—the only mother he had ever known—to live with his biological father and mother, a woman who willingly gave him up for adoption at birth and even told his father he was dead. *Chicago Tribune* columnist Bob Greene wrote of the day Richard left his home:

> "Please, Mommy, don't make me go alone. Please go with me, Mommy."
>
> The four-year-old child known as Richard was sobbing so convulsively he seemed barely able to breathe. His adoptive mother was holding him inside the home in Schaumburg where Richard had lived his whole life. This was just before 3 P.M. on Sunday.
>
> "I don't want to go." The boy tried to scream through his sobs, but the words were choking him. "Don't make me leave."
>
> There was no way for the woman he had always known as his mother to answer him. She was sobbing, too. "We'll love you forever," she managed to say.[23]

Why did Richard have to endure this most wrenching and heart-breaking of separations? Five Illinois judges had ruled that he was not entitled to a "best interests of the child" hearing because the rights of his biological father were absolute.[24]

"I'll be good," sobbed Richard to his adoptive mother. "Don't make me leave. "I'll be good."[25]

What a tragedy! Though one of the most celebrated cases, Baby Richard is hardly alone; the courts are seeing more and more cases of biological parents seeking to reclaim children they abandoned years before. Recently, the *Washington Post Magazine* profiled area resident and pediatric nurse Diane Hendel who took in abandoned twins with severe health problems. After devoting two and a half years to loving, soothing, and healing the anxious children, Diane lost them to their biological mother, a former substance abuser. In their efforts to reunite mother and children, social workers even paid the mother's rent so that she could regain custody. Said Diane, the mother left behind:

> Goodbye to their toys. Goodbye to their drawings. Goodbye to their bedroom. Goodbye to everything. Just like that. And then, goodbye to Diane, who leaves the children, as ordered, so they can say hello a moment later to their new mother, who is the woman who conceived them, and abandoned them, and was charged with neglecting them, and now $3^{1}/_{2}$ years after they were born, and $2^{1}/_{2}$ years after Diane took them in with the hope of adopting them, has been declared legally fit to take them with her to a new place, a strange place, their true home.
>
> Just like that.
> Goodbye.
> Hello.[26]

When told about the twins, Marilyn Benoit, a child psychiatrist and executive director of the Devereux Children's Center in Washington, D.C., said:

You have now disrupted the emotional development of
these children. . . . You, the court, have created a new
abandonment. You have deliberately interjected separation
and loss into their lives. What we know that does is disrupt
development. You have depression. You have regression. You
undermine a sense of trust. You introduce a sense of
powerlessness. Children that age, what they want to develop
is a sense of mastery, and you have done everything to thwart
that, and you have really compromised that child's ability to
move on.[27]

While these children and little Richard may become compliant
and give their new parents little trouble, in some corner of their souls
they will probably feel that to love is to lose—forever. And this belief
will color all their later intimate attachments.

HOSPITALIZATION

There are additional separation experiences that are difficult for children. In *Necessary Losses*, Judith Viorst described her reaction to three
months of separation due to hospitalization when she was four years
old. Since hospitals at that time did not welcome on-site parents,
Viorst saw her mother only briefly during the three months. Later she
developed separation anxiety manifested by sleepwalking, a pattern
that continued well into her teens. Perhaps that's why Viorst writes
with such sensitivity about the high cost of separation from mother
that some young children pay. "Absence makes the heart grow frozen,
not fonder," says Viorst.[28]

Another woman recalls a trip to the hospital that occurred over
four decades ago. "How vividly I remember the day I stopped crying,"
said fifty-one-year-old Sue Huml, a mother of two grown children and
a lactation consultant in the Midwest. Sue spent two weeks in the hospital as a three-year-old because of recurring ear infections. Since this

was 1949, Sue's parents were not allowed to see their young daughter even once during this time. "The doctors and nurses felt it was better for children not to see their mommies and daddies," said Sue, "but it was just easier for them if they didn't have to deal with screaming children once the parents left."

Sue remembers that she stayed in a ward with eight other children who, like her, slept on narrow cots. Because she was too young to understand that her absent parents would return, Sue believed that she would never see them again. Distressed, she wet her bed frequently. One night when a nurse came to change her sheets, she accused Sue of being a "very, very bad little girl."

"Does this mean I'll never see my mommy and daddy again?" asked Sue.

The night nurse uttered a terse "yes" and left the ward.

"That's the moment I stopped crying," Sue said.

Not until her parents came to take her home did Sue cry again. Then she sobbed brokenheartedly and wouldn't let her mother out of her sight. "My mother started to cry when we got home and said to my father, 'This is awful; how could we have allowed this to happen?'"

Because of the trauma caused by the hospital stay, Sue Huml has become a woman with a mission. She now works as a volunteer with La Leche International because she wants every mother to know that "she is her baby's world." That's why, when some women in midlife are throttling back, playing bridge, or going on cruises, Sue is committed to mentoring younger mothers. "I want to help them see life through their baby's eyes."

John Bowlby's research confirms Sue's response to separation from her parents. In the 1950s, Bowlby and his colleague James Robertson studied young children of two and three years of age who were temporarily separated from their mothers due to hospital visits or stays in a residential nursery. They found that the children typically progressed through three stages: protest, despair, and detachment.[29] When a mother first left, her baby or small child cried loudly in protest; then when she failed to return, he lapsed into despair. Finally, to preserve his fragile sense of self, he began to detach from those around him. And when his mother returned after weeks or months, her child was sometimes cold and rejecting, acting as if she were a total stranger. According to Bowlby, a child might intensely cling "to the mother for weeks, months, or even years" or he could reject his mother temporarily or forever.[30] This detachment is a mask for feelings of rage at having been abandoned, and it may become a defense "against the agony of ever loving, or ever losing, again."[31]

BETH'S STORY

Children who are subjected to disruptive separations may grow up subject to chronic depression and intense separation anxiety. One of my friends is just now, at age forty-seven, beginning to deal with the fallout from a four-month separation from her mother when she was eight months old. Beth believes she has experienced chronic, low-grade depression, or dysthymia, all of her life. Attractive, with long blond hair and a rakish smile, Beth is a warm, affectionate wife and mother, as well as a competent high school teacher. No one would suspect that when she's away from her husband and four sons she feels terror, fearing that they may be killed and she will be left utterly alone *again.* On the summer day I interviewed Beth, I was struck by how many times she spoke of warding off a terrible sense of loneliness "again."

Beth told me that her mother left her in the care of extended family when she was eight months old to nurse a relative with a life-threatening disease. "It was a life or death situation," said Beth, "so I have no anger at my mother. What do you do when life presents you with such a dilemma? She obviously felt that she could not care for the relative and an infant at the same time."

Beth, of course, has no conscious memory of being dropped off at a relative's house or of seeing her mother walk out the door. As young children, what we remember are the feelings that loss generates. "What stays with us," writes Judith Viorst, "is what it surely must have felt like to be powerless and needy and alone. Forty years later, a door slams shut and a woman is swept with waves of primitive terror. That anxiety is her memory of loss."[32] So it is with Beth, whose sons are just beginning to leave home. These current tensions and losses take her back to an earlier place and time when her safety net gave way and she plummeted headlong into a sea of anxiety and sorrow.

My friend says that while she may outwardly seem "together," she feels emotionally fragile. "I do have a sense of belonging when all of my props are there: my family, parents, friends. But I'm like a little tree. Remove the props, and the tree isn't strong enough to stand on its own. Any wind can come and blow it over. And then the feelings I have are intense and powerful. Scary. Sometimes I am overwhelmed by feelings of fear, dread, and a choking kind of panic. I come up with scenarios in my mind of what could happen to Tom and the boys." She adds with a gravelly voice, "As a baby, I wasn't in control. I feel now like maybe it will happen all over again, and I'll be alone and desperately lonely."

Beth's brain buzzes with questions that those who have had secure beginnings would seldom, if ever, ask. "What will happen to me if I lose my family? Will I be lonely in old age? Will I ever belong? Who will be there for me when I really need someone? Will I ever be happy? Will I ever feel normal?"

From conversations with her therapist, Beth has learned that the grief she experienced as a baby has been transmuted into depression and anxiety. Her inability to trust others, her hypervigilance, and her sensitivity to rejection all have their roots in her infancy. Like others who have experienced maternal absence when they were too young to cope, Beth had academic and social difficulties growing up. "I didn't get the A's my siblings got, and I can remember being the last one picked for a team. Some kids were really resilient and could handle this, but it crushed me. Once again, I felt unwanted."

Beth considers herself fortunate to have a sensitive, nurturing husband but admits that while God has brought healing to her life during the past fifteen years, there are still parts of her that need His healing touch. For one thing, she wants to be able to handle life with greater peace when she's alone. And she wants to be able to let her children grow up and leave home.

As a mother of four attractive, optimistic sons, Beth isn't quite sure how her early history has affected them. She says she hasn't been overly fearful with them or overprotective but admits that she takes out her anger on her boys on occasion. "I keep all the anger pushed down until the volcano erupts. It's like I go through the day and there are petty annoyances, but I'll say nothing. Then something insignificant will set me off, and one of my boys will say, 'Mom, what was that all about?'" She worries about the unpredictability of her anger and its long-term effect on her children.

In spite of the early separation, Beth loves her mother dearly and feels emotionally close to her now. She describes this vivacious, talented seventy-five-year-old as a powerful role model and trusted friend and is convinced that her mom would never have left her in the care of others had she known about the long-term, profound consequences of early separation. But Beth admits that her need for her mother in her adult life has been unhealthy. "Until I was forty-two, I could not have continued to exist if my mother had died. She was my lifeline."

According to Judith Viorst, "Loss can dwell within us all our life."[33] And when it does, it colors the entire emotional landscape of our lives.

WHEN YOU MUST LEAVE A YOUNG CHILD . . .

What can you, as a sensitive mother, do when you must, at times, leave your young children?
• Explain what's going to occur, even though a child under two or three will have trouble understanding that you will return.
• Tell your child good-bye and hold him. If possible, be matter-of-

fact and cheerful. *Never* slip away without letting him see you; this will heighten his distress.

- Spend face time with your child when you return and listen to his verbal and nonverbal messages. Hold and comfort him until he's ready to leave your lap.
- If he is clinging, angry, or inconsolable, understand that the separation has been hard for him and that it's a sign he loves you and needs you. Be patient as you work to reestablish an emotional connection.
- Try to minimize separations during the first three years, especially those longer than a few days. Why not take your baby or young child with you?
- When you leave your child for hours or days, always leave him with someone he knows and loves, never with a stranger. Make an attempt to provide him with a loving and consistent caregiver, since he suffers when baby-sitters he loves quit and move on.
- Monitor the impact of your daily separations, especially in the first year. If you must work outside your home, opt for part-time, flex-time, or tag-team parenting.

The evidence shows that our physical and emotional presence is as essential for our babies and young children as food, air, or water. "At first I, too, was uninformed of the cost of separation," wrote Barbara Latterner about separation from her baby, Emily. "Frightened by the intensity of her response to my absence, I gave heed to her cues. Ashamed that my insensitivity to her needs had caused her such pain, I refused to impose further separation. *I stopped listening to the voices of those who cautioned against dependency, and I began listening to my heart*" (italics mine).[34]

Indeed.

CHAPTER 8

The Power *to* Impart Faith

When Stacey, twenty-nine, was in elementary school, she worked hard on Saturday mornings. In addition to cleaning up her room, she and her siblings had three hours of family chores to complete. Some Saturdays she mowed the lawn, raked leaves, baked bread, or washed the hardwood floors. After Stacey finished her chores, her mother gave her a weekly allowance of four dollars. Soon Stacey had saved fourteen dollars, a tidy sum to this young girl; it meant some candy and a movie or trinkets from a trip to the mall with her girlfriends.

One day when her mother handed her the cash, she challenged Stacey to tithe on her earnings. "Give God the first fruits of your labor," she told Stacey, "and He will bless you more than you can imagine." Inspired by her mom's words, Stacey decided to give God more than the usual 10 percent. Instead, at church the next Sunday, she put the entire fourteen dollars into the offering plate.

What happened? Within two to three weeks, checks rolled in from various relatives who didn't ordinarily send money. Stacey remembers,

"I'd go to the mailbox each afternoon with great excitement and be amazed when I tore open the envelope to see a check inside." Her total haul: eighty dollars, nearly a 600 percent return on her investment.

Now Stacey and her husband tithe faithfully. It's hard. She and Seth, who works for an accounting firm, have chosen to live on a single income. A lot of their discretionary income is spent buying their three kids things they need, like school clothes and soccer shoes. Stacey and Seth can seldom afford to go to the movies or eat dinner out. But they never consider stinting God. And He never shortchanges them. Some months may be tight, but the couple is buying a small house, thanks to a twenty-nine-thousand-dollar inheritance from Seth's grandmother, which came unexpectedly. And when they can't afford clothes for the newest addition, little Ben, doting grandparents often buy outfits or older friends offer hand-me-downs. Or Stacey shops at discount stores and consignment shops.

By God's cosmic accounting and their own, Stacey and Seth have clearly come out ahead. Both say they daily experience the truth written in Malachi 3:10: "'Bring the whole tithe into the storehouse, that there may be food in my house. Test me in this,' says the LORD Almighty, 'and see if I will not throw open the floodgates of heaven and pour out so much blessing that you will not have room enough for it.'"

And the lessons of faith, instilled early on by a God-fearing mother, have generated blessings for this young couple who live frugally and have zero credit-card debt.

IMPARTING FAITH TO YOUR CHILDREN

As a mother, you have enormous influence in your children's lives, especially in the arena of faith. For eighteen years you have a front row seat, and backstage passes for many more. These years provide you with valuable time and opportunities to teach your kids about God through Scripture, rituals, and your own all-important actions.

The Old Testament states that after Moses gave the Ten Commandments to the children of Israel, he instructed them not only to obey all of God's commands but to teach their children to fear the Lord as well. Here are Moses' words as he prepared the Israelites to possess the Promised Land:

> Hear, O Israel: the LORD our God, the LORD is one. *Love* the LORD your God with all your heart and with all your soul and with all your strength. These commandments that I give you today are to be upon your hearts. *Impress* them on your children. *Talk* about them when you sit at home and when you walk along the road, when you lie down and when you get up. *Tie* them as symbols on your hands and bind them on your foreheads. *Write* them on the doorframes of your houses and on your gates. (Deuteronomy 6:4-9, italics mine)

Notice that Moses' language is rich in verbs: *love, impress, talk, tie, write.* These are action words, indicating that we're to be proactive in imparting our faith to our children. And our daily lives provide us with ample opportunities to do this.

Caitlin James, a thirty-two-year-old sales executive, says her father often took her and her sister out for breakfast on Sunday mornings and had "little devotionals" with them. "I liked it," says this attractive young woman with long brown hair. "I especially liked hanging out with my dad."

She adds: "For years my mother led a Bible study for women. During the summers, my sister and I would go, even after I went to college. We chose to; Mom didn't make us. We loved hearing her teach. She always used a lot of real-life examples."

We are to teach our children about God in the car, at the park, as we take walks, bake cookies, camp out, go shopping, play sports. I'm not suggesting that we take a robotic approach to this but that we seize teachable moments throughout the day. Judy Dungan, a St. Louis mother of three, says, "We use everyday living opportunities to teach our children about faith. Around the dinner table we discuss various situations and how a Christian should react. We're not real good about a specific family devotion time, but we are good at using situations for teaching. We also pray about being a witness to others."

Judy said that one night she, Mark, her husband, and seven-year-old Mark Jr. were coming home from a birthday party. Some of Mark Jr.'s friends were in the car. "The other kids were using words like *stupid* and *butt*," says Judy. "Then Mark Jr. turned around and said that we didn't use those words in our family. I told him later that I was proud of him for standing up and saying that."

Northern Virginia mom Carlie Dixon, who has three sons, agrees that mothers need to seize teachable moments. "At our house, we talk about praising God. What does that mean? To be kind, to be honest, not to take anything that isn't yours, to be respectful to adults. My son Peter knows the Ten Commandments by heart, and he has them in his room."

What a child inscribes on his heart will become foundational for his belief system as he grows into manhood.

When my girls were very young, I read aloud from a children's Bible storybook that is now out of print. Then we graduated to *The Children's Bible*, published by Golden Press. Young children under five will enjoy *The Beginner's Bible*, which has timeless stories told by Karen Henley. For children ages five to eleven, Robert Morgan's Gold Medallion winner, *The Child's Daily Devotional Bible*, is a must. Little ones and growing children alike profit from hearing us read all the wonderful Bible stories about Noah, David, Abraham, Moses, Ruth, Esther, and other biblical greats. Through their triumphs and heartbreaking mistakes we learn how to follow and love the Lord.

THE POWER OF RITUALS

In addition to teaching your children about God through Scripture and the power of words, you can help their journey toward faith by establishing family rituals. It's important to supplement Bible reading by attending church together. Most of the women interviewed for this book felt that family involvement in church was essential. For example, Margie Johnson, mother of six, said, "We take our children to church right from the time they are born. And they stay with us during the three hours we meet on Sundays. That way, our children know from the start that faith is an important part of our lives."

Another mother, Ann Gadanyi, says she and her husband feel that worshiping God is so important that they attend daily mass. "Faith in God is such an integral part of our lives," says Gadanyi, "that I don't want Emily and Juliana to think it's something we set aside for Sundays. It's something we live each day. When we wake up, our first impulse of the day is to worship together. So we all go to mass as a family at 8:45 A.M." It's only after they return home that Ann begins home-schooling her children.

Our family has always attended church together, and both girls were involved in the high school church youth group. I felt this was important because my own mother, tired from her full-time employment, didn't attend church with me. Sunday was the day she cleaned our apartment. I can remember going to church alone, dressed in my best Sunday dresses, black Mary Janes, and white cotton gloves. Fortunately, next-door neighbors took an interest in my spiritual well-being and drove me to church for a while, but the morning I went forward to commit my life to Jesus Christ, no family member was present. That was a lonely experience for me.

Never underestimate the power of your presence as you sit in the pew with your children. You serve as a role model who says by her actions, "Worship is important to me," and shows her child that faith is best lived out in the community of other believers.

One regret I have is that Don and I didn't attend Sunday school ourselves or take the girls on early Sunday mornings. We chose to sleep in. So Holly and Kristen missed out on the richness of that experience, though it was in Sunday school that I learned the order of the books of the Bible and heard all those compelling Bible stories about the great men and women of God.

A young friend who volunteers as a leader for Pioneer Girls, a national outreach program for elementary schoolchildren, said recently, "It's important for children to learn about God from as many people as possible—their parents, other adults at church, friends' parents. It strengthens the impact of Christianity on their young lives." So get your children involved in Boys Brigade, Pioneer Girls, AWANAS—all those Christian organizations that have programs in churches across the country to mold children's values at an early age.

In addition to reading the Bible daily with your children and attending church, it's important to make praying with them a daily habit. Heidi Brennan says, "We pray together every night as a family, and the older children are very comfortable with this. We didn't make the eighteen-month-old kneel, but one day he simply fell to his knees. And we always say grace, even at McDonald's. Sometimes the baby will come up after everyone has eaten, and I'll hear 'anya, anya, anya,' which is his way of saying 'amen' as he pats his hands together."

One of my favorite memories is of praying with each child just before she dropped off to sleep at night. After a nightly conversation in the dark, our sleepy voices would intone our prayers. Sometimes when I got up to leave, I was reminded of what sixteenth-century theologian Martin Luther said: "It is amazing that a poor human creature is able to speak with God's high majesty in heaven and not be afraid."[1] How good it feels to climb up into the heart of God with our children and thereby teach them that prayer is as vital as breathing. As we make prayer an essential part of child rearing, our children will feel free to come to us spontaneously to ask us to pray for a soccer match, an exam, or a painful relationship with a friend.

LET'S WALK OUR TALK

Finally, we need to make sure that our lives—our choices, words, actions—are congruent with what we say we believe, since children are aware of any dissonance. We need to walk our talk, or else all that we say will fall on deaf ears.

"My dad always encouraged me to think, 'What would Christ do in this situation?'" says Joanna Rice, a single thirty-two-year-old economist who lives in Virginia. "During our dinner conversations we talked about Christ's life and what we were called to do." Joanna listened to what her father and mother said about faith, because they were devout Quakers who lived lives full of integrity. "We spent a lot of weekends on our boat, and Dad would always stop to help those who needed it, even if it meant an hour and a half of towing them back to shore. He'd always refuse payment, too, even though some people were quite aggressive about trying to give him money."

Since Joanna's parents were actively engaged in helping others, when they talked about living lives of compassion, she didn't dismiss them. She listened.

On the other hand, a man whose father was a minister said it hurt his own journey of faith to have a father "who trivialized Christianity." This minister father never prayed with his only son except to say grace at meals. "I was never sure my dad actually believed the words he said in his sermons," said this sixty-year-old businessman.

At the opposite end of the spectrum are those parents who live out their faith, even when it costs them a great deal and they're hurting. Says Caitlin, "My parents always acted with integrity. When I was a teenager, my parents were taken advantage of by business associates. They lost everything: their house, their savings, the car. It was a really hard time, but they prayed for peace and asked for grace that they wouldn't become bitter. To this day, even though they're still digging their way out of debt, they're friends with one of the people who hurt them. That's amazing to see. It's real forgiveness in action."

LET'S GET SPECIFIC

Here are some practical suggestions on how to improve your family's spiritual life:

- Establish a family quiet time. Assign a different child to read Scripture out loud each morning or evening. Ask your kids what they learned from the biblical passage and how they can apply its teaching to their lives. As your kids translate eternal principles into solutions for dilemmas, they will grasp the relevance of the Bible for all ages.
- Keep a prayer list—missionaries, friends and their problems, people who need to come to know God, family goals and needs. Monitor answers to prayer; write them down and date them so your children can see God at work and remember His deeds.
- Frame important verses and hang them in your kids' rooms so they can look at them daily.
- Buy or make little cards with individual Bible verses. Encourage your children to memorize Scripture, and reward them for doing so.
- Use life as a morality lesson. Discuss how to handle possible transgressions of God's laws that arise in your child's life and your own, whether the issue is clear-cut or ambiguous. What does God think about cheating, shoplifting, underage drinking, and sexual temptation, and why?
- Bring up spiritual matters with your children. Ask them how they stand with God and what would help them on their journey of faith.
- Make sure your own life mirrors the qualities you want your child to emulate. If you need to make changes, do so: Curb an angry temper, edit out the words and phrases you wouldn't want your child repeating, spend your time doing the things you think are

worthy and pleasing to God. Children learn more from what we do than from what we say.

- Use downtime—long car trips, family days, vacations—to sing praise songs, read Bible stories, memorize the books of the Bible or the Ten Commandments.
- Help your teenager find a youth group or Bible study he likes. Listen to his comments and complaints, and be responsive. It's okay for a child to dislike choir but love weekend soccer matches with church pals. There are many excellent Christian organizations for youth and college students, such as Young Life, Youth for Christ, Campus Crusade, Youth with a Mission, and Fellowship of Christian Athletes. Help your child find a group where he feels comfortable and can thrive among fellow Christians.
- Help build a house with Habitat for Humanity. Interacting with families that need real, practical help in the form of shelter can be an eye-opening experience for children from middle- and upper-class families.
- Save for a trip to the Holy Land. Walk where Jesus walked, taught, and suffered. This will bring the Scriptures to life for you and your child. Many churches offer study programs and two-week tours of the places where Jesus performed miracles and engaged in His ministry. You may find yourself wondering why you didn't journey to Jerusalem years ago.

We serve as lights in a dark world, not only to our neighbors but also to our children. Through our words, priorities, and actions we show our kids a lot about the state of our own spiritual lives and what we believe about God.

Is God worthy of our submission? Is He a loving God? Can I trust Him with all my needs and desires? Are His teachings relevant in a complex, morally bewildering age? How does God want me to handle money? These are questions we answer through our words, actions, and choices.

IF OUR CHILDREN HAVEN'T YET COME TO FAITH

What about those sons and daughters who aren't yet believers? Some of us, after we've taken our children to Sunday school and church, and after we've read the Bible and prayed for them for years, must wait patiently for our children to come to the place where they surrender their hopes, dreams, and lives to God. Jane Whitman, a fifty-nine-year-old writer and editor who lives in Asheville, North Carolina, is the mother of two grown sons she respects and admires. One is an airline pilot, and the other works for an ad agency.

Jane says that she has a "rich" relationship with both sons, who call her weekly. "They share their thoughts, lives, and dreams with me, and they're interested in my writing, my life." She adds that she prayed for her sons when they were young and she prays for them now. As for sharing her faith, Jane believes that once a mother has done all she can she must respect her children and trust in the sovereignty of God. "You can't hound your children to death. Once you've done your work it's up to the Holy Spirit to draw them to the Lord." She adds: "In terms of imparting our faith to our children, there are no formulas, no pat answers. It's a process. Ultimately, it's all about God's power and His ability to work in our children's lives."

As we wait for our children to come to faith, we must never forget that we cannot see the whole picture. Sometimes we have no idea what God is doing in our children's lives. During those times when we "walk in darkness without a gleam of light," we have to rely on God, who loves our children dearly. And we have no idea how our lives, our spirituality, will influence those who come after us.

Recently, Don and I were invited to the State Department, along with a number of other people, to see Phil Lader sworn in by Vice President Al Gore as the new American ambassador to the Court of St.

James. This is America's most prestigious ambassadorship. Phil's wife, Linda, has been a friend of mine for many years. As Linda and their two daughters stood beside Phil, listening attentively, he spoke about the honor conferred on him by his country. Then he added that he and his family were experiencing this blessing in some measure because of the faith of their parents. He mentioned Linda's father, the late Len LeSourd, who once worked as an editor for *Guideposts*; Linda's stepmother, the late Catherine Marshall; and last, but not least, Linda's stepgrandmother, also deceased, who was the prototype for the character of Christy in Marshall's novel by the same name. It was exciting and moving to watch CNN's cameras roll and to hear Phil give credit to the faith of those who had lived before and had prayed earnestly for him and Linda.

In the arena of faith, the blessings of the generations roll on.

CHAPTER 9

The Power
to Hone a Conscience

T he three boys came to steal a Big-Wheel tricycle; they stayed
to hit, kick, and punch a vulnerable five-week-old baby who
slept peacefully in his bassinet. The baby, whose parents were
shopping, was in the care of an eighteen-year-old stepsister who happened to be in the bathroom when the boys pushed open the unlocked
front door. She didn't hear them enter. She didn't hear them beat the
baby, nor did she see the boys grab the Big-Wheel and flee. Fortunately, a neighbor saw the boys leave the house and reported them to
the police. And if the baby, little Ignacio Bermudez Jr., should die,
these three boys—two of whom are eight, and one is six—may be the
youngest defendants tried for attempted murder in California's
history.[1]

In London, two eleven-year-old boys were found guilty and sentenced to indefinite detention for the murder of a toddler. They lured
James Bulger away from his mother's side in a shopping mall, then
stoned him to death, and left his body to be run over by a train. In sen-
tencing these boys, Justice Michael Norland said that these children

had committed "an act of unparalleled evil and barbarity."[2] He also described both boys as "cunning and very wicked."

In July 1996, sixteen-year-old Billy Sovonn told a Maryland jury how he had plunged a knife into fourteen-year-old Tatia Brenman's back. As Tatia begged him to let her go, Billy's classmate stabbed her in the stomach.[3]

Our hearts reel when we read such news, hoping that each case is an anomaly. But the facts prove otherwise. Acts of youthful violence are on the upswing. From California to the East Coast, we are witnessing an unprecedented epidemic of juvenile crime. As we read or hear about each new incident of violence among our youngest citizens, we can no longer believe, if we ever did, in the guilelessness and innocence of youth. At increasingly early ages, children are committing acts of barbaric savagery that make William Golding's novel *The Lord of the Flies* look tame.

Why are we witnessing such brutality and heartlessness among some of our nation's youngest? As a psychologist, I believe such acts are motivated by weak or absent parental attachments; many children who are neglected, abused, or rejected by their parents develop profound rage. For decades we, as a society, have pursued our own self-fulfillment and asked our children to rear themselves. We're about to reap a bitter harvest.

WHAT'S COMING, AMERICA?

On July 18, 1996, U.S. Senator Dan Coats chaired a Senate subcommittee on children and families in Washington, D.C., to examine solutions to juvenile crime. Experts in juvenile crime assembled to talk about how to combat this newest societal cancer.

Senator Coats opened the meeting with some disturbing statistics. He noted that between 1965 and 1992 the arrest rates for violent crimes committed by juveniles have tripled. And while arrest rates for adult homicides rose 11 percent between 1985 and 1994, the arrest rate for homicides committed by juveniles soared by 150 percent. Senator Coats spoke of the despair, anger, and rage behind this increase in juvenile violence. "The mind-set driving the violent juveniles is deeply troubling," he said. "The depth of their anger is matched only by their lack of remorse."[4]

One of the criminal justice experts who testified that day, James Fox, is a media luminary who is also dean of the College of Criminal Justice at Northeastern University in Boston. Fox has forecast crime waves for years. At the hearing, he predicted that a massive crime wave will crest in 2005, when the current bumper crop of children—some 39 million currently under ten years of age—hits adolescence.[5] This generation of children is "better armed than any generation before it" and less supervised. According to Fox, "Fifty-seven percent of children in this country lack full-time parental supervision; they are either living with a single working parent, who works full-time, or in a household where both parents work full-time."[6]

Many juvenile crimes do not occur in the dark of night or the wee hours of the morning; they occur after school. According to Fox, some 40 percent of crimes occur between 3:00 and 7:00 P.M., when no parent is at home to converse, comfort, or supervise.[7] "We have about five years to invest in these kids, to reinvest in these kids," said Fox. "And we had better act now or we will *all* be in trouble" (italics mine).[8]

CLOSE TO HOME

While most of us do not harbor a youthful offender in our homes, we do have children who walk the hallways of elementary schools or high schools. Our children are often fearful of their angry or violent peers, some of whom couple emotional unpredictability with using drugs or bearing weapons. Juvenile crime, like any crime, cuts across socioeconomic boundaries. And if James Fox is accurate, soon we will have no place to hide.

Even rural areas are not immune to this dramatic increase in juvenile crime. In rural Ohio, for example, Nancy Slaven Peters's two-and-a-half-year-old daughter was killed by two young boys, ages six and ten. This mother became so outraged when authorities refused to give her any information about her daughter's killers that she and others are now crusading to open up the traditionally secret juvenile court process.[9]

All around us the culture is unraveling, and we can't put our heads in the sand. Rather than deny what's happening to kids both here and abroad, we need to rear moral, compassionate children who can help repair our torn society. But before we look at how to instill a conscience in children, we need to define our terms.

WHAT IS CONSCIENCE?

The word *conscience* comes from the Latin word *conscientia*, meaning "to be conscious of guilt." The Hebrew word for conscience is *leb*, which is usually translated "heart" in the Old Testament. In the ancient Hebrew mind, conscience was at the core of all it meant to be human.[10] The Bible clearly indicates that conscience is an innate capacity we humans have that enables us to distinguish right from wrong. The New Testament suggests that everyone is born with a conscience that sometimes accuses, sometimes defends. It's as if the laws and requirements of God are written upon our hearts (Romans 2:15). Yet the apostle Paul indicated that it's possible to develop a moral insensitivity and hardened heart, or in other words, a deadened conscience (Ephesians 4:17-19).

So how do we develop moral sensitivity? God places us in families to help Him shape our innate, embryonic consciences.

ATTACHMENT: THE ROOT OF CONSCIENCE

Our ability to shape our children's consciences depends greatly on the strength of the emotional bond they have with us. If we've held them close since birth and given them consistent messages about their worth and our love for them, they will love us and want to please us. In *The Moral Sense*, Stanford moralist James Q. Wilson wrote that conscience "acquires its strongest development when those attachments are strongest."[11] He added, "People with the strongest conscience will not be those with the most powerfully repressed aggressiveness, but those with the most powerfully developed affiliation."[12]

Wilson believes that a child's conscience is rooted in the soil of a warm, affectionate attachment with both parents, but particularly with the mother. Simply put, because he is loved and learns to love in response, a child wants to please first his mother and then his father.[13] Later, these attachments are "expanded by the enlarged relationships of families and peers."[14] It is from this "universal attachment" with each parent that a child develops a sense of empathy, fairness, and self-control.

FIRST ATTACHMENT, THEN DISCIPLINE

Together, both parents help to plant, build, and cultivate their children's conscience. While this book is about mothering, I want to affirm that a father's presence as an authority figure in the home is extremely important for both sons and daughters. In fact, studies show that when children are reared by mother alone, they are more likely to be suspended or expelled from school, to have emotional or behavioral problems, to display antisocial behavior, and to create single-parent families themselves.[15] Fathers establish secure emotional bonds with their children so that they will want to please and obey; fathers also instruct their children in family rules and discipline them with firmness and affection. Thus, both parents play key roles in developing a moral child.

While a father usually institutes rules and discipline, a mother, by virtue of her presence, must often enforce them. Every mother of a fledgling toddler knows that she must bank on her child's innate wish to please her to control his behavior and teach him family rules. If she's too often emotionally or physically absent, she will find the "terrible twos" harder to deal with than the mother who has spent her hours and days getting to know her child and forging a warm, affectionate bond.

A friend told me about a recent power struggle with her twenty-two-month-old daughter. One day the child climbed onto the dining room table, hands akimbo on her little hips, and dared her mother to tell her to come down. "I was prepared to pick her up and put her on the floor," said her amused mother, "but she and I have quite a bond. So I told her firmly, 'Annie, get off the table, or Mommy *will* take you off.' Then I laughed. She smiled, thought for a long moment, and clambered down. 'I love you, Mommy,' she said."

As my friend, who has a secure attachment relationship with her charming daughter, has learned, she is into a new phase of child rearing—one characterized by defiance and limit-testing. This phase will ebb and flow until Annie leaves home in late adolescence. To help her shape her child's conscience, behavior, values, and will, my friend will need to learn the skills of consistency, patience, and clear communication. In addition, she and Annie's father will need to be firm and loving and apply consistent discipline across the years.

DIFFERENT PARENTING STYLES

Have you ever wondered what parents need to do to rear engaging, responsible adults?

All children need open communication, consistent discipline, warmth, and affection to become responsible people. If we're either permissive or harsh in our discipline, our children will have great difficulty controlling their behavior and thinking well of themselves.

Child-development expert Diana Baumrind, who has studied different parenting styles, assessed four dimensions of child-rearing behavior that I believe have a bearing on the development of conscience.

They are parental control, clarity of parent-child communication, maturity demands, and nurturance.[16] Baumrind defined parental control as "strict discipline"; clarity of communication as "listening to the child's opinions and giving him reasons for any punishment or restriction"; maturity demands as "parental encouragement to do well intellectually, socially, and morally—in other words, 'live up to your abilities'"; and nurturance as "parental warmth and engagement."

Basically, Baumrind identified three parenting styles: *authoritarian, authoritative*, and *permissive. Authoritarian* parents were controlling but lacked warmth and good communication skills. *Permissive* parents, on the other hand, gave plenty of nurturance and communication but demanded little of their children and therefore had little control of their offspring. *Authoritative* parents were the stars. These parents maintained high control with the kids and had high maturity demands but were also high in nurturance and clarity of communication.[17] Get the picture? Ask a lot, but also be prepared to give a lot.

How do parents get what Baumrind calls "high control"? The answer is no longer popular: discipline. Parents need to shape their children's behavior by using methods that get results. The public debate on discipline leads some parents to shun any form of corporal punishment because they're afraid of damaging their children's psyches. Now a parent has a new obstacle in implementing discipline: Some schools have begun to tell students to call 911 if they feel their parents are in any way abusive. One of my colleagues told me an amusing story about her eight-year-old son, Rick. The family had been attending an older brother's basketball game when Rick became obnoxious and surly. As she and her son headed for their car, Marcy grabbed his arm and reprimanded him.

"Don't do that," he said, jerking his arm away. "If you do that again, I'll turn you in."

"What do you mean?" she asked.

"Well, today my teacher said that we kids don't have to take any abuse from our parents. We can call 911."

"You do that," said his bemused his mother, "and you'll be finding yourself a new place to live."

Since discipline is a hot topic in our culture, it's important to clarify our terms. What do I mean by *discipline? Discipline is a firm response to your child's disobedience that produces a desired change in his or her behavior.* It can take many forms, from a simple warning to a light swat on the bottom or a harder spanking; from time-out to grounding or revoked privileges. Whatever the form, discipline should always be handed out rationally and calmly; it should be undertaken in love. It's important that as a parent you explain family rules to your child and the repercussions for breaking them. Sound logic, not anger, should drive discipline.

At this point, I need to state what discipline is not. It is *not* physical violence, such as kicking, punching, hair pulling, or beating. Nor is discipline emotional abuse such as screaming, cursing, belittling, or demeaning a child. Discipline must not be undertaken at times of great anger when wrong decisions or hurtful words can scar a child's self-esteem.

Also, discipline must be age-appropriate. It should begin when a child is quite young but vary with each age bracket. We can't expect to employ the same methods with a pre-rational toddler that we use with a verbal adolescent. And not all offenses merit the same punishment. Eating cookies before dinner is not the same as hijacking the family car for a forbidden night out. Age-appropriate discipline not only shapes behavior and teaches self-control, it is also critical to developing your child's conscience. Above all, we need to avoid harshness and inconsistency when we discipline.

A child's will only grows stronger as his or her mind and body matures. Heaven help us if we lose control of our children when they're toddlers! What we refuse to deal with when our child is two years old will assert itself with greater strength when he is three and four. A wise older friend told me, "If you create a solid foundation for discipline before your girls are six years old, you'll have a much easier time thereafter." Marty was right. We ignore our young children's bad behavior at great cost to them and to us. The book of Proverbs says, "Discipline your son, and he will give you peace; he will bring delight to your soul" (Proverbs 29:17).

How to Rear a Bully

In his bestseller *Emotional Intelligence*, psychologist Daniel Goleman wrote about a study of 870 children from upstate New York who were tracked from age eight to thirty. The most belligerent children had parents who were harsh and inconsistent in their discipline. As these boys and girls grew up, they punished their own children with severity. Goleman, who noted this cross-generational legacy, said, "The parents were not necessarily meanspirited, nor did they fail to wish the best for their children; rather, they seemed to be simply repeating the style of parenting that had been modeled for them by their own parents."[18]

Haphazard discipline creates a model for violence, says Goleman. In writing about kids who later become violent, he stated, "If their parents were in a bad mood, they would be severely punished; if their parents were in a good mood, they could get away with mayhem at home. The punishment came not so much because of what the child had done but by virtue of how the parent felt. *This is a recipe for worthlessness and helplessness and for the sense that threats are everywhere and may strike at any time*" (italics mine).[19]

In some sense, psychologists can predict future problems from early behavior. In fact, researchers have been able to forecast how teenagers will behave based on their behavior as small children. Studies show, for example, that children who are aggressive in preschool have a hard time with self-control, peer relationships, and education as teenagers. "Studies that have followed children from the preschool years into the teenage ones find that up to half of first graders who are disruptive, unable to get along with other kids, disobedient with their parents, and resistant with their teachers will become delinquents in their teen years."[20]

Patrick Fagan of the Heritage Foundation agrees. Fagan believes that the failure of a child to forge a warm and secure emotional bond with his mother early on is one of the key precursors of criminal behavior. According to Fagan, children are likely to become future criminals when they do not have an emotionally secure relationship with their mother; when they are abandoned by the father; when they have transient caregivers; when they show aggressive behavior; or when they have witnessed repeated acts of violence between their parents.

Even at age five, children may be on a trajectory for later violence and criminality. According to Fagan the future criminal is "both hyperactive and difficult to endure," often hitting his mother and others.[21] Goleman cites one study of children in a Montreal kindergarten who were rated for hostility and troublemaking. Those with the highest scores at age five had a far greater evidence of delinquency just five to eight years later, when they were in their early teens. These hostile children were about three times more likely than other children to have beaten up someone, shoplifted, stolen a car, or been drunk before the age of fourteen.[22]

WHEN TO BEGIN

How can you shape your child's conscience so that he will be a responsible, moral adult? The key is to discipline your child firmly and consistently across the years.

Psychologist Burton White says that it is important to "begin to establish a picture of solid and effective discipline during phase one (between eight and fourteen months) in order to prepare for more difficult challenges when the child is a bit older."[23] White suggests that parents of infants and toddlers repeat their messages once; if the child refuses to comply, they should move him to another situation, remove the forbidden object, or distract him. The main thing, says White, is to follow through once you insist a child stop doing something.[24] Inconsistency undermines further attempts at discipline and makes a parent's work tougher.

Whatever form of discipline you choose for your child, you need to start early and get the results you want. If the method you are using doesn't work, don't stay with it. Be pragmatic; find new tactics that work. Margie Johnson, mother of six, said she tried spanking her first daughter, who told her mom that her swats were "too soft." "Since that didn't work," said Margie, "I switched to time-outs. I would say, 'If you don't do what I say, then I'm going to pick you up and carry you to your room.' She knew I meant what I said, so she actually went herself." This is a pretty remarkable thing since Margie Johnson is a petite woman.

"We haven't had a lot of problems with discipline," Margie told me. "I credit that to the fact that I'm home to monitor my children's actions. I know their dispositions. I know what they think they can get away with. What I will allow. Basically, our kids know I'm not a punitive person but that I do have my limits. I want them to experiment and explore within wide limits. However, they know that if I make a limit, I mean it."

Kristie Tamillow, mother of a thirteen-year-old son and an eleven-year-old daughter, agrees that children need firm limits and consistent discipline. "When my children were young, they got spankings. I made sure there were limits. So much of your conscience has to do with whether there are really sound limits and boundaries. That's when your children learn, 'Well, I can't go past that line.'"

Kristie told me a story about her son, Matt, to illustrate the effectiveness of firm but loving discipline.

When Matt was six, he loved Hot Wheels, and I could tell that he wanted this little boy's Hot Wheel that he played with on a regular basis. I could tell this was a real temptation for him. One day after we had been over at his friend's house, this little boy was missing some toy cars. I knew my son had taken them. So I went to him and I said, "Matt, I'm going to ask you some questions, and I need you to be really honest because if you're not honest, you're going to get in trouble. But if you are honest, you won't get in any trouble whatsoever." And I asked him if he took the Hot Wheels, and he thought about it and said, "Yes." I said to him, "Well, we have to make this right."

I really wanted to leave a lasting impression on my child. And I knew that to do that, rather than just punishing him, I needed to make him accountable. So I said to him, "You will have to go to Mrs. Steskins (the little boy's mother) and tell her what you've done and ask her to forgive you, and then you need to give the Hot Wheels back to her son." And he pleaded, "Can't I just give them to *him*?" I said, "No, you have to give them to her." So he got them out and gave them back, and I've never had another serious character issue with him.

WHAT ABOUT SPANKING?

Since I've raised the issue of spanking, I want to deal with it forthrightly. Of all forms of discipline, spanking is surely the most controversial; it serves as a lightning rod for media and public criticism. In the popular mind, spanking has even become equated with child abuse. During the writing of this book, I appeared on the *Diane Rehm Show*, a syndicated radio program, to debate a psychologist who had written a diatribe against spanking. The blurb on his book implied that any parent who spanked his child was a potential child abuser or murderer. Now, spanking is *not* my hot topic—attachment is—but I felt that the author was wrong to link *all* spanking categorically with child abuse, so I agreed to appear with him.

I had a rousing hour. The author, who had joked about the Religious Right upon entering the studio, railed against corporal punishment of any kind. And he kept saying, "I just don't understand how Dr. Hunter could say that." I tried to present my point of view calmly and rationally: Sometimes it's appropriate to spank a defiant younger child. I also knew something about this man. I had read his book and learned that he'd had a physically abusive father. As a therapist I believe this psychologist has made a *cause célèbre* out of his own woundedness. I chose not make this connection on the air, but I also did not allow his views to go unopposed.

Ironically, when used correctly, spanking works as well or better than other forms of discipline. By defining spanking as abusive, we rob parents of an effective means of disciplining and controlling younger children. The book of Proverbs clearly supports the idea of corporal punishment:

> The rod of correction imparts wisdom, but a child left to himself disgraces his mother. (Proverbs 29:15)

> Folly is bound up in the heart of a child, but the rod of discipline will drive it far from him. (Proverbs 22:15)

The idea that children's behavior may sometimes need to be shaped by corporal punishment is centuries old. As for the current rhetoric that links spanking to child abuse, Harvard psychologist Burton White observed:

> Firmness does not mean abuse. . . . There is no evidence that children who have been spanked (not abused) when they were young become either aggressive older children or abusive parents. Indeed, the long-term research to test this thesis has never been done. Nevertheless, I can state that some two-thirds of successful families we have observed from all levels of society have used occasional mild

physical punishment with their children after they entered the second year.[25]

Psychologist Diana Baumrind says that the "notion that children can or should be raised without using aversive discipline . . . is utopian."[26] She does, however, advocate the "judicious use of physical punishment." According to Baumrind, most parents spank their preschoolers occasionally, but the use of physical punishment tapers off by age nine. Then, only a third of parents spank their children as often as once a month. And by adolescence, physical punishment is rare.[27]

What about those experts and parents who argue that logic is enough? White states that simply explaining what you want may not be enough for a young child; rational explanations do not work at all with toddlers because they simply lack the linguistic ability to understand all a parent is saying.[28] Baumrind concurs; she believes that simply reasoning with a young child without "the display of power" teaches the child that his parent is indecisive.[29] So it's important to insist on obedience. Otherwise, you're wasting your breath and teaching your children that you are wishy-washy and not to be heeded.

Please understand that I am *not* advocating hitting babies who don't comprehend the meaning of the word "no" and who are too young to defy a parent. But when our children reach the age of fifteen to eighteen months, they understand "no." If they can be moved to another place or distracted, so be it. But when a three-year-old puts her hands on her hips and defies her mother, smirking, a single swat on the bottom and a repeated "no" may get good results.

I spanked my girls when they were young. When the spanking was over, I held them on my lap and explained why their defiance merited swift punishment. Then I told my children I loved them and they would need to learn to obey me. As they grew, I switched to other means of discipline, but none proved as uncomplicated as a simple spanking.

Was I a child abuser? No. Did I ruin my children? No. I tried to mold their behavior and their consciences, teaching them right from wrong, by disciplining defiant behavior so they would grow up to be law-abiding, self-controlled, honest people. That has happened. Therefore, I believe that spanking can be an effective tool. It should, however, be used wisely and infrequently and never when a parent is angry or uncontrolled.

AS CHILDREN GROW OLDER

Of course, as children grow older, they can begin to experience the consequences of their actions in other ways. We can begin to allow them to experience the results of their wrongdoing as early as five, six, or seven years old; when they become adolescents, this may be the best way to discipline them.

According to psychiatrist William Glasser, who wrote the international bestseller *Reality Therapy*, a child needs to learn at home and at school to be a responsible individual early on.[30] Glasser used an example from his own life to illustrate his point. One night Glasser asked his five-year-old son if he wanted to splash and play in the family's big tub. After saying no, the little boy said he'd prefer playing in his smaller tub. "He wanted to assert his independence of our wishes, a very common but trying five-year-old characteristic," says Glasser. At this point, the boy's ten-year-old sister shed her clothes and popped into the big tub. "Immediately the five-year-old started to scream that he really wanted to bathe in it himself," wrote Glasser. So what did this father do? He picked up "fifty pounds of tantrum" and placed his son in his own small tub where he continued to wail. Then Glasser told his son, "Let me give you some advice. Do you know what advice is?" When the boy said yes, his father taught him a golden truth, "Never say 'no' when you mean 'yes.'"[31]

According to Glasser, if we want to rear a responsible child, we must first be responsible parents who are emotionally engaged with our children. In referring to the bathtub incident, Glasser wrote about his son, "If I had given in to his tantrum, he would have learned nothing. In his attempts to find out if I really cared, he judged me first by what I did, then by what I said, much as all psychiatric patients do with their therapist."[32]

Don and I believed in letting the girls experience the consequences of their actions once they entered grade school. One day, when Kristen was seven years old, she told me that she had cheated on a test. Kristen felt guilty because of what she had done. Don and I decided that the best course of action was for Kristen to call her teacher and tell her what had happened. Trembling, Kristen dialed the teacher's number and said, "Mrs. Newton, I'm calling to say I cheated on the test today. I copied an answer from Candace's paper."

As we had hoped, the teacher handled Kristen beautifully. She thanked Krissy for the call, then said, "I know that other children cheat, but you're the first to call and confess. Thank you for your honesty and courage." I've always felt that this experience was important in helping Kristen become a more responsible human.

Later, when Holly was seventeen, she got a speeding ticket. Just as her sister had paid for library fines out of her allowance, so Holly paid for the ticket from the earnings of her part-time job. These examples may sound pretty simple, but I know parents who continue to pay for their children's mistakes, year after year. Even when their kids are adults, parents send in balances due, only to have their adult children max out credit cards again. Other parents bail kids out of jail only to have them break the law again. And still others buy their children new cars when their previous cars were totaled under suspicious circumstances. The result? These children never really grow up and assume responsibility for their lives.

TEACHING TEENS ABOUT CONSEQUENCES

In *Parenting Teens with Love and Logic*, psychiatrist Foster Cline and educator Jim Fay challenge parents to allow their teens to experience the consequences of their actions by allowing them to "hurt from the inside out."[33] Cline and Foster believe that "the best solution for any problem lies within the skin of the person who owns the problem."[34] To illustrate their point, the writers describe the following scenario:

Phil's seventeen-year-old daughter, Tiffany, comes home with alcohol on her breath. Should Phil talk to her about it immediately or in the morning? *Morning.* With anger or sadness? *Sadness.*

"Oh, I felt so sorry for you last night," Phil says the following morning. "I smelled alcohol on your breath. I'm starting to worry about you and alcohol. What would you guess about using the family car right now?"

"I guess I might not get to use it," Tiffany replies.

"Good thinking," Phil says.

Did Phil set a limit? Yes. Is Tiffany going to try to talk him out of it? Absolutely. Can she? No. Because no matter what Tiffany says, Phil can say, "Probably so."

"But I won't do it again," Tiffany begs.

"Probably so."

"Well, all the other kids get to do it."

"Probably so."

"Well," says Tiffany, trying to draw her father into an argument, "so you've got a big problem over alcohol, Dad, and now I can't drive and I've got to look like a dork at school because—"

"Probably so."

"Well," she persists, "how am I supposed to get to work at the jewelry shop?"

Now Tiffany's trying to give her problem to her dad.

If Phil gives her an answer, will she like it? No. It would be better for Phil to say, "I don't know. I was going to ask you the same thing."

"Well, I'll get fired!"

"Probably so."

Phil knows that if he gets angry with Tiffany, he will strip the consequences of her drinking of their power. By expressing anger he will insert himself into the process and impede the logic of the consequences from taking effect. By using "probably so" and keeping the focus on the effects of drinking and driving, Phil prevented Tiffany from focusing her anger on him. Instead, she was continually forced into facing the lesson taught by the consequences of her drinking.[35]

Because of the way this father handled his teenager, I believe she will think twice about drinking and driving again. As a parent, I would take the discussion further and address the legality and morality of drinking—the girl was under age, thereby breaking the law, and this becomes a moral issue. At each level there are consequences for Tiffany to consider.

LEARNING TO OBEY GOD

One thing is certain: If our kids won't obey us, they'll have a tough time obeying God. Years ago I discovered a book at the Library of Congress, long out of print. It was entitled *Marriage to a Difficult Man* by Elizabeth Dodds and chronicled the marriage of Jonathon and Sarah Edwards, which produced eleven accomplished children. Jonathon Edwards was a famous Puritan clergyman and theologian who lived in the 1700s. He was at the forefront of the Great Awakening, a religious movement that began in New England in the 1730s and swept the American colonies.

According to Dodds, Sarah was a disciplinarian who spoke once, and her children obeyed. We parents of the nineties, accustomed to truculent toddlers and snarling adolescents, would marvel at such a response in our own children. So how did Sarah Edwards do it? By treating her children with love and respect. Her "system of discipline was begun at a very early age and it was her rule to resist the first, as well as every subsequent exhibition of temper or disobedience in the child."[36] Her motivation? She believed "that until a child will obey his parents, he will never be brought to obey God."[37]

One of the most sobering accounts of parental discipline gone awry is related in the Old Testament in the book of 1 Samuel. The corpulent priest Eli had renegade sons, Hophni and Phinehas, who had "no regard for the Lord." They treated the sacrifices offered to God with contempt and were sexually promiscuous. Poor Eli. When he heard about his sons' contemptible behavior, he rebuked them. But it was too late. They were adults who did not listen. So what did God do? Because Eli "failed to restrain" his sons, God told him they would die on that same day and that God would judge Eli's family forever. No longer would they serve the Lord as priests. Moreover, all of Eli's descendants would die in the prime of life.[38] That was bad news for Eli and his descendents indeed. This account shows that God does not take the area of parental discipline lightly.

THE POWER OF STORIES

Discipline becomes easier if we begin to teach our children positive values and principles when they are very young. And what better way to instill virtue than through the power of story? When our children are young, we can read great literature with them and let the content of the stories help to mold and shape their character. The phenomenal success of William Bennett's *Book of Virtues* attests to the fact that millions of parents recognize that stories can have a powerful influence on children.

William Kilpatrick, professor of education at Boston College and author of *Why Johnny Can't Tell Right from Wrong*, says, "Stories help make sense of our lives; they also create a desire to be good."[39] Plato, one of the world's most famous moralists, thought that children should be brought up in such a way that they would fall in love with virtue. He believed that stories and histories were keys to sparking that desire. According to Kilpatrick, Plato felt that no amount of discussion or dialogue could compensate if the desire to embrace morality was missing.[40]

What are some stories that can inspire your child's desire to be good? Kilpatrick suggests that beginning readers start with *Aesop's Fables, Beauty and the Beast*, and *The Children's Bible in 365 Stories* by Mary B. Atchelor. Other fine books are *The Children's Homer: The Adventures of Odysseus and the Tale of Troy*, and Laura Ingalls Wilder's *Little House in the Big Woods*, among others.

For middle-school readers, Kilpatrick recommends Anna Sowell's *Black Beauty*, Carol Ryrie Brink's *Caddie Woodlawn*, C. S. Lewis's *The Chronicles of Narnia*, Johanna Spyri's *Heidi*, and Esther Forbes's *Johnny Tremain*, to name a few.

Kilpatrick encourages older readers to sample Mark Twain's *Huckleberry Finn*, Rudyard Kipling's *Captain Courageous*, and Jack London's *Call of the Wild*. For fun, he recommends Frank Gilbraith Jr.'s *Cheaper by the Dozen*. These are the years to enjoy J. R. R. Tolkien's *The Hobbit*, Louisa May Alcott's *Little Women*, and Herman Melville's *Moby Dick*. Kilpatrick also includes one of my favorites in his list: Fred Gipson's *Old Yeller*, as well as books I once taught to my high school students: Charles Dickens's *Oliver Twist* and *Great Expectations*.

WE ARE OUR KIDS' BEST ROLE MODELS

A final thought. None of our tutelage really works if we fail to model self-control, honesty, morality, and integrity before our children. As psychiatrist William Glasser said, "Parents who have no self-discipline cannot successfully discipline a child."[41] Since we are the most powerful role models in our children's lives, we need to examine our own consciences and hearts daily before God to see how we may have violated His rules for living responsible, honest lives. Know this: All of our rebellions affect our children. If, as single mothers, we sleep with our boyfriends, it will do little good to tell our teenagers to be chaste. If we cheat on our income tax or fail to pay the full tab at a restaurant or store because somebody made a mistake in our favor, then telling a child not to steal will sound false to him. Conversely, each time we own up to our shortcomings, our children learn how to correct their misdeeds.

Your children are cognizant of your moral triumphs and failures. And because they model their behavior after yours, their ship is torpedoed each time you take the easy way out. I've talked to numerous mothers who were sexually immoral in the sixties and seventies who later had daughters follow in their footsteps. One mother recently "celebrated" the fourth marriage of her thirty-five-year-old daughter. The daughter lived with each man before she married him and conceived a child out of wedlock. The mother, a sixties hell-raiser turned conservative suburbanite, expressed considerable regret for her past.

Holly and Kristen have sometimes been vulnerable to temptation in those areas where Don and I have been weakest, and strongest in areas where we would not compromise. I've learned from hard experience that to hone my child's conscience I must first work on my own. I've failed many times to be an exemplary mother. At those times I confess my failures and sins to God, asking Him to forgive me and put me on my feet again. Then I go to my children and work things through with them.

And when your children come to you to confess their wrongdoing? Listen, forgive, and help them make restitution if necessary. It's not wise to get angry, judgmental, and say cruel things. Rather, hear them out, ask where they feel they went astray, and help them plan any restitution. Then they will grow strong in those areas where formerly they were weak.

"HOMELESS, HEARTHLESS, LAWLESS, STATELESS"

Successful parents rear kids who possess a well-developed conscience amid a sea of kids without a conscience. The latter are those unattached souls who, never having been close to either mother or father, may wreak havoc in our culture in the coming years. In Homer's chilling words, they are truly "homeless, hearthless, lawless, stateless." Even though these unattached kids without a conscience will run amok, you can rear children who work to mend a battered and torn society. What a challenge! But they will become those who "stand in the breach," helping to restore our nation. As mothers, we are makers of the men and women who can confront the coming generations with love and righteousness.

CHAPTER 10

The Power
to Create Empathy

In the summer of 1942, Shmulek, a Jewish boy of twelve who had been hiding in a squalid ghetto for two months, suddenly appeared at the home of a Polish peasant woman named Balwina. "For heaven's sake, what are you doing here?" she asked. "It's very dangerous. Where did you come from? Hurry, come on in."

After Balwina heard the boy's story, dried his tears, and fed him, she hid him in her attic for several days. Then she gave him a new name, Jusek Polewski, and taught him the Polish catechism and how to read Polish. Later, Balwina masterminded his survival by helping him hire himself out to Polish peasants. This boy who survived the Holocaust later became a professor of sociology at Humboldt State University in California. Along with his wife, Pearl, Shmulek, who has taken the Americanized name Samuel Oliner, wrote a book called *The Altruistic Personality* about ordinary men and women like Balwina who risked their lives for their Jewish neighbors.[1] Men and women who were empathic toward their suffering neighbors.

Oh, the power of empathy. How we need the intuitive

understanding and help of others when we stand at the edge of a precipice. I know. Months ago I began an unplanned experiment on the subject of empathy. It happened this way. On Good Friday I went to bed after the evening service, eager for sleep. I rolled over, casually touched my right breast, and felt a large, hard lump. Instantly jarred from a state of sleepiness to sheer terror, I nudged my husband and asked him to feel my breast. "Do you feel a lump," I whispered, "or is it my imagination?" Slowly Don said, "Yes, there's a lump there." Needless to say, I hardly slept that night or subsequent nights.

Struggling to contain my terror until Monday morning, I called my gynecologist's office at 9:00 A.M., only to learn that she was on vacation. Her partner agreed to see me and ordered a mammogram. It confirmed what I already knew—the lump was large, hard, and movable. With a sinking heart, I listened as the radiologist told me that my lump was in the upper right quadrant of my breast where about 50 percent of all breast cancers occur. Not a comforting thought! Later that week the surgeon told me he was pretty sure the lump was malignant.

As I told friends and family about my predicament, I received a wide variety of responses, ranging from denial and gallows humor to sympathy and concern. Exquisitely vulnerable to whatever people said, I flinched at the negative responses and desperately mined all others for some degree of hope and encouragement.

The worst comment came from a woman who should have known better. A physician, she palpated my breast and said quietly, "Hmmm, this looks suspicious. By the time a lump has gotten this large, it has usually metastasized."

"Don't say that," I groaned. "Can't you give me a little hope?"

Grudgingly she added, "Well, it's movable," meaning, I later learned, that the tumor had not eaten into the chest wall. By the time I left her office, I was beside myself. Referral slip in hand, I stumbled to my car only to find a twenty-five-dollar ticket on the windshield. Since Holly was at the university, I called Kristen as soon as I got home. My sweet, lovely girl, seven months pregnant, agreed to accompany me to the radiologist. Then I called a close friend to give her the news. She was preoccupied with her own concerns and detached. Well, I didn't need that, so I hung up and in despair went to the kitchen to prepare some lunch. My husband was somewhere between our home and Charlotte, North Carolina, driving my mother back after her Easter visit; I remembered that he wouldn't call until later that night.

I soon heard Kristen's car drive up our driveway. My warm and empathetic daughter prayed for me, bestowing a comforting presence.

During those terrifying days, I experienced anew the reality that hope is fragile. Without thinking, a person can squash it, like the one who cheerily said, "Well, at least you're not dead yet." In retrospect, I understand that some people simply didn't know what to say. Fortunately, there were also kind friends who fortified me for the battle ahead and invariably strengthened my hope. Shirley, who had breast cancer and a radical mastectomy over twenty years ago, told me, "I understand how you feel. I was tormented during that period of waiting. But then one day I felt the peace of the Lord settle on my shoulders, and I knew that whatever happened I would be okay." What a gift! As I hung up the phone, I had my first peaceful sleep in days, for I had internalized the thought that God could give me the same reassurance He gave Shirley—that I, too, would be okay.

I KNOW HOW YOU FEEL

What is empathy, and why do some humans seem to have an abundance of this quality, while others are clueless? Empathy is a complex human emotion that bears explaining. The best definition I have encountered is offered by psychoanalyst Heinz Kohut, who defines empathy as "the capacity to *think* and *feel* oneself into the inner life of another person" (italics mine).[2]

Empathy, then, is the capacity to participate in other people's feelings, even when their experiences are foreign to our own. We do this with a complex emotional response to another's pain that has two parts to it: a feeling (affective) component and a thinking (cognitive) component. The feeling aspect of empathy refers to our inner capacity to respond to another's joy, fear, or distress. The thinking, or cognitive, aspect consists of understanding the other person's perspective and discerning his emotional state, or role-taking.[3]

While a child's rational capacity for empathy is nurtured in his early experience of mothering, the feeling part of empathy is innate. Even day-old babies cry sympathetically when they hear another baby cry. Sympathetic feelings and responses are the earliest expression of empathy and become the foundation for what the experts call "pro-social behavior." It's the cognitive component of empathy that develops as we mature.

Martin Hoffman, a noted child-development expert, pinpoints three stages a child progresses through as he develops his capacity for empathy. In stage one, a child has a global feeling of discomfort that exists when others—mom, dad, another child—are distressed. This stage occurs between one and two years of age as children begin to form a sense of self and realize they are separate and distinct from others. But even our youngest can make wise decisions based on empathic feelings. For example, a thirteen-month-old can fetch his mom to comfort his friend who is in distress.[4]

When a child reaches two years of age, the second stage begins. At this point, he can begin to understand that others possess different emotions than he does. He can put himself in another person's place and even begin to offer aid.[5] A two-year-old who sees his mommy cry, for example, will often say, "Mommy cry. Poor Mommy," and run to fetch a Kleenex.

Hoffman believes that children enter a new stage of maturation between ages six and nine. At stage three, children can empathize with another's joy or sorrow and also express sensitivity to the poor, the handicapped, and the socially needy.[6]

ATTACHMENT SECURITY AND EMPATHY

Heinz Kohut believes that children begin to develop, or fail to develop, the capacity for empathy in infancy based on the way their mothers respond to their cries. If a mother panics and withdraws when her baby cries, then her baby is deprived of the experience of her comforting presence and feeling her move from mild anxiety to calmness. If this happens too many times, the child may wall himself off, develop an "impoverished psychic organization"—a fragile inner core—and have difficulty expressing empathy to others.[7] Responding to a baby's cries is not only important for attachment security but for development of empathy. On a positive note, Kohut also believes that adults can correct early deprivation and privation by finding a therapist who provides the "empathic resonance" he or she failed to experience in childhood.[8]

Our capacity for empathy, like our feelings about intimacy, is rooted in our earliest attachment relationships. And once again, emotional security is a huge asset. According to author and clinical psychologist Robert Karen, the securely attached child possesses a far greater capacity for empathy than either the ambivalent or avoidant child. In *Becoming Attached*, Karen describes studies that show that secure preschoolers possessed more empathy for other children in distress than did insecure children. Children classified as ambivalent were simply too preoccupied with their own neediness to have empathy for others. And the avoidant? They often became bullies or teasers who "seemed to take pleasure in another child's misery."[9] What's going on here? According to Karen, ambivalent and avoidant children have little if any inner reserves of compassionate and empathic feelings to draw on.

Discussing his research, Alan Sroufe, psychologist and attachment researcher at the Institute of Child Development at the University of Minnesota, explained it this way: "We found that a number of ambivalent kids had difficulty maintaining a boundary between themselves and the distressed child. That's customary for really young children—two-year-olds would do this—but these kids [in his research] were four and five. So, for example, a little girl fell and hurt her lip, and one of the ambivalent kids immediately put his hand to his own mouth and went and got up on a teacher's lap. It was as though it had happened to him. In the same situation, an avoidant child would do something like call her a crybaby. Whereas a secure child would get a teacher and bring the teacher to the child or stand by and look concerned."[10]

This makes sense. As we send our children out into their world of school and friendships, they will give to others what we have given to them. And if we want them to be empathic, sympathetic, and compassionate humans, then they must first receive these golden responses from us.

CAN YOU TEACH YOUR CHILDREN EMPATHY?

Is empathy taught or caught? Alan Sroufe believes that parents help their children become empathic by the way they treat them. "You get an empathic child not by trying to teach the child or admonish the child to be empathic; you get an empathic child by being empathic with the child. The child's understanding of relationships can only be from the relationships he's experienced."[11]

In fact, the research shows that greater maternal warmth is connected with greater empathy in toddlers. Of course, we need to talk to our children about empathy. Those mothers who discuss emotions and point out the harmful consequences of hurtful behavior tend to have more empathetic children, whereas mothers who control their children by anger have children with less capacity to empathize.[12]

If you want empathic children, you need to deal compassionately with your children's emotions—joy, tears, needing to cuddle. Sroufe believes that the way children treat other children has its origins in what happens when they bring their neediness to their mothers. A mother who ignores or rebuffs her child will hamper his ability to be empathic with his peers' cries for help and pleas for compassion.

Describing Lucy, an avoidant four-year-old who antagonized a playmate with a stomachache by hitting her in the stomach, Sroufe said, "It's unlikely that the child's [Lucy's] mother actually hit her in the stomach when she had a stomachache, but she [Lucy] has had countless experiences with what happens when a person is poor and needy. Does a partner exploit that vulnerability? Is a partner rejecting because you're feeling vulnerable? If that's been my experience of what a partner does, that's what I know to do as a partner when I'm in that situation."[13] Sroufe's reference to a partner in this instance refers to the child's mother. When a child is vulnerable, if he meets with rejection and abuse from his mother, he is liable to beat up kids on the playground.

On the other hand, if a child has a confident, affectionate mother who encourages empathy and discourages aggression, he will become empathic toward others. Heidi Brennan told me about an incident with her youngest of five children, two-year-old Jeep, that illustrates how she encouraged an empathic response and discouraged aggressive behavior. "I was playing a face-to-face game with Jeep when he reached out his fist and hit me in the nose. He wasn't sure how to react. I said, 'Hurts.' Then I said, 'Pat, don't hit.' Later that day he turned to me and put his fist on his nose and said, 'Hit, no hurt' and got a concerned look on his face." Brennan's toddler is working on controlling his aggressive impulses and developing empathy in his relationships. And he's learning his first lessons from his mother. "Helping a child become loving and compassionate takes feedback," Heidi says. "Without your love and tutelage, your child will be clueless."

As mothers, then, we need to help our sons and daughters own their emotional responses and express them appropriately. As we show empathy and compassion to our children, they will learn that they can count on us and will become empathic toward others.

Marian Gormley, the mother of seven-and-a-half-year-old twins, has worked with Jake and his sister, Tara, in deepening their empathic understanding. One day Jake called home from the nurse's office at school to ask his mother to come and get him. He had a sore throat and felt sick. On that particular day, Marian was scheduled to have lunch with a friend whose husband had recently died. "Are you still having lunch with Wendy?" Jake asked. When Marian said yes, her son told her not to break her date because he could wait in the nurse's office. "Wendy really needs you, Mom," said this little boy, who has already learned that he can count on his mom's empathy and concern and that others sometimes need it too.

Recently Ginny Grimes took eight-year-old Sarah to visit Rosa, a new friend in a nursing home. That particular day, Rosa, a plucky African-American who is pushing ninety-two, lay in bed fully dressed with her tennis shoes on. Although she had lived an active life and reared three children, Rosa had outlived her spouse, her sons, and her friends. That day, Rosa, who was generally cheerful, spoke of her loneliness. "Don't nobody come to see me much anymore," she said, coughing. "I get pretty lonely in this place, even though there's plenty of nurses and other people around. Somebody is always in the hall screaming. Poor souls."

Later, when Ginny and her daughter walked out of the nursing home, Sarah said, "Mommy, can we invite Rosa to come to our house for dinner? She's sad and lonely, and she doesn't have any children to visit her. She needs for us to be her friends." Her mother assured her they could indeed do that. She was pleased that her desire to expose Sarah to the lonely and needy had paid off; her young daughter had "heard" Rosa's loneliness and had responded with empathy.

MOTHERS AND SONS

While many mothers work with their daughters in the area of empathy, these same moms may neglect their sons because of societal conditioning that teaches them to prize toughness and lack of emotion in men. Studies show that boys consistently score lower than girls on measures of empathy. But our sons, as well as our daughters, need to learn from us that our emotions are innate and God-given and can be understood as well as regulated. It's not wise to teach our sons to repress their feelings while we encourage our daughters to be expressive. Little boys shouldn't have to swallow their tears or disown their sadness. If they do, they may grow up to become adult men who seldom or never cry. I know one man who cries only at sad movies, though his life has tragic overtones, and another in his seventies who hasn't cried for forty years. When a man can't on occasion express sorrow and pain through tears, it follows that he can't experience joy either. And what an impoverished emotional life we will have if we exist on some safe but emotionless plateau, unable to experience the extremes of joy and sorrow.

WHEN NO EMPATHY EXISTS

Empathy—giving and receiving it—is part of the continuum of human behavior that we accept as normal. Some human beings, however, are incapable of empathetic feelings. They are the psychopaths who, possessing no conscience, maim or torture others; when their victims cry out for mercy, they feel no compassion or remorse. Human beings who possess little or no empathy because they were not attached to either parent are time bombs waiting to explode and hurt others, like the two teenagers in New Jersey who decided to murder a total stranger "just to see how it would feel."[14] They phoned for a pizza and then shot and killed the two delivery men when they arrived, one of whom was the father of a four-year-old girl.

In another hideous crime, two fifteen-year-olds killed a forty-four-year-old real estate agent in Central Park. One of the killers was the daughter of a wealthy East Side businessman, and the other was an altar boy who attended an expensive private school. The crime was especially ugly and heartless. Daphnene Abdela apparently urged Christopher Vasquez to cut off the victim's hands after he had been stabbed forty-four times and disemboweled so his body would not float. (It did.) Then the pair returned to Daphnene's expensive apartment to wash the blood off themselves and call 911. Why? To report that "a friend" had fallen into the Central Park lake.[15]

Where does this brutal heartlessness, this total absence of empathy and compassion, come from? Just as we are witnessing the emergence of a bumper crop of kids without a conscience, we're also seeing that they're heartless and cruel in a way that is inconceivable to many of us. But the absence of empathy, as well as the absence of conscience, flows from the lack of human bonds or attachments. If we want our children to be empathic, then we need to be there, giving them empathy and modeling compassion toward others.

If the psychopath is cruel and remorseless in an inhuman way, at the other end of the spectrum is the altruistic person. Studies show that the individuals who fed and hid the Jews in Europe during World War II were emotionally close to their parents and that they had learned to be empathic at their mothers' knees.

Samuel and Pearl Oliner in *The Altruistic Personality* reported that those who rescued Jews were significantly more likely than non-rescuers to say they had close early family relationships, particularly with their mothers. And they were close to their fathers. Their parents taught them to care for others within the family and beyond. Not surprisingly, the rescuers possessed a high sense of social responsibility. According to the Oliners, "The rescuers in our study did not differ from non-rescuers with respect to generalized emotional empathy. However, they did differ from non-rescuers with respect to emotional empathy for others' pain."[16]

Those individuals who rescued the Jews during World War II did not just feel another's pain, they acted on their convictions. They felt a sense of responsibility for, and commitment to, the poor and the weak. Like securely attached children, rescuers believed they had significant internal control over the events of their lives.[17] This produced high self-esteem and feelings of empowerment. Rather than being passive or uninvolved, these individuals chose to make decisions that put themselves in danger because they understood and felt compassion for the desperate need of others.

One rescuer, Stanislaus, who was emotionally close to his mother and saved the lives of many Jews, said, "I learned to respect the world from my mother." His mother modeled compassionate behavior for her son, often filling up their household with assorted friends or relatives who needed help.[18]

PRESENT-DAY ROLE MODELS

When I read the stories in the Oliners' book, they remind me of a present-day rescuer, my friend Susie Hamilton, the wife of Will, a general practitioner in Asheville, North Carolina. They have five children, ranging in age from ten to twenty-three. I have known Susie and Will for over twenty-five years. In fact, Holly and Kristen were in their home wedding in London when the girls were three and five years old. (We all remember how Krissy, the youngest flower girl, somersaulted down the last few steps of the staircase.)

Years ago, a minister appeared at Susie's door in deep winter and asked if she would take in a teenager whose father had thrown her out of the family trailer. That first night the girl slept next to the cows in the nearby pasture just to keep warm. Susie and Will opened their home to Linda, as they have to others, and she ended up living with them for five years. Now Linda is a single mother with a charming toddler, and Susie is still involved in her life. When I saw Susie and Will recently, Susie, a petite fifty-year-old with a long blond ponytail, said, "I spend almost as much time with Linda as I do my own children." Then she told me of the practical help she gives this single mother.

In addition to Linda, Susie has housed dozens of visiting students from around the world. Visitors stay weeks, months, or even years.

Where does Susie get her concern for others and her drive to help them? From her parents, particularly her mother. Susie once told me that when her high school friends ran away from home, they often ran to her parents' spacious farm, a rambling white house with black shutters that used to be a stagecoach inn where Thomas Jefferson had once stayed.

Today, as Susie reaches out to others, she models a compassionate, empathic life for her children. In fact, this past summer when I had dinner at her home, I arrived to see single mothers picking up their children. (Susie has long provided on her farm free after-school care for children of divorce.) And Susie said she had just received a call from the school principal to take in another student. "I don't know how I'll do it," she said, "but my heart has grown too big to turn a child away." The result of Susie's empathy and compassion? "My children," says Susie, "are always reaching out to help others."

BABY KRYSTAL

Margie Johnson, a mother of six who has housed two pregnant teenagers needing a place to stay, says that the most powerful force in shaping empathy in the lives of her children was the death of their baby sister, Krystal, her fifth child:

> When she was born, I felt as though it was a miracle. But I noticed the night before I was to leave the hospital that her face looked a little bit dusky. The nurse said that sometimes babies forget to breathe for a little while, and when they get like that, just tap their feet. I did mention this to the doctor, and he suggested keeping her for twenty-four hours to observe her. So they kept her for twenty-four hours and couldn't really verify any problems aside from the fact that she had a slow heart rate. They did a battery of tests on her and she ended up there for two weeks. I felt like a mother

tiger. I knew she needed time with our family and she needed to be home. I had a sense of urgency with her.

Krystal brought an unexpected joy to our home. My nine-year-old son would guard her door—he would lay at her door and protect her. He begged us to let her sleep by him at night. The three-and-a-half months she was with us were literally a time when our home was so much like heaven. We had a family night before she died. We put in a pan all the ingredients that go into a cake, except for the flour. Everyone agreed the cake probably wouldn't taste very good without the flour. We said the family is very much like this—each person is an essential ingredient to the family.

The night before she died I wrote in my journal about how much I felt I had grown and developed as a mother. The next morning when I went to her crib, she was gone. I picked her up and tried CPR with her. I called 911 and my husband. My children heard the ambulance as the bus was taking off for school. . . . When the autopsy report was given, they felt it was SIDS—they didn't find any sign of infection. She had been coughing and congested, and the doctor told me to run the humidifier. Later, the primary cause of death was rewritten as bronchial pneumonia.

I asked the Lord for comfort and it came like a warm, soft blanket. For about three months the Holy Spirit's comforting presence stayed with me. Soon after Krystal died, my husband got us together and we had a family meeting and talked about heaven and how wonderful it was that Krystal was perfect enough to return to God. One of the things I marveled at is that the Lord is the giver and taker of life. I had prayed to know that it was His will that she be with Him and not with us. And so I trusted His decision implicitly.

We went to her grave shortly after her funeral—she died

January 10. We went in March, and the grass seeds that had been planted had started to grow. When we got back into the car, my nine-year-old looked very sad, and I had him sit on my lap. He had his little fist closed up and he had blades of grass in them, and he buried his head in my chest and cried softly.

He is a very talented artist and spends a lot of time drawing. In his college years, I went to visit him, and he had on his drawing board a picture of him holding his three-and-a-half-month-old little sister. She is very much a part of my children's consciousness.

How has this experience enlarged this family's capacity for empathy? Margie, who was aware of God's empathy and compassion for her, feels that Krystal's death has deepened her capacity to identify with other mothers who have lost children. She has stood in their shoes. She knows how they feel. And because God comforted her, and this experience deepened her spiritually, Margie is able to pass on hope and encouragement to those in similar situations. The loss has worked a similar alchemy with her children. Because Margie was empathic with her family, they dealt openly with Krystal's loss. Margie says her six children share a deep concern for each other and they've become more sensitive toward their peers.

WHAT IT MEANS TO BE HUMAN

We've discussed the fact that as mothers we help our children become human in the best sense of the word. From the strong attachment we share with our children, they hone a conscience and develop a capacity for empathy. Without our presence, our love, our empathy, many of our children will grow up emotionally handicapped, unable to say a timely word to a hurting friend or to reach out to the less fortunate.

Others—and their number is increasing—may even become brutal, remorseless killers.

Our children cannot effectively raise themselves, nor can they grow a heart without our empathy and wise tutelage. It takes years of on-site training, of watching their parents reach out to the world around them, for children to become compassionate, wise healers. The reward is a generation that knows how to bind the wounds of the hurting rather than add to their pain.

It has moved me deeply to be the recipient of my daughters' love and care during these past months when I've struggled with cancer. "Mummy, how's my vulnerable little mom?" said Holly over the phone one day recently. "I usually think of you as hearty and competent, but this breast cancer scare has changed that. How are you doing?"

"I'm terrified, Holly," I replied. "After taking the cancer survivors course at Johns Hopkins University, I know too much about this disease."

During these scary and difficult days, my family's love, empathy, and tenderness have meant the world to me. While friends and others are sometimes empathic, I always feel safe with my immediate family and have experienced Don's tenderness and Greg and the girls' care.

The morning after surgery, when my surgeon told me the tumor he excised was two centimeters in size and was indeed malignant, I felt as if the bottom had dropped out of my stomach. I called Kristen, and within an hour the five of us gathered at Kristen and Greg's townhouse for a lunch-feast of grilled fresh salmon, red and green peppers, onions, red potatoes, sourdough bread, spinach, and succulent strawberries. When I thanked Kristen and Greg for the sumptuous and expensive meal, Kristen said, "Mom, if you had wanted zebra today, I would have found it."

Oh, the power of empathy.

CHAPTER 11

The Power *to* Build a Brain

M arty Larson and her physician husband, Elliott, have taken the education of their five sons seriously. Marty, a fifty-six-year-old high school Spanish teacher, and Elliott, a fifty-seven-year-old internist, have five accomplished sons who for years have listened to their father read from the Bible at breakfast and their mother read from children's classics at night. "I elected to feed the children early," says Marty, who ate dinner with Elliott when he returned from the London hospital where he worked until seven or eight o' clock at night. "I learned that if I fed the children at five o'clock, I could forestall any fighting during the next two hours. For me, that was wonderful! So the children were a captive audience as I read aloud poetry, history, and novels."

When asked what she would advise younger mothers to do, Marty, who has one son still at home, says, "Hug your children, and read to them almost every time they ask. In addition, get down on the floor and play with them." She believes it's important for a mother to be widely read so she can answer her children's questions with depth and breadth.

Whether they were in Afghanistan or London, Marty and Elliott chose to have "an open home," entertaining numerous people from diverse backgrounds. "That way," says Marty, "the children were able to participate in discussions with people who held differing viewpoints on a wide range of issues." In their large, rambling house in a suburb of London, they often had missionaries living in their second-floor flat, as well as frequent houseguests from America.

Marty says one of the best things she and Elliott did for their family was to create "Sunday choice." On Sunday afternoons, family members took turns choosing an activity that the other six had to engage in. Says Marty, "That meant that the father who hated board games had to play Monopoly, and the child who didn't like museums had to visit one occasionally. The only thing a child couldn't choose was to go off on his own and engage in a solo activity."

In addition, each son was encouraged to play a musical instrument, to become proficient in at least one sport, and to do well academically. Today their eldest son, Eric, who graduated from West Point, is a member of the army's elite Special Forces. Mark, who won a first in economics at Cambridge University, is married and works in London as an economist. Paul is a premed student at Gordon-Conwell; his twin, Scott, a junior at St. Johns College, just spent six months working in an orphanage in India. Carl, who like his brothers enjoys acting and singing, will soon graduate from high school.

While Elliott has guided his sons' education and been an exemplary role model as a doctor, preacher, and counselor, Marty has had a more hands-on, on-site role in educating her sons. Twenty-eight years ago I watched Marty make replicas of Montessori toys when Eric was a baby. And when she and Elliott went to Afghanistan as missionaries, Marty took along cartons of books to educate the boys. Not only did she homeschool three of them for a few years, she also compiled an extensive list of the books she had read aloud across the years called "Books

Too Good to Miss," which she passes on to other mothers who cross her path. A friend since college days, Marty had a profound influence on my life as a young mother, encouraging me to read aloud to my children and to be actively involved in their intellectual development.

New Brain Research

When my daughters were babies, I didn't know what researchers have only recently discovered: that at birth, babies' brains contain 100 billion neurons—about as many "nerve cells as there are stars in the Milky Way."[1] Nor did I understand that my children's environment would shape or prune the synapses, or connections, between the neurons in their brains and that once these were pruned, they would be gone forever. I did know, however, that I had a unique role in influencing my children's intellectual development through the environment I created, although I didn't understand just how powerful this influence would be.

While my first husband and I did not provide the girls with the marital stability and emotional security they needed in their earliest years, I worked hard as a single parent to stimulate and educate them. And when Don and I married, he discovered that he loved tutoring them in history and math, as well as encouraging them athletically.

Studies have proven that mothers and fathers are critical in building their children's brains, especially in the early years. Research supports what many mothers know intuitively: The brain is quite plastic early on and mom is her baby's first toy and the creator of his world. If a baby's brain is to flourish, a mother needs to be actively involved in providing a stimulating and rich milieu.

"You cannot see what is going on inside your baby's brain," wrote Sharon Begley in *Newsweek*. "You cannot see the electrical activity as her eyes lock onto yours and, almost instantaneously, a neuron in her retina makes a connection to one in her visual cortex that will last all of her life."[2]

Although we can't see the electrical activity in our child's brain, neurobiologists can measure it through positron-emission tomography (PET). PET scans measure activity in different parts of the brain, watching one region after another turn on "like city neighborhoods having their electricity restored after a blackout."[3]

Scientists have recently discovered that the brain is still in the process of forming after birth; unlike other organs, it's not merely growing larger but is creating vital connections that are "responsible for feeling, learning, and remembering."[4] In fact, it's what the baby experiences *after* birth that determines the wiring of his brain. Although as little as fifteen years ago scientists thought a baby's genetic endowment was chiefly responsible for his brain, they now know that what he experiences in his early years determines how the "intricate neural circuits" are actually wired.[5]

In the first months of life, the brain will produce one thousand trillion synapses, or connections, between these neurons. Then it's up to early experience and environment to determine how many of these synapses the baby will keep: "Synapses that are not used will wither away in a process called pruning."[6] The evidence is that once those synapses or connections are pruned, they are gone forever. Interestingly, the formation of synapses and their pruning does not occur all at once but over time as different skills emerge. For example, synapse formation peaks in the visual cortex at three months, whereas at eight or nine months, a fully functional hippocampus allows your baby to file away memories.[7]

WHAT HELPS THE BRAIN DEVELOP?

You Are Your Baby's Best Toy
How can you strengthen your baby's synapses and help him become a brighter child?

The new wave of brain research emphasizes the strategic importance of your baby's "environment"; babies, say the scientists who conducted the research, need a rich and varied world that stimulates their early brain development. What happens when babies don't have a stimulating setting or environment? They simply have smaller brains. In fact, researchers at Baylor College of Medicine found that children who were rarely touched or played with had brains that were 20 percent to 30 percent smaller than normal. "Rich experiences, in other words, really do produce rich brains."[8]

Who can provide that rich experience better than you? Your baby needs you to be an attentive, engaged mother who loves to spend most of her baby's waking hours with him, singing, chatting, smiling, and playing simple games of peekaboo and pat-a-cake. *You are your baby's best toy.* In fact, you are the architect of his world. As you interact with him and provide the gentle stimulation he needs (let him set the pace), you help his brain flourish. Love—not flashcards or expensive toys—undergirds your baby's brain development. As your baby feels loved, he is maximally prepared to learn. The famous child psychologist Jean Piaget said that emotional development is the gas that runs the car which is intellectual development.[9]

Talk to Your Baby

One of the best ways you can stimulate your baby's brain is just by talking—talk to him as you stroll with him or as you take him with you on simple outings to the park, the grocery store, or a friend's house. Go ahead and use that melodic, high-pitched, singsong voice—you're speaking "motherese." Babies around the world love motherese and respond by cooing and babbling.

Recently Don and I watched a thirtysomething mother push her baby along in a carriage in a local mall. As her pink-clad baby of five or six months looked up at her, this mother leaned toward her baby and began to speak in the universal language of motherese. "You are such a beautiful baby," the mother cooed. "I just love you sooo much."

Completely oblivious to passersby, this mother was locked in an intense, adoring exchange with her baby, who rewarded her with a dazzling smile.

As you converse with your baby or toddler, you not only communicate your pleasure in his company, you enhance his language development and build his vocabulary. "The size of a toddler's vocabulary is strongly correlated with how much a mother talks to her child," wrote Sharon Begley.[10] Even at twenty months of age, toddlers who have talkative mothers have 131 more words than children of less chatty mothers. By twenty-four months of age, this gap has widened to 295 words! A mother can increase her child's vocabulary by using complex sentences beginning with words like *while* and *although*. Her toddler will mimic this more complicated sentence structure and advance linguistically more quickly than his peers.[11]

Can television teach language to your young child and help him increase his vocabulary? The research says no. Studies show that only "live" language enlarges a child's vocabulary. So, technology can't replace a mother's presence and active engagement. According to new brain research, what children need is instruction "embedded in an emotional context."[12] You and the activities you and your child engage in provide that "emotional context" par excellence.

Breast-feed Your Baby

You can also maximize your baby's brain by breast-feeding him. Researchers have discovered that breast-feeding a baby helps boosts his brain development. Scientists are now calling breast milk "nature's brain food." Breast milk not only contains antibodies that help fight ear and respiratory infections and even protect against certain cancers later on, but evidence is rolling in that there can be an eight-point IQ difference between breast-fed and bottle-fed babies.[13] Consequently, the American Academy of Pediatrics recommends that babies be fed breast milk for the first twelve months. As a mother, it's important that you know that no formula can match the marvel of breast milk. "Breast milk gives you things we don't even know about," says Dr. William Goldman, medical director of Wyeth Nutritionals International.[14]

While nursing a baby may seem inconvenient to a mother who has many obligations in her life—other children, a job, a house to care for—it can be a relaxing and enjoyable time for mothers, if they let it. Said the mother of a five-month-old daughter, "I love it when Sally pulls away from my breast and looks at me and smiles." I found that nursing the girls for nine months was a wonderful experience. Nursing deepened the emotional closeness I felt for my babies, and it has helped keep my children healthy throughout their lives. I would strongly encourage any mother to make time in her life for this special experience. You will be giving your baby a healthy start in life, and you may also help him to become smarter. As Daniel Glick, a writer for *Newsweek*, said, "Wouldn't it be something if mother's milk turns out to be, ahem, the mother's milk of intelligence?"[15]

Minimize Trauma and Stress, and Provide Comfort When Needed
Your baby's wonderful brain, while acutely open to learning, is also vulnerable to trauma and stress. "Experience may alter the behavior of an adult," says Dr. Bruce Penely of Baylor College of Medicine, but it "literally provides the organizing framework" for a child's brain.[16] What happens when a child repeatedly experiences fear and stress? His neurochemical responses to those emotions alter his brain. For example:

- Trauma causes stress hormones such as cortisol to increase; these stress hormones are like an acid wash on the brain. In abused children, for example, the cortex and limbic system are 20 to 30 percent smaller than in normal children. These areas also have fewer synapses.
- Because of increased cortisol levels, abused adults have a smaller hippocampus than nonabused adults.
- If a child has high cortisol levels between birth and age three,

he will become hyperaroused and vigilant. His brain stays on "hair trigger alert," meaning that the slightest stress will produce a surge of stress hormones.[17]

Since stress is such a powerful force in shaping a child's brain, we need to know what causes stress for our youngest children and minimize it. Obviously, we would agree that the death of a parent, parental divorce, or physical or sexual abuse produce a lot of stress. But what about brief daily separations? As we saw in the chapter on separation, when a baby is around nine months old, even a thirty-minute separation from his mother increases the level of cortisol in his saliva. So we need to be sensitive to our baby's cries and try, whenever possible, to reduce his stress by being a comforting, reliable presence who is both physically and emotionally available.

When I had my first bone scan and was dealing with my own stress, in another part of the room a ten-month-old baby was lying on his stomach while a lab technician pressed down on his little body. Later I was told that the baby had a reflux problem—he vomited up his food—and the technician was taking films to see if something was wrong anatomically. During the procedure, the little boy sobbed helplessly. While this noninvasive procedure didn't actually hurt, it was stressful for him, even though his mother stood beside him, trying to soothe and comfort him with her voice.

Although most of us may worry when we sense that our babies are stressed, occasional stress will not produce permanent damage, especially if we're available to soothe and comfort. It's *repeated* stress or trauma that literally shapes the brain. But we need to understand that what may be okay for us, like a two-week absence on a cruise, may be intensely stressful for our baby, particularly between six and twelve months, when attachment is in the making.

Touch and Cuddle Your Baby

While trauma and stress powerfully impact a baby's developing brain in a negative way, human touch is a baby's lifeline. Just how important is touching and cuddling a baby? Frederick II, the thirteenth-century emperor of the Holy Roman Empire, discovered in a tragic way that touch is essential for human development. Because he wanted to learn what language young children would naturally speak without parental influence, he took a group of babies from their parents and hired nurses to feed and bathe them. He gave these nurses strict orders— they were not to sing or talk to the babies, nor were they to hold them. What was the result of this early experiment? All the babies died. Not one survived without the tenderness and comfort of human touch.[18]

By the same token, doctors and nurses today use touch when conventional medicine fails. An intensive-care nurse at the Medical Center Hospital of Massachusetts, Gayle Kasparian, tried a variety of medical techniques to calm baby Brielle Jackson but to no avail. Baby Brielle, who weighed only two pounds at birth, had dangerously low blood-oxygen saturation levels. Only when she was placed in an incubator with her sister, Kyrie, did Brielle's condition stabilize as she snuggled up to her twin.[19]

Holding, cuddling, and stroking a baby's soft face and little legs comfort him and stimulate his central nervous system. In addition, touching a baby strengthens his immune system and causes weight gain. Psychologist Tiffany Field of the University of Miami's Touch Research Institute has studied the power of touch in the lives of premature babies. She found that when preemies were given a daily massage, they gained 47 percent more weight than nonmassaged preemies, and they were discharged from the hospital six days earlier. Follow-up studies found that massaged preemies also had a higher IQ score on the tests for a baby's response to social stimulation.[20]

I observed a mother nurse her six-month-old baby girl and listened as she recounted her experience of early motherhood. As she breast-fed her baby, this mother instinctively stroked her baby's legs and massaged her bare feet. The baby responded by thrusting her chubby legs in a pumping motion, almost as if she were riding a bicycle. Not once during the five hours I was with this duo did the serene baby cry.

In their 1994 study of full-term babies, researcher Tiffany Field and her colleagues found that those babies who received daily massages cried less and had lower levels of cortisol in their saliva.[21] Stroking and touching your baby will lower his stress level and help keep him happy.

HOW TO MASSAGE A BABY

The best way to stroke a baby, says Dr. Tiffany Field, is with firm, gentle, slow strokes. If the touch is too light, it may stimulate or tickle your baby; if it's too hard, it may hurt. So be careful and take the time to learn what your child likes best. Heed his cues. Does he coo or pull away? Remember: If you want to soothe your baby, lightly massage his back and legs, and if you want to stimulate him, simply stroke his face, belly, or little feet.[22]

TOUCH AND OLDER CHILDREN

How does touch affect older children? Field and her colleagues found that daily massages helped preschool children fall asleep faster and have more restful naps; massage also helped asthmatic children breathe better and experience fewer attacks. And autistic children who were given daily massages were less distracted, more attentive, and more sociable.[23] Even teenagers respond to soothing backrubs. In fact, touch research shows that anxious adolescents with sleep disturbances sleep better after five days of thirty-minute massages.[24] Researcher Tiffany Field, who says, "Kids in general aren't getting as much touch as generations past," rubs her sixteen-year-old daughter's back and shoulders each night.[25]

What's good for a child is good for a mother too. I remember holding and stroking my babies' little arms and legs. I loved those chubby

little limbs with their fat rolls. Since I had grown up in an environment with limited touch—I usually got hugged only when I came
home and when I left—I found that carrying and holding my little
girls was quite pleasurable. I relaxed when I touched and played with
my babies. In fact, I believe some deep, elemental skin hunger within
me was satisfied as I carried, bathed, and held my babies.

You will find that touching your babies and older children is pleasurable and makes you feel emotionally closer to them. All of us need
appropriate skin-to-skin contact. And if we didn't get enough touch
growing up, something inside can be healed as we nurture and touch
our babies.

THE BRAIN MATURES

At this point you may be wondering how long you have to grow your
child's brain. The evidence is that the brain's marvelous growth spurt
ends at about ten years of age. Over the next several years your child's
brain will ruthlessly destroy its weakest synapses, "preserving only
those that have been magically transformed by experience."[26] Then,
until age eighteen, while the brain declines in plasticity, it increases in
power. That's when all those talents that have been nurtured—musical, artistic, athletic—burst into flower. As J. Madeleine Nash wrote in
Time, "Potential for greatness may be encoded in the genes, but
whether that potential is realized as a gift for mathematics, say, or a
brilliant criminal mind depends on patterns etched by experiences in
those critical early years" (italics mine).[27]

If you want to maximize your baby or young child's chances for
optimal brain development, ignore the media hype for higher quality
day care and the myth that anyone can provide as wonderful an environment as you can. Simply decide that nothing has greater urgency
than protecting your baby's brain from stress and helping it grow. How
can you ensure this, except by providing your on-site presence? After
all, how can any mother know how much stress her baby experiences

when she's not with him during the day? Too much maternal absence may create more stress or trauma than your child can cope with. As Sharon Begley concludes, "Babies are born into this world with their brains primed to learn. But they cannot do it alone."[28] Nor do older children learn as well alone.

SHAPING THE OLDER CHILD'S BRAIN

Mothers have always shaped their children's intelligence and functioned as their first, and sometimes most important, teacher. Abraham Lincoln said he owed much of his intellectual development to his mother, Nancy Hanks, who died when he was ten years old. Nancy taught young Abe to read, walking miles to secure books for him.[29]

The French poet Alexis François Desroys said this about his mother:

My education was wholly centered in the glance, more or less serene, and the smile, more or less open, of my mother. The reins of my heart were in her hands. I drank in, as a plant from the soil, the first nourishing juices of my young intellect from the books carefully selected by my mother. But I drank deep, above all, from my mother's eyes, I felt through her impressions, I lived through her life.[30]

British art critic and writer John Ruskin learned to read the Bible at the knee of his Scottish Presbyterian mother. As an adult, he wrote:

My mother's influence in molding my character was conspicuous. She forced me to learn daily long chapters of the Bible by heart. To that disciplined, patient, accurate resolve, I owe not only much of my general power for taking pains, but the best part of my taste for literature.[31]

Another mother of famous sons, Susanna Wesley, chose the Bible as the first book her children would ever read. Susanna, who had studied Greek, Latin, French, logic, and metaphysics, daily taught her ten children (among them the famous John and Charles). Her tactics? When a child reached the age of five, she took him into her school-room and taught him the alphabet. Then each child plunged into reading the Bible, starting with Genesis 1:1. Susanna, who ran a busy household, taught her children from 9:00 A.M. to noon and 2:00 P.M. to 5:00 P.M. each day.[32]

Kristie Tamillow, who lives in Fredericksburg, Virginia, is an ener-getic and gregarious teacher and mother of thirteen-year-old Matt and eleven-year-old Meggie. She has taken an active role in shaping her children's brains. She began teaching her children through everyday activities when they were very young. Says Kristie, "We would go to the grocery store when my kids were five and seven, and I would say to Matt, 'Tell me which item is the better buy.' Since Meggie was younger and not as developed mathematically, I would tell her to look for sodium content—she was in charge of making sure we weren't buy-ing anything that was high in sodium. And that's how I trained them to read labels and to take an interest in nutrition. You have to look for opportunities to teach your children. You have to be awake, aware, and have a method."

Kristie, who homeschooled her son for five years and her daugh-ter for four, also turned at-home tasks into opportunities for learn-ing. Kristie recounts, "We had charts everywhere for chores. When they didn't know how to read, the chart would have little laundry tags or a picture of a bed. When they finished their tasks, they would turn over the tag so that Mom or Dad would know they'd completed their chores for that day. When Meggie was two, she learned how to sort clothes. By three, she knew her colors from helping me sort laundry."

Kristie used positive reinforcement to reward her children when they completed their tasks. She made up coupons for "hugs and kisses or an ice cream cone at McDonald's" and left them on their bed pil-lows. Now that her children are older, Kristie is reaping the rewards.

She says, "Now when I tell my children to do something, they can go and do it. They can clean the entire house; they can do laundry and clean bathrooms. Matt's dad spent all of Matt's twelfth year teaching him how to edge, mow, and clean out a gutter. Now Matt has his own business mowing lawns. All of this takes a lot of work, and you have to be systematic about it, but if you do it when they're young, your kids will be able to go off on their own and be really productive when they're teenagers."

Kristie and her husband, Mike, have also used family time in the evenings to train their children in table manners and social graces. "We taught manners with a manners basket," says Kristie. "Each night the children would take a piece of paper out of the manners basket, and that's what they would work on that night—things like not talking with their mouths full, asking to be excused at the end of dinner, or having a polite conversation." Laughs Kristie, "That meant that Matt wouldn't talk about blood and gore or the frog he had just smushed with his bike that day."

Kristie says that while she's been disciplined and focused in teaching her children, she's also learned not to push them too hard. "You have to watch your child. When my kids were no longer able to do something, I would stop. Now they have a love for learning, and it's not a high pressure thing for them. It's just part of their life."

CREATING A STIMULATING ENVIRONMENT

You have enormous power in developing your children's intelligence during all their years at home. The mother who reads aloud to her children and keeps challenging books and magazines around the house, the mother who takes her children on excursions into the larger world, cultivates the art of conversation, and invites interesting people to dinner will likely have more precocious children than the woman who parks them in front of the television, has few if any books and magazines around, and talks to her children seldom, if at all. While one mother creates a magical and stimulating world, the other provides a barren and sterile place in which to grow up.

If you want to help your children develop their intellectual potential, you need to stay several steps ahead of their intellectual pursuits. When my girls were very young, I bought all the books I could afford as a single parent; for several years I let the girls purchase a paperback a week. When they showed an interest in a particular subject, I helped them pursue it avidly. For instance, like most preteens, Kristen fell in love with horses as an eleven-year-old. I encouraged her to read all of Walter Farley's *Black Stallion* books as well as those by Marguerite Henry. Don and I also provided her with as many horseback riding lessons as we could afford.

Later, when Holly wanted to take a college class after tenth grade, I drove her to Drew University to register for a summer course in microbiology. She was later told that this experience was partly the reason she was chosen to be the only girl from her high school to attend Virginia's Governor's School for the Gifted, a select summer program for upcoming high school seniors. And when the girls confronted the SAT exam their junior year, I cheered each one on. While Holly worked on her own with a SAT review book and index cards for vocabulary, gregarious Kristen needed extra motivation to prepare. I held my own SAT review class for her and her five girlfriends every Wednesday afternoon. They raided my refrigerator, but this plan worked. Not only did it help Kristen, but the other girls felt they performed better as well.

HELP YOUR CHILDREN PURSUE THEIR DREAMS

As we help our children build their brains and grow intellectually, it's also important to encourage their dreams. One of my favorite poets, Langston Hughes, wrote:

Hold fast to dreams
for if dreams die

life is a broken winged bird
that cannot fly.[33]

We need to teach our children to soar. It doesn't matter if we have plenty or live in poverty, we can nurture our children's dreams.

The late writer Catherine Marshall encouraged me to dream through her books. In *Adventures in Prayer*, Marshall wrote about her desire to attend Agnes Scott College at a time when her minister father earned little money. What to do? "One evening mother found me lying across the bed, face down, sobbing. So she sat down beside me. 'You and I are going to pray about this,' she said quietly." Marshall's mother told her it was right for her to go to college and said, "I believe God planted this dream in you." Within a few weeks, Marshall's mother had received an offer from the Federal Writers' Project to write the history of the county; her salary helped defray her daughter's college expenses.[34]

As an eighteen-year-old with dreams but no money, I was encouraged by Catherine Marshall's story. Many of the adults in my family thought I should attend a vocational school, but my interests lay elsewhere. Fortunately, my high school teachers and principal encouraged me to attend college and pursue my dreams. As it turned out, I received a full scholarship to Duke University in North Carolina, and admission-only to Wheaton College—Billy Graham's alma mater. Wheaton gave me absolutely no assurance that I would ever receive any financial help to defray costs. What a dilemma! When I decided to attend Wheaton because I felt God was leading me there, my granddaddy thought I had lost my mind. "Why go into debt when you have a free ride at Duke?" said this intelligent man who had an eighth-grade education.

Why, indeed? What Granddaddy didn't understand was my conviction that God would pay my bills at Wheaton. As it turned out, individuals I barely knew—a local factory owner, a surgeon, my high school Bible teacher, and two elderly women in another state—heard that I was "going to college on faith." Each semester they sent money to pay my tuition. But when I rejected Duke's offer, I didn't know this. Since I didn't want to incur debt, each semester as I signed a deferred payment statement, I prayed, "Father, you know what I need, and I believe you brought me here. I'll work hard, but I can't possibly earn all I need. And if I can't pay my bills in a timely fashion, I'll leave school. You've told me to 'owe no man any debt except the debt of love.' And I'm standing on that promise." As it turned out, I graduated from Wheaton without a penny of debt.

During my last semester, when most of what I earned went to pay for my upcoming wedding, I struggled with an unpaid balance. One day when I checked my mailbox, I learned that an anonymous benefactor had paid my debt. Years later a former roommate told me that her father's boss had heard about me from her father and had decided to help a struggling college student. He had his secretary call Wheaton and write a check for the balance of the semester's tuition bill. His name? S. S. Kresge of K-Mart fame.

Those of you who have teenagers longing to go to college but lacking the funds may take heart from my story. While it's frightening to take the less trodden path and trust God, the rewards are tremendous. We learn lessons of faith that we couldn't possibly master any other way. Out of my own life experience, I've always encouraged my daughters to "hold fast to dreams," to pray, to expect God to work in their lives.

AGAINST ALL ODDS: SONYA CARSON AND HER SONS

Sometimes a mother's ability to help her child to dream has results beyond her wildest imaginings.

The speaker at the 1997 National Prayer Breakfast, attended by President Clinton, senators and congressmen, and numerous Christian luminaries, was himself extremely distinguished. Dr. Ben Carson, the chief of pediatric neurosurgery at Johns Hopkins Hospital, created a technique used worldwide to separate Siamese twins. His medical talents have brought him considerable acclaim and financial success. In addition, this surgeon was the subject of a play, *Ben Carson, M.D.*, which has run for the past two years in his native city of Baltimore. Anyone studying Dr. Carson's life would probably assume that he had parlayed a childhood of financial and social privilege into adult accomplishments. Right? Wrong!

Ben and his brother, Curtis, were born to a teenage mom. Married at thirteen, Sonya Carson had two sons by a husband who soon deserted her. With only a third-grade education, Sonya worked two or three jobs at a time to support her sons, leaving them alone for long hours. But she was determined they would not experience the fate of other fatherless boys who succumbed to the lure of the streets. According to Dr. Carson, his mother prayed and asked God for wisdom. She felt led to give her sons reading projects.

Although her sons didn't realize it, Ms. Carson couldn't read. Yet she assigned Ben and Curtis the task of reading the book of Proverbs to her and explaining its contents. Her sons were allowed to watch only two television programs a week, and they had to spend the rest of their spare time reading.[35] They read two books each week and wrote weekly book reports. "They didn't like that very much," said Sonya.[36]

But Sonya needed to do something and do it immediately. Before his mother's intervention, Ben was getting zeroes in math class. In fact, one of his classmates told him he was "the dumbest person in the world."[37] In one year, however, he shot up from the bottom of the fifth grade class to the top of the sixth grade. "When that happened," Carson told the National Prayer Breakfast audience, "my classmates asked, 'How did you do that?' And I said, 'Sit at my feet!' "[38]

Although his academic performance was improving, Ben still had serious emotional problems. He had a terrible problem with rage, due to his father's abandonment and the emotional deprivation he experienced. He beat up other children and even went after his own mother with a knife. At age fourteen, Ben stabbed a classmate, and only the other boy's belt buckle saved him from serious injury and Ben from going to jail.[39] After the incident, Ben went into the bathroom to cool down. He knew he would never become a physician—his dream—unless he got his temper under control. He fell on his knees and prayed, "Lord, I cannot control my temper, so I'm giving it over to you." Desperate, he turned to the book of Proverbs for guidance and read it through in three hours. "I've never had a problem with rage since," said Carson, who admitted to the National Prayer Breakfast audience that he might "have been sent to San Quentin prison but for the grace of God."[40]

No psychologist would be surprised at Ben Carson's problem with rage. Not only was his father absent, but his mother—due to her several jobs—was also absent. Carson's story is testimony to the power of God, who is a father to the fatherless, and to the influence of a mother who prayed and cared passionately about what was happening to her boys. In spite of her daily absences, Sonya tracked her sons' academic performance, turned off the television, and insisted they read and write—two powerful keys to academic achievement. When children read great literature, they not only enlarge their vocabulary and knowledge base, but they hone their writing skills as well. I always told my high school students, "If you want to be a good writer, you have to read avidly." Sonya's plan, inspired by her faith in God, worked.

Ben and Curtis were such high achievers that each went to college on a full scholarship. While Curtis studied engineering at the University of Michigan, Ben was an undergraduate at Yale before earning an M.D. at his brother's alma mater.

Because of his history, Dr. Carson feels a deep sense of compassion for other fatherless black boys. Stating that more young black males go to jail than attend college, he remarked, "All of our ancestors came in different boats. But we're all in the same boat now. If one part sinks, the whole boat will, too."[41] Upbeat, Carson stated that since he made it, others can too. He added, self-deprecatingly, that he's living proof of "what the brain is capable of."[42]

How does Sonya—who has since learned to read, has attended college, and has been awarded an honorary doctorate—feel about her accomplished sons? She credits her sons' success to God's intervention rather than her own child-rearing practices. But she adds, "My children are everything I hoped they'd be."[43]

Suggestions for Honing Your Child's Intelligence

How can you help your children excel intellectually?

- Become an on-site consultant, and answer your children's questions about life, the world, and how things work. (If you don't know the answers, go to the library with the kids and discover them together.)
- Talk to your children a lot, using increasingly complex words to expand their vocabularies, and post a "word for the day" on the family fridge.
- Create a home that is filled with interesting books, magazines, people, kits, and tools. If you can't afford subscriptions to magazines, buy used classics or write the magazine publishers and explain your financial situation and ask for a "scholarship" for the children.
- Model intellectual curiosity by learning something new every day, and then share this new thing with your children at mealtimes.
- Turn off the television and play challenging games.
- Prepare and sample ethnic cuisine as a way of introducing your children to new cultures.
- Use family excursions—to church, the gas station, the grocery store—as laboratories for learning.
- Foster friendships with older adults and children from different backgrounds.
- Instill financial responsibility and planning by giving your kids graduated allowances that increase as they age. Give them a

clothing allowance at age twelve, and teach them to shop sales, garage sales, and discount stores.

- Plan trips to local zoos, libraries, parks, art galleries, historic sites, outdoor craft fairs, and markets.
- Teach your children to do work, starting by having toddlers empty wastebaskets and later having teens cut the grass or clean the house. Work with them across the years. This cuts down on their resentment and allows you to mentor and teach.
- Encourage them to pursue new language skills by enrolling them in courses offered by local universities, adult education courses, embassies, or ethnic interest groups.
- Interest them in nature with botany books, night sky-watching sessions, bird-watching excursions, and visits to planetariums.
- Challenge your teenagers by providing summer camp experiences, Outward Bound or athletic specialty trips, travel, interesting employment, or college courses.
- Reward them for exploring new interests with resources— chemistry kits, model airplanes, botany guides, kites, baking dishes, sewing machines—that allow further pursuit.
- Help your sons and daughters learn about interesting careers by setting up internships or informational interviews.
- Let them choose a sport to pursue, and attend meets, play-offs, and tournaments to encourage their perseverance.
- Play classical music, and interest them in learning an instrument.
- Use summers to expose them to art and dance camps.
- Read aloud every day—from the Bible in the mornings and great literature at night before bed.
- Build independence by allowing older children to take solo plane or train trips to visit relatives or friends.
- Encourage them to dream dreams, and then show them how to build foundations for those dreams through a personal faith in God.

A FINAL THOUGHT

What a privilege and responsibility it is to shape a child's brain, starting in infancy. Few tasks could ever prove more rewarding. And we don't need to be teachers or psychologists to do our job well; we just have to possess an inquiring mind, patience, and a heartfelt desire to help our children excel. As one friend said, "Just imagine you and your children are adventurers, and each day you happily set off to explore your world together."

CHAPTER 12

The Power
of Time

B renda Barnes, one of the highest ranking women in corporate America, created quite a stir when she quit her job as president and chief executive of Pepsi Cola North America.[1] The attractive forty-three-year-old former executive had given Pepsi twenty-two years of devoted service—half her life. Why did Barnes leave the fast track when headhunters predicted she would be a first choice as CEO for any number of consumer companies? She said she wanted to spend more time with her family—her husband, former treasurer of PepsiCo, and her three children, ages seven, eight, and ten.

Barnes, who acknowledges she struggled with her decision "for a long time," said she had "made a lot of trade-offs" for Pepsi—hectic travel, dinner meetings, living in a different city from her husband as both scaled the corporate ladder. And missing her children's birthday parties. It was the latter that helped Brenda Barnes finally make her decision to come home. When she discussed with her children the possibility of leaving PepsiCo, one of them said she could stay "if you can keep working and promise to be home for all our birthdays."[2]

Barnes, who never expected PepsiCo to cut her any slack when it came to demands on her time, said, "You have to make your choices. Maybe I burned at both ends too long."[3]

Time. Brenda Barnes, mother and fast-track corporate superstar, apparently realized she was finite, that she couldn't be in two places at the same time, that attending her children's birthday parties had to become a top priority. So she chose to give her family more of herself. She chose to give them the gift of time.

THE FINITENESS OF TIME

Today many mothers in America are grappling with the finiteness of time. *Washington Times* business editor Anne Veigle is another high-profile mother who left her job to spend more time with her two young sons. Veigle wrote in her *Washington Times* column: "After four years of struggling to balance my loyalties between motherhood and the newspaper, I made the toughest decision of my life: to leave a job I love to devote more attention to nurturing two young minds."[4] She admits that her long workday often had her arriving home just as her husband was tucking her sons into bed. Things got so bad that two years ago at a preschool conference a teacher told her, "Your son talks about you all the time. Is there any way you can spend more time with him?"[5] While Veigle didn't act on this advice immediately, she finally decided to work at a more leisurely pace from home when she confronted the fact that the pace of her professional life would never change and someone else—a Bolivian nanny—would raise her sons.

These two mothers are not alone in realizing they can't give their all to child rearing and work at the same time. A Pew Research Center study of more than one thousand women found that 56 percent thought their mothers did a better job of parenting than they were doing.[6] Commented Sandra Watson, a mother of an eighteen-year-old son, "I think that parenting has taken a backseat to our lives, and that should not be. A lot of kids are somewhat having to rear themselves."[7]

THE MYTH OF QUALITY TIME

We owe much of the modern neglect of children to the myth of quality time. Where, oh where, did this insane concept of "quality time" come from? Apparently it emerged in the 1970s as a result of a now famous study by psychologist Alison Clarke-Stewart. She wrote a book on day care, which she dedicated to her young son who spent his early years in other-than-mother care. In her study on quality time, Clarke-Stewart discovered that babies of mothers who cooed and sang to them had better cognitive and social development than babies of disengaged mothers. Sounds like common sense, right? Yet somehow the myth of quality time emerged from this particular study and changed cultural attitudes in the process.[8] Soon quality time became a national mantra.

In the intervening years, Clarke-Stewart has attempted to set the record straight. She says, "To be able to have that high quality time, you have to invest a certain amount of *pure time* [italics mine]. It's not just ten minutes a week."[9] But what is this mythical high quality time? And how do we measure it? How much "pure time" must parents put in before they mine gold? Over the years, parents have used their own discretion in defining quality time. No one has ever said whether quality time is ten minutes per day with each child or thirty minutes a week. Consequently, many children have been neglected and have received inconsistent discipline and training, like this six-year-old son who accompanied his mother, a tired New York lawyer, to a local grocery store one night.

> Suddenly there was her son, whooping and tearing around
> the store, skidding the length of the aisles on his knees. *This
> can't be my child*, she thought in horror. Then the cashier gave
> a final twist to the knife. "Oh," she remarked, "so *you're* the
> mother."[10]

The cashier's comment was the final straw for this mother. She realized that she and her husband, also a busy lawyer, were rearing two "brats" because their carefully scheduled quality time simply wasn't working. She finally acknowledged, "It's not that sitters do a bad job, but sitters don't raise kids. Parents do."[11]

Simply put, quality time doesn't work. It never has. Says Ronald Levant, a psychologist at Harvard Medical School, "Children need vast amounts of parental time and attention. It's an illusion to think they're going to be on your timetable and that you can say, 'OK, we've got half an hour; let's get on with it.'"[12]

For the past two decades, in books and speeches, I have tried to debunk the myth of quality time. I believe children need enormous amounts of *quantity* time with at least one parent to achieve their potential. And as I've said for years, *quality time grows out of the soil of quantity time.* We need to be with our babies, toddlers, preteens, and adolescents for hours or even days before we experience those fleeting golden moments known as quality time. When our children are confident they have our full attention and empathy, then and only then do they open their hearts.

HECTIC LIVES, HARRIED MOTHERS

Even though the gift of time is one of the greatest gifts we give our children and undergirds all others, the reality is that many of us live frenetic lives, trying to juggle professional responsibilities along with Little League games, grocery shopping, housecleaning, bill paying, and our kids' homework, not to mention time with our husbands. Said a friend who has three sons and who works full-time, "My life is exhausting. My husband and I work all week and spend our evenings and weekends driving our kids to church groups, practices, and their friends' houses. We're never alone. When we are, we either fight or have sex."

Another busy mom, Lynda Obst, producer of the movie *Sleepless in Seattle*, describes her life this way:

There's never any one thing to address at a given time. . . .
I've been out with a director or another of my projects and
then my beeper goes off, and I find out my son is *in extremis*
and needs to be picked up from school immediately, and
then I get call waiting on my cell phone, which means I have
to cut off the director, which is bad because directors like you
to be available to them at all times, and it's the head of
production at the studio telling me I have to cut the budget
of a movie or cancel a shoot.[13]

Like Obst, many of us feel pulled in numerous directions at once.
When that happens, we feel stressed to the max. Forget juggling. Forget quality time. The name of the game is survival.

THE OFFICE IS WHERE THE HEART IS

Home life in America has become so harried, so overscheduled, that
many moms now view the office as their personal sanctuary. So writes
sociologist Arlie Hochschild in her recent book *The Time Bind.*
Hochschild, who studied a corporation she calls "Amerco" for three
years, discovered that many of the workers she interviewed were superstressed at home. Writes Hochschild, "Family time, for them, had
taken on an 'industrial tone.' . . . And they felt they had to be as efficient at home as in the workplace."[14] Too often the moms and dads
that Hochschild interviewed complained of rushing through dinner so
they could head out for baseball games or drama practice, only to
return home exhausted. Then they had to do the laundry, walk the
family dog, and make tomorrow's lunches. Eileen O'Donnell, mother
of a young son and daughter, says, "On weekends, I feel like a taxi service. It's as bad as work can be some days. You're just torn in so many
directions."[15]

Although most individuals would probably say they hate being overscheduled, Manhattan-based psychologist Arlene Kagle argues otherwise: "Today people revel in being busy. It's the hair shirt of the '90s."[16] The bottom line, though, is that many of us have created untenable lives replete with schedules that are completely upended at the first sign of trouble, whether it be sick children, urgent work deadlines, demanding in-laws, or mechanical failures. How can we possibly live with the frenetic schedules we've created?

Hochschild found that the parents at Amerco often coped by withdrawing from their families and investing themselves in their jobs. According to Hochschild, the parents she interviewed "'emotionally downsize' life—convincing themselves that spouses and kids just don't need all that much attention."[17] While home is a crazy place, "the office, by contrast, is where Amerco employees get to socialize, feel competent, and relax on breaks."[18] Not surprisingly, Hochschild found that many mothers lengthened their workdays because they enjoyed the time spent with their colleagues. "Now work is where the heart is."[19]

Our children pay an inordinately high price when we are harried, exhausted, and emotionally disengaged. "Experts say that many of the most important elements in children's lives—regular routines and domestic rituals, consistency, the sense that their parents know and care about them—are exactly what's jettisoned when quality time substitutes for quantity time."[20]

ONE MOM'S TAKE ON QUALITY TIME

I'd like to share an anonymous mother's perspective on quality time that was published in the *Seattle Times* in 1979—long before we were well into the grand social experiment called "letting kids raise themselves." I've held on to this article because of its poignancy, honesty, and contemporary feel.

> I do not support the quality-care-after-work theory, the quality-care-on-the-weekend theory. I was a working mother for seven years, and I speak from experience.

I had to return to work for financial reasons when my son was eight weeks old. I went to work that first day in tears and was told not to worry, he would know his mother; it was instinctive. But I didn't believe it.

I sang to him each morning on the way to the sitter. "I'm your mommy, Mommy loves you." I hoped, somehow, the tiny face would remember the song all day long until Mommy could pick him up.

So in the evenings, the quality care comes in. It somehow eluded me. Evenings I prepared dinner, shopped for groceries, did small cleaning jobs, visited with my husband, bathed, ironed, and prepared to go to work again the next day.

Weekends then must become your quality time with the child. But Saturdays I had to do the large cleaning jobs which I could not fit in week nights.

Also, at least one night we enjoyed a dinner out, a movie, a drive. Friends dropped by, relatives were visited, errands attended to.

Summers were the worst. Other neighborhood children slept in on those long, hot days. My child was up as usual at 6:30 A.M. to hurry and dress, have breakfast, and proceed to the sitter.

. . . I would drive off to work, tears wetting the steering wheel.

Ah, but he will grow to be an independent, self-reliant little person! Yes, that has happened. But he also has become withdrawn, too independent and unemotional, surrounding himself with a wall I am only slowly penetrating.

Yes, I gave him hugs and kisses when I left him at 7:00 in the morning. I gave lots more when I picked him up at 6:00 at night. But what happened when he desired a hug or kiss at 10:00 or 3:00, or in between?

He fell down, and psychologists say it is well that he learned to pick himself up. *But my little boy picked himself up so many times that now it is hard for him to accept a helping hand, an outstretched bridge to another human being* [italics mine].

I am a full-time housewife now. Besides my nine-year-old son, I have two babies at home. I am not a perfect mother. I may not even be a good mother. But I am always handy to dry a tear when they stumble.

Every morning I send my nine-year-old to school, and I am there when he gets home. Dinner is on the table when my husband gets home; my housework is completed. We relax together during the evenings, and on the weekends, we play.

But is this quality care? Does my quantity care automatically become a quality product? Of course not. Maybe in years to come I will be able to judge the quality versus quantity method of child rearing. I unconsciously will compare my day-care child with my full-time housewife children.

I am scared that I will find a difference. I am afraid that I failed him in those early years. Perhaps I could have tried to squeeze more quality time in. I hurt for the times he needed me and I wasn't there.

My nine-year-old no longer seems to want the ritual of hello and good-bye kisses. Perhaps they remind him of a coming-and-going mother he'd just as soon forget.

I spend my time slowly trying to break through the wall that he feels protects him. I try to show him that he can really depend on me. I try to love him as best I can [italics mine].

No one ever will convince me he received enough quality time as a child. No one ever will convince me that a lot of quantity time wouldn't have helped him now to face his world.[21]

While other psychologists might dismiss this woman's poignant statement as purely anecdotal, I believe she's a sensitive mother who has picked up on real differences between her quality-time-reared child and her other quantity-time-reared children. And she struggles to deal with the fallout of her choices.

1,342 GAMES

Fortunately, many mothers have always known intuitively that the concept of quality time lacked the ring of truth. Margie Johnson, for example, never bought into the myth of quality time. "If we're spending ten hours at the office, do we think our kids don't notice? How can we forget that for them time is equated with love and devotion? I don't see how you can fool a child."

Margie, whose husband is a contractor, has raised their six children on quantity and quality time. Trim and petite, she used to sing with a big band, the Bicsiman Orchestra, but gave it up when she felt her children needed more of her time. "I loved it, and I'm probably going to return to it little by little," says Margie, "but I backed off because of my kids' schedules. They're all athletic."

Margie is proud of the fact that she has attended all of her children's athletic events: 1,342 in total. "I have tried to attend every event—football, basketball, baseball, and wrestling," she says, adding that her family has only two weeks a year without any athletic events. "My oldest child won the state championship in wrestling twice; that was a marvelous family time. They can always tell I'm rooting for them. I have this whistle I learned in sixth grade, and I can whistle louder than a man. I wanted my kids to know that whether they won or lost, I was always behind them. No matter what, I wanted to be there for them."

Margie also homeschooled one son when, as a fifth grader, he faltered, lost his confidence, and had trouble in school. "It was very difficult, and I felt inadequate. But my son regained his self-confidence when I tried to help him see his strengths rather than his weaknesses. Because of that, he's done wonderfully ever since."

DAD CUTS BACK

While Margie Johnson has never missed her children's athletic events, one father quit his job because he missed too many Little League games. Washington, D.C., was aghast when Bill Galston, President Clinton's domestic advisor, quit his superdemanding job which exacted twelve-hour days, to return to teaching at the University of Maryland.[22] Why? Galston wanted to spend more time with his ten-year-old son, Ezra. He said, "Fatherhood for me has been the most deeply transformative experience in my life. Nothing else is a close second. It is a prism through which I see the world."[23]

While working at the White House, Galston was so wrung out when he got home at eight-thirty in the evening. that he was only "technically" present. Sensing his own house was in disorder and "sand was running through the hourglass" of Ezra's childhood, Galston decided to cut back. Then came a letter from Ezra, saying, "Baseball's not fun when there's no one there to applaud you." Ezra ended his letter saying that baseball would be fun if only his dad were there to watch him play.

YOU CAN'T RAISE A KID ON SPEED-DIAL

Galston, and others, have learned that it takes an inordinate amount of time to truly know your children—what they're thinking, feeling, doing. Whether you're learning to dance with your baby or struggling to decode a ten-year-old's sadness or attempting to get a seventeen-year-old to confide in you, all of this takes time and emotional energy.

Some mothers may think it takes more time to parent a baby or toddler than a teenager. While this is true on one level—we don't feed

our teenagers several times throughout the night—our adolescents
need us just as much as our babies but for different reasons. While babies are forging emotional bonds, developing their brains, and learning elementary lessons about love and empathy, teenagers are making
life choices about drugs, sex, and academic achievement. Notes the
Carnegie Council on Adolescent Development: "With the exception
of infancy, no time of life compresses more physical, intellectual, social, emotional, and moral development into so brief a span."[24]

Even though this is true, parents often spend far less time with
their teenagers than with younger children, because they're hitting
their peak in their careers or they mistakenly believe their teens don't
need them at home. When the National Commission on Children
surveyed 1,700 parents in 1990, only 34 percent of the parents of
fourteen- to seventeen-year-olds played with their child once a week,
compared to 90 percent of the parents of children five and under. A
senior at a private Washington, D.C., girls' school said of her family,
"We used to eat family dinners together until I was in the fourth or
fifth grade. Then that stopped. Now I go home about 4:30—in the
carpool or the bus, and eat dinner alone in front of the television."[25]

Many of us realize just how important our presence is in our teen's
life, and we make adjustments and even sacrifices to be home when
the teenager is home. Like Kay Hickman, a commander in the Coast
Guard and longtime working mother. Kay was sitting in her family
room at three in the morning when she realized her teenage son, Andy,
needed more of her time and presence. As she monitored her contractions, awaiting the birth of another child, the phone rang. A police-
man said she and her husband needed to come down to the police
station, pronto. Andy was in trouble.

While her husband went to get Andy, Kay evaluated her family's
life together. "I was leaving home at six in the morning and getting
home at six in the evening. My family was crashing and burning
around me. I was scared to death."[26] What did she do? She took a

two-year sabbatical from the Coast Guard. "The key to raising a teenager is being available, and you can't be available if you're running by each other all the time."[27]

That is true. That's why I tried to be home when Holly and Kristen were home during the high school years. It wasn't easy. I was in a doctoral program, and though their high school day ended at two o'clock, I didn't always know when the girls would be home. Some days they ran track or attended club meetings after school. Other days they came home early—ready to go shopping or chat. Their variable schedule created a lot of pressure, but I chose not to provide just another empty house in a neighborhood already full of empty houses. So I scheduled my graduate school classes in the mornings and became either counselor mom, buddy mom, or vigilante mom as the situation required. And on those rare days when I was absent and one of the girls was home alone, she complained. Even when Kristen was a senior and tore up our driveway in our old Subaru, she wanted me to be around when she came through the door.

Sound selfish on her part? Sacrificial on mine? After all, what about my agenda? What about exercise? Self-fulfillment? A leisurely lunch out? Shopping? Actually, being available to my children has long been my agenda and a great source of fulfillment.

What all of us have to do is figure out how we're going to invest our time and if we're going to try to parent our kids well over the long haul. Since 40 percent of our teenagers' time is discretionary, they will fill up all those available hours with or without us. The question is, do we like the way they spend their time? If we don't, then we need to make adjustments in our schedules so that we can attend their games, help with homework, or just hang out in the kitchen. The payoff? They will probably do better academically and say no to drugs. In fact, researchers at the University of Southern California surveyed four thousand ninth graders and found a correlation "between unsupervised care after school and susceptibility to cigarette, alcohol, and marijuana use, depressed mood, risk taking, and lower academic grades."[28]

A SEASON FOR EVERYTHING

The book of Ecclesiastes says: "There is a time for everything, and a season for every activity under heaven":

> A time to be born and a time to die,
> A time to plant and a time to uproot,
> A time to kill and a time to heal,
> A time to tear down and a time to build,
> A time to weep and a time to laugh,
> A time to mourn and a time to dance.
>
> Ecclesiastes 3:1-4

I would suggest that there's a time to expend our energies in mothering our children, and once they're in school we have all those golden hours to develop our gifts or pursue employment on a flexible schedule. And when they need us less or leave home? We have yet another season of our lives to pursue myriad activities.

What if we choose to make our children pay the piper because we sacrifice our presence and the gift of parental time? They will suffer. Currently, rates of depression among children in this country are skyrocketing, and some authorities believe this is tied to parental neglect. The *Wall Street Journal* states that in 1996 some 580,000 children and adolescents received a prescription for Prozac, Paxil, or Zoloft.[29] Indeed, kids comprise a controversial new market for the makers of antidepressants. At a time when the adult market for antidepressants is slowing down, the children's market is rising.[30]

I'm alarmed and saddened by this trend. It's often easier for busy parents to find a mental health professional to medicate away a child's hostility and sadness than it is to make the lifestyle changes that would allow more on-line attention, love, and comfort.

No Second Acts

A week ago today I had a mastectomy, and as I sit and write, I am on painkillers that make me drowsy and nauseated. I have two drains extending from my armpit to my waist that collect fluid in plastic vials. For six weeks now I have lived with the realization that I, a basically healthy person for most of my life, have breast cancer. And as I've struggled with terror, sadness, and grief, I have also become acutely aware of the *reality of time*. Cancer survivors, I've learned, live in a different time warp. Instead of casually counting on longevity, they say, "Every day is a good day." And they learn to "live moment by moment."

As I confront my mortality, I reflect on the concept of time—how I've lived in the past, how I want to live in the future. Do I have regrets? Of course. I regret that I haven't spent more time alone with God. I regret that Don and I have spent too much time working and too little time playing. I want to laugh more, work less, and enjoy simple pleasures with those who matter most to me. But as I think of my children, I have few regrets. I gave my daughters oceans of time. I gave them myself.

Lee Atwater, former chairman of the Republican National Committee, on the other hand, knew what it was to be swamped with regret. When he lay dying of brain cancer, Atwater became philosophical about what really mattered in life. He said, "I acquired more wealth, power, and prestige than most. But you can acquire all you want and still feel empty. What power wouldn't I trade for a little more time with my family? What price wouldn't I pay for an evening with friends? It took a deadly illness to put me eye to eye with that truth, but it is a truth that this country, caught up in its ruthless ambition, can learn on my dime."[31]

Time. When it was too late, Atwater yearned for more time with his family. With his friends. And like many who confront a life-threatening illness, he saw that power, prestige, and toys never provide the fulfillment we yearn for. That fulfillment lies closer to home. It's often in our own backyard.

It's an illusion to think we can cheat our children of our love and presence now and make it up to them later. The season for child rearing is when our children are growing up in our homes before our very eyes. That's the time to give them hugs, kisses, and abundant time. That's the time to teach them values and deliver up to them our humanity. And if we elect to spend our valuable but fleeting time otherwise? One mother said it well, "There are no second acts with children."

PART THREE

THE LEGACY OF MOTHER LOVE

Ah, the legacy of mother love.

How it stretches and swells across the generations, uniting mother and daughter, fleshing out a new mother's identity and femininity, shaping her personality and the life of her child in ways our culture, with its emphasis on achievement and narcissism, has long forgotten.

Mother love is ultimately a love song, a siren's call, luring women not to self-destruction but to new realms of being . . . of sacrifice and being turned inside out. And if we can surrender to its love song, not only will our own lives be blessed and stretched, but we will affect future generations long after our names are forgotten and we are gone.

Ah, the power of mother love.

CHAPTER 13

The Journey
to the Heart

Former *Washington Post* reporter Sally Quinn created quite a
furor in 1992 when she wrote an article for the *Post* that was
picked up by many other newspapers. In the article, Quinn
said that feminism was dead and that its "hypocritical leaders" had
killed it.[1] Quinn went on to compare feminism to the Soviet Union's
failed experiment in communism and indicated that the movement
had not only outlasted its present usefulness but also had overlooked
"the deepest, most fundamental needs of its constituency."[2] While
Quinn was not explicit about what these needs were, she did say that
feminism made women feel ashamed to be housewives and full-time
mothers and that new leaders were needed who would speak to the real
concerns of women and acknowledge "the human factor."[3]

I've thought a lot about Quinn's article over the years, and I've con-
cluded that feminism doesn't need new leaders. What this country
needs now is for women everywhere to band together to reclaim the territory they have ceded—the terrain of the heart. Feminism as we have
experienced it in the past three decades needs to die. Most recently, the

world watched as the National Organization of Women launched an outrageous attack against the October 4, 1997, Washington, D.C., gathering of Promise Keepers. When these million-plus men gathered to confess their sins and shortcomings as husbands, fathers, and brothers, and prostrate themselves on the Washington Mall before God, asking for His forgiveness and mercy, Patricia Ireland railed against the organization as a threat to women's rights and equality.

Fortunately, most of us who watched the news that day and listened to the speakers looked through the feminist haze to see men doing soul work. We felt moved, humbled, and encouraged. God is using Promise Keepers to encourage men around the globe to reclaim the territory they have ceded as husbands, fathers, servants. What woman wouldn't rejoice about that?

We can't see what God is doing in the hearts of our men without looking deeply into our own hearts as well. So what do we need to do? *Washington Times* columnist Jonetta Rose Barras says we need to become "kinder, gentler women." She argues that women have "ventured so far away from a woman's geography and into the foreign terrain of men, that we have lost ourselves; forgot the habits, expressions and values that made us different but no less equal to men. The lawlessness of our children, the destruction of our communities, and the escalation of the divorce rate lend credibility to the charge that our wanderings have been devastating."[4]

We have lost ourselves. Our children are lawless. Our marriages lie in ruins. These are strong charges to lay at women's feet. But I agree with Barras. Women have always been the dreamers, the stokers of the communal family fire, the angels in an increasingly soulless culture who care for the poor, the sick, and the dying. And if we are not doing our job, who will? Feminists have long tried to draft men who perversely insist on being fathers, not mothers. Now the thrust is to get the federal government to fund better quality day care, train caregivers, and thus provide the "village" that will somehow nurture our children, shape their character, hone their brains, form strong attachments, and deepen their empathy.

But the contemporary feminist agenda must ultimately fail. Why? Because it has ignored women's overwhelming desire to mother their children. In ignoring the "m" word—*motherhood*—feminism has failed to address a major part of female identity. Women are different from men in a multiplicity of ways, and the power of mother love will ultimately prevail in their lives and hearts. The jet stream of mother love will always be a greater force in most women's lives than the lust for achievement or the hunger for personal power. Even as I write, I sense that a new and powerful grass-roots movement is stirring across this land—a movement fueled by love instead of narcissism. A movement undergirded by the Holy Spirit. A movement of the heart.

THE LEGACY

In concluding this book, which has become for me an intense personal journey, I'd like to share what some of the women I interviewed said they wished to leave as legacies to their children. At the end of every interview, I asked each woman a question that often made her pause and reflect. Sometimes it made her cry. This was the question I asked: *"What do you want your children to hear you saying in their hearts and in their minds long after you're gone?"* The responses I heard were invariably tender.

> *Margie:* "That I loved them more than anything else and dedicated my time to them because I knew it was God's will and I wanted to do that more than anything else."

> *Marian:* "I want my children to remember they were the most important people in my life and that they can do anything they want to do. I want them to respect their uniqueness and that of other people. I tell them often that

they've changed my life and made me the happiest person I could be."

Carlie: "I want my three sons to see me as someone who gave them the tools of character to handle whatever life has to offer. I want them to learn from my husband and me that anything valuable requires work and sacrifice. I want them to hear me saying, 'Try to always do the right thing, no matter what the consequences. Lead a life of integrity. Don't go looking for easy answers or take the easy road.'"

Melissa: "I want all three sons to grow up feeling unconditionally loved. I want them to always hear me saying, 'No matter what, I'll always love you. You speared your brother with a stick today, but there's nothing you could ever do that would make me not love you.'"

Judy: "I want them to hear that I love them and accept them, regardless of what they do, and that Christ loves them and accepts them as well. He wants to have a relationship with them. That's why He created them."

Kristie: "More than anything else I want my kids to have wisdom from God. I want to pass on to them the sense that the Bible and their relationship with God are more important than anything else. Sure, I've taught them some really important things, but after they are grown, they've got to be willing to submit to God and learn about Him. So I hope they hear me saying, 'Have a thirst and a hunger for God.'"

WHAT ABOUT YOU?

What do you want your children to remember about you when they're grown and gone? What central message do you wish them to internalize from all the years spent in your presence—the essence of who you were as a mother, what you believed, stood for, sought to give to them? And what do you want them to carry in their heads and hearts? Our children will someday leave our presence with core messages about their worth, whether positive or not. And these messages will influence every important decision they make, as well as their capacity to nurture their children.

What I want my daughters to remember—and I am crying softly just as the other mothers did—is that I've always loved them with a singular passion I have felt for no other human being. While I've loved two men dearly, no man has ever inspired the fierce protectiveness, the constant concern, the sheer joy that my children have given me just by existing. I wasn't a perfect mother, and some days, especially when they were teenagers, I wasn't even a particularly good mother. But their needs, their well-being, their dreams were never far from my mind.

So what do I want them to remember after I've left this earth? (And with a breast-cancer diagnosis, this question becomes less hypothetical.) I want them to hear me whisper:

> *I love you dearly. You have been my life's greatest gifts. Strive to*
> *live moral, responsible, compassionate lives. Love God with your*
> *whole heart and others as yourselves. And when you have*
> *children, love them as passionately as I have loved you.*
> *Remember that no achievement, no corporate title or graduate*
> *degree will ever compensate for lost moments or stolen memories.*
> *So love your children well.*
>
> *Remember, it's all about heart.*

Postscript

Finally, the long-awaited day arrived. Kristen had her baby!

It happened this way. Three weeks after I had a modified radical mastectomy, and one week before her due date, Kristen and I sat on my back patio in the afternoon summer sun, talking. We talked about my struggles with all the physical and emotional pain of cancer and her difficulty in dealing with this during her last trimester. Then in a happier, lighter vein, we discussed her desire to have her baby *soon! Krissy wanted to get her body back.* Dressed in a maternity blouse and black skirt, my daughter looked oh, so uncomfortable. Her bulging abdomen made it difficult for her to bend over or find a comfortable position for sleeping. Since she got up every hour to go to the bathroom, she was exhausted as she moved slowly through each day.

"I saw my obstetrician today, and he told me I could have this baby at any time now, but so far there's no sign it's going to happen soon," she said wearily.

Anxious to be available when the baby was born, I expressed some concern that I couldn't get in to see my oncologist or get an appointment for a second opinion at Johns Hopkins. I felt I needed to make a treatment decision right away so I could have a free mind as a grandmother.

Kristen listened and then said, "Mom, I wish I could have this baby this weekend. You have all next week free, and you could come and stay with me. Plus, you wouldn't be so preoccupied with cancer."

I agreed. "Well, I've been reading about the power of the mind-body connection. So why don't you just tell your body to have this baby tonight?"

Kristen smiled and changed the subject. But several hours later she started cramping, and by nine o'clock the next morning, she and Greg were at the hospital, monitoring her contractions, which came every four or five minutes. Greg called our house midmorning to say the baby's birth was imminent. "I'll keep you posted," he said as he quickly hung up the phone.

Don and I waited throughout the afternoon with great excitement. Finally, we came in from working in our yard at about four o'clock only to discover that Greg had called and left a message. In a strong voice, my son-in-law had said, "Krissy just had our baby. I'm not going to tell you what she had. You'll just have to come to the hospital and find out." He added, "She'll be in room 627 after five." Then, almost as an afterthought, he stated, "The mother and baby are fine."

Don and I quickly changed our clothes and raced to the hospital. While he parked the car, I took off past the information desk in the hospital lobby at a dead run. Carrying a basket full of Kristen's favorite flowers—purple irises, daisies, yellow day lilies—I strode briskly into room 627 only to discover she wasn't there. The nurse told me that both mother and baby were still in the recovery area. When I finally found the right room, I pushed open the door and there was my younger daughter, propped up in bed, cradling a tiny, still baby swaddled in a blanket, wearing a stocking cap. Don stood by her bed, smiling, and I could tell by looking at him that he already knew the sex of the baby.

"Would you like to hold your new grandson, Austin Gregory Blair?" asked Krissy, sounding for all the world as though she were introducing Britain's future prime minister.

I took my new grandson in my arms and examined him. Such a sweet little face he had. His eyes were closed, and I could barely see his microscopic eyelashes. His rosebud mouth was tiny. Gently I unwrapped the blanket as one unwraps a present and discovered a perfect little boy, replete with tiny fingers and toes.

"What a beautiful baby," I exclaimed, knowing that I was about to become an adoring grandparent, as silly in her devotion as some of my closest women friends. "Just look at those little fingernails." As I reluctantly shared Austin with Don and Holly, Greg and Kristen recounted the tale of the labor and delivery. All had gone well until Austin's heartbeat dropped dramatically as his mother's contractions came faster and faster. Quickly, the nurse slapped an oxygen mask on Kristen and gave her a shot to slow down the contractions. The obstetrician then carefully inserted an internal fetal monitor into the birth canal and attached it to the baby's head. "I was so scared," said Kristen. "I prayed that nothing bad would happen to the baby." Fortunately, several hours later little Austin was born, safe and serene.

What wonderful, healing moments those were for our entire family. The past two months had been grim, filled with my surgeries and cancer's death statistics. All of us felt ravaged. Now we could bask in the joy and wonder of a new life. Here was a baby, a gift from God. The hope of things to come. By his mere arrival little Austin had conferred new roles to all of us: mother, father, aunt, grandmother, grandfather. We were thrilled.

Then I remembered the dream God had given Kristen about this baby months before she even conceived. In the dream she had held a son and nursed him. And though her doctor would later tell her that her baby's rapid heartbeat signaled a girl, Kristen believed in her heart that God would give her a son. And she was right.

In the weeks since Austin's birth I have enjoyed watching my daughter's evolution as a mother. She had a week of euphoria following the birth, in part because Greg and I were there to help her. "That was one of the happiest weeks of my life," she told me. Soon, however, the sleepless nights took their toll, and Kristen looked exhausted. She nursed her baby faithfully every one or two hours but lost her joy. Now at six weeks postpartum, Kristen is feeling much better. She is sleeping for longer intervals between feedings, and Austin has gained almost three pounds. She tells me she loves her "darling" baby and has grown fiercely protective. As I witness the legacy of love and nurture that my daughter gives her baby, I know something of what I gave her is being poured into this little boy.

What has this baby's birth meant to me? In the midst of severe suffering, this child gives me hope and a renewed will to live. I want to be alive to see this baby become a man, and I try to visualize him in my mind's eye, striding across a stage to get his college diploma and waiting in the front of a church for his bride to walk down the aisle. As you can see, I am, like King Hezekiah in the Old Testament, asking the Lord for more years. Also, the day after I held Austin, about 50 percent of my mastectomy pain evaporated. I had greater range of motion in my semi-invalid right arm where fifteen lymph nodes were removed. When I think about it, I do not believe the convergence of a cancer diagnosis, the writing of this book, and this baby's birth are coincidental. Instead, I feel that God, in His goodness, has carefully orchestrated the timing of everything. Austin's birth not only heralds the dawning of a new day for his parents, it gives me even more reason to fight for my life.

Already I love this sweet little baby. Sometimes I hold him in my arms as his eyes flutter when he goes to sleep, and I talk to him in high-pitched motherese. With his eyes closed, he makes little grunts and moaning sounds. "He's talking to me," I tell my daughter who smiles indulgently, knowing her baby has captured my heart.

Notes

CHAPTER ONE: THE POWER OF MOTHER LOVE

1. Pam Lambert and Cynthia Wang, "Bringing Up Babies," *People*, 8 July 1996, 84.
2. Jeanne Hendricks, "The Mother/Child Connection" (Garland, Tex.: American Tract Society, n.d.).
3. Louis M. Notkin, ed., *Mother Tributes from the World's Great Literature* (New York: Samuel Curl, 1943), 117.
4. Lisa Jones Townsel, "Shaquille O'Neal: Superstar Pays Tribute to His Supermom," *Ebony*, May 1996, 27.
5. As quoted in Eileen Simpson, *Orphans: Real and Imaginary* (New York: Weidenfeld and Nicholson, 1987), 19.
6. Mary Frances Berry, *The Politics of Parenthood* (New York: Viking, 1993), 5.
7. Berry, *Politics of Parenthood*, 3.
8. Jeanne Safer, *Beyond Motherhood* (New York: Pocket Books, 1996), 7.
9. Safer, *Beyond Motherhood*, 7.
10. Anna Borgman, "Out of Death, A Cherished Life," *Washington Post*, 12 March 1995, A1.
11. Borgman, "Out of Death," A14.
12. Borgman, "Out of Death," A14.
13. Bill Hewitt, Gail Cameron Wescott, and Don Sider, "Tears of Hate, Tears of Pity," *People*, 13 March 1995, 78.
14. Cynthia King, "Childless by Choice," *Harper's Bazaar*, June 1996, 134.
15. Linda Burton, "The Bad Days," in *What's a Smart Woman Like*

You Doing at Home? ed. Linda Burton, Janet Dittmer, and Cheri Loveless (Vienna, Va.: Mothers at Home, 1992), 41.

16. Sigmund Freud, *Outline of Psychoanalysis*, SE 23 (London: Hogarth Press, 1940), 188.

CHAPTER TWO: THE POWER TO TRANSFORM A LIFE

1. Anthony Violanti, "Wynonna: Country's First Daughter Finds Her Balance," *Buffalo News*, 17 November 1996, 1F.
2. Violanti, "Wynonna," 1F.
3. Violanti, "Wynonna," 1F.
4. Amy Herrick, "Mortal Terrors and Motherhood," *Washington Post Magazine*, 11 May 1997, 16.
5. Herrick, "Mortal Terrors," 18.
6. Herrick, "Mortal Terrors," 18.
7. Herrick, "Mortal Terrors," 18.
8. Herrick, "Mortal Terrors," 19.
9. Herrick, "Mortal Terrors," 19.
10. Herrick, "Mortal Terrors," 19.
11. Samantha Miller, Lorenzo Benet, et.al., "MA-MA-MA-VOOM," *People*, 26 May 1997, 88.
12. Byron Egeland and Martha Farrell Erickson, "Rising Above the Past: Strategies for Helping New Mothers Break the Cycle of Abuse and Neglect," *Zero to Three*, December 1990, 29.
13. Michel Odent, M.D., "Why Laboring Women Need Support," *Mothering* no. 80 (Fall 1996): 49.
14. Odent, "Laboring Women," 50.
15. Odent, "Laboring Women," 50.
16. Heidi Brennan, "Transitions," *Discovering Motherhood*, ed. H. L. Brennan, P. M. Goresh, C. H. Myers (Vienna, Va.: Mothers at Home, 1991), 2.
17. Brennan, "Transitions," 2.
18. Brennan, "Transitions," 3.

19. Brennan, "Transitions," 3.

20. Antoinette Clyde, "Motherhood as a Most Unselfish Act," *Newsday*, 3 September 1996, B16.

21. "A Mother's Poignant Note Left with Abandoned Baby," *Washington Times*, 10 December 1996.

22. John Bowlby, talk given to physicians at the American Psychiatric Association convention, Washington, D.C., May 1986.

CHAPTER THREE: THE POWER OF SURRENDER

1. Iris Krasnow, "Surrendering to Motherhood," *Washington Post*, 22 November 1994, D5.

2. Krasnow, "Surrendering," D5.

3. Krasnow, "Surrendering," D5.

4. Krasnow, "Surrendering," D5.

5. Krasnow, "Surrendering," D5.

6. Krasnow, "Surrendering," D5.

7. Cornelia Odom, "What About You?" *Discovering Motherhood*, ed. H. L. Brennan, P. M. Goresh, and C. H. Myers (Vienna, Va.: Mothers at Home, 1991), 78.

8. Mary Eberstadt, "Putting Children Last," *Commentary*, May 1995, 44-50.

9. Eberstadt, "Putting Children Last," 46.

10. Eberstadt, "Putting Children Last," 46.

11. Eberstadt, "Putting Children Last," 46.

12. Eberstadt, "Putting Children Last," 46.

13. Eberstadt, "Putting Children Last," 48.

14. Eberstadt, "Putting Children Last," 48.

15. Mary Amoroso, "The Pull Toward Home Is Strong for a Working Mom," *The Record*, 7 April 1996, taken from Lexis-Nexis, an electronic database service.

16. Krasnow, "Surrendering," D5.

CHAPTER FOUR: THE POWER OF SIMPLICITY

1. Sarah Ban Breathnach, *Simple Abundance: A Daybook of Comfort and Joy* (New York: Warner Books, 1995), foreword.
2. Anne Roiphe, *Fruitful* (New York: Houghton-Mifflin, 1996), 11.
3. Richard Lorr, "What Do Moms Really Want?" *Parents*, May 1996, 38.
4. Lorr, "What Do Moms Really Want?" 40.
5. Danielle Crittenden, "The Mother of All Problems," *Saturday Night*, April 1996, 46.
6. Crittenden, "Problems," 46.
7. Crittenden, "Problems," 47.
8. Breathnach, *Simple Abundance*, reading from May 8.
9. Breathnach, *Simple Abundance*, reading from May 8.
10. Diane Fisher, "Mothers at Home," *New Beginnings*, September/October, 1996, 135.
11. Fisher, "Mothers at Home," 133.
12. Fisher, "Mothers at Home," 134.
13. Fisher, "Mothers at Home," 135.
14. Breathnach, *Simple Abundance*, foreword.
15. Angela Neustatter, "Children: Ingredients of a Happy Childhood," *The Independent*, 16 August 1992, 52.

CHAPTER FIVE: THE POWER TO HEAL

1. Selma Fraiberg with Edna Adelson and Vivian Shapiro, "Ghosts in the Nursery: A Psychoanalytic Approach to the Problems of Impaired Infant-Mother Relationships," *Selected Writings of Selma Fraiberg*, ed. Louis Fraiberg (Columbus, Ohio: The State University Press, 1987), 100.
2. Fraiberg, "Impaired Infant-Mother Relationships," 134.
3. Fraiberg, "Impaired Infant-Mother Relationships," 135.
4. Fraiberg, "Impaired Infant-Mother Relationships," 135.
5. Fraiberg, "Impaired Infant-Mother Relationships," 135.

6. Diane Benoit and Kevin Parker, "Stability and Transmission of Attachment Across Three Generations," *Child Development* 65 (1994): 1444.

7. Victoria Secunda, *When You and Your Mother Can't Be Friends* (New York: Dell Publishers, 1990), 377.

CHAPTER SIX: THE POWER OF ATTACHMENT

1. Joseph Campos, et al., "Socioemotional Development," in *Handbook of Child Psychology,* ed. Paul H. Mussen, vol. 2 (New York: John Wiley & Sons, 1983), 783-917.

2. John Bowlby, *Attachment,* vol. 1, *Attachment and Loss* (New York: Basic Books, 1969), xi.

3. Alan Sroufe and Everett Waters, "Attachment as an Organizational Construct," *Child Development* 48 (1977): 1186.

4. Michael E. Lamb, "The Development of Mother-Infant and Father-Infant Attachment in the Second Year of Life," *Developmental Psychology* 13 (1977): 637-48.

5. Frits A. Goossens and Marinus H. Van IJzendoorn, "Quality of Infants' Attachments to Professional Caregivers: Relation to Infant-Parent Attachment and Day-Care Characteristics," *Child Development* 61 (1990): 832-37.

6. John Bowlby, address given at the American Psychiatric Association, Washington, D.C., 10-16 May 1986.

7. Bowlby, address given 10-16 May 1986.

8. Bob Greene, *Good Morning, Merry Sunshine* (New York: Penguin, 1985), 102-3.

9. Ross Parke and Barbara Tinsley, "Family Interaction in Infancy," *Handbook of Infant Development,* ed. Joy Osofsky (New York: John Wiley & Sons, 1987), 591.

10. Parke, "Family Interaction in Infancy," 591.

11. John Bowlby, *A Secure Base* (New York: Basic Books, 1988), 10.

12. Bowlby, *A Secure Base*, 11.

13. Robert Karen, *Becoming Attached* (New York: Warner, 1994), 146-64.

14. Karen, *Becoming Attached*, 176.

15. Douglas Teti, D. S. Messinger, D. M. Gelfand, R. Isabella, "Maternal Depression and the Quality of Early Attachment: An Examination of Infants, Preschoolers and their Mothers," *Developmental Psychology* 31, no. 3 (1995): 364-76.

16. Karen, *Becoming Attached*, 159.

17. Karen, *Becoming Attached*, 160.

18. Karen, *Becoming Attached*, 159-60.

19. Virginia L. Colin, "Human Attachment: What We Know Now," *Infant Attachment Literature Review for the U.S. Department of Health and Human Services* (28 June 1991): 119.

20. Judy F. Rosenblith, *In the Beginning* (Newbury Park, N. J.: Sage, 1992), 473.

21. Rosenblith, *In the Beginning*, 473.

22. Rosenblith, *In the Beginning*, 473.

23. Roy Maynard, "The Ezzos Know Best: Controversial Parenting Curriculum Is Sweeping the Church," *World Magazine* 2, no. 8 (May 25-June 1, 1996): 18-19.

24. Gary and Anne Marie Ezzo, *Preparation for Parenting* (Chatsworth, Calif.: Growing Families International, 1995), 24.

25. Maynard, "The Ezzos Know Best," 18.

26. Ezzo, *Preparation for Parenting*, 26.

27. Ezzo, *Preparation for Parenting*, 49.

28. Ezzo, *Preparation for Parenting*, 151.

29. Ezzo, *Preparation for Parenting*, 152.

30. Ezzo, *Preparation for Parenting*, 153.

31. Robert Karen, "Becoming Attached," *The Atlantic* (February 1990): 37.

32. Evelyn Thoman and Sue Browder, *Born Dancing* (New York: Harper & Row, 1987), 168.

33. Silvia Bell and Mary D. Salter Ainsworth, "Infant Crying and Maternal Responsiveness," *Child Development* 43 (1972): 1171-90.

34. Thoman and Browder, *Born Dancing*, 168.

35. Thoman and Browder, *Born Dancing*, 112.

36. Bell and Ainsworth, "Maternal Responsiveness," 1171-90.

37. Bell and Ainsworth, "Maternal Responsiveness," 1171-90.

38. Thoman and Browder, *Born Dancing*, 170.

39. Thoman and Browder, *Born Dancing*, 169-73.

40. Bowlby, *A Secure Base*, 28.

41. Carol Smaldino, "Tossing and Turning Over Crying It Out," *Mothering* (March 1995): 32.

42. Smaldino, "Tossing and Turning," 32.

43. Burton White, *The First Three Years* (New York: Simon & Schuster, 1993), 242-3.

44. Correspondence from Focus on the Family, 9 October 1997.

45. Dr. Robert E. Hannemann, interview by author, Washington, D.C., 23 October 1997.

46. Teti, "Maternal Depression," 364-76.

47. Teti, "Maternal Depression," 373.

48. Ellyn Satter, "The Feeding Relationship," *Zero to Three* XII, no. 5, National Center for Clinical Infant Programs (June 1992): 4.

49. Bowlby, address given 10-16 May 1986.

50. Karen, *Becoming Attached*, 442-3.

51. Karen, *Becoming Attached*, 442-3.

52. Robert Munsch, *Love You Forever* (Ontario, Canada: Firefly Books, 1986). Used by permission of the author.

CHAPTER SEVEN: THE POWER OF SEPARATION

1. Jay Belsky, Testimony, Presidential Commission on Assignment of Women in the Armed Forces, 9 June 1992, 323.

2. Belsky, Women in the Armed Forces, 302.

3. Judith Viorst, *Necessary Losses: The Loves, Illusions, Dependencies*

and Impossible Expectations that All of Us Have to Give Up in Order to Grow (New York: Simon & Schuster, 1992), 21.

4. Viorst, *Necessary Losses.*

5. Lee Salk, *What Every Child Would Like His Parents to Know* (New York: Warner, 1973), 30-1.

6. Selma Fraiberg, *Every Child's Birthright: In Defense of Mothering* (New York: Bantam, 1977), 34.

7. Julia Duin, "Day Care Study Provides 'Cautionary Note' to Mothers," *Washington Times*, 5 April 1997, A3.

8. Mary C. Larson, M. R. Gonnor, and L. Hertsgaard, "The Effects of Morning Naps, Car Trips, and Maternal Separation on Adrenocortical Activity in Human Infants," *Child Development*, 1991, 62, 362-72.

9. Jay Belsky, "Infant Day Care: A Cause for Concern," *Zero to Three* (September 1986): 6.

10. Jay Belsky, "Risks Remain," *Zero to Three* (February 1987), 22.

11. Brenda Hunter, "Storm Clouds or a Drizzle? A Look at a New Study on Child Care" (Washington, D.C.: Family Research Council Report, 1996), 1.

12. Elizabeth Mehner, "Child Care No Risk to Infant-Mother Ties, Study Says," *Los Angeles Times*, 21 April 1996.

13. Jonathon Freedland, "Child Care Report Backs Working Moms," *The Guardian*, 22 April 1996.

14. "Infant and Child Care and Attachment Security: Results of the NICHD Study of Child Care," Symposium, International Conference on Infant Studies (Providence, R.I.), NICHD Early Child Care Research Network, 20 April 1996, 15.

15. "Results of the NICHD Study of Child Care," 15.

16. "Study Says Babies in Child Care Keep Secure Bonds to Mothers," *New York Times*, 21 April 1996, 2.

17. Suzanne Fields, "What a Day (Care) This Has Been," *Washington Times*, 2 May 1996.

18. "Results of the NICHD Study of Child Care," 15.

19. Hunter, "New Study on Child Care," 4.

20. Susan Chiva, "Study Says Babies in Child Care Keep Secure Bonds to Mothers," *New York Times*, 21 April 1996, 1.

21. Duin, "Day Care Study," A3.

22. Duin, "Day Care Study," A3.

23. Bob Greene, "Wrenching Day for 'Richard': 'Don't Send Me Away,' Boy Begs at Separation," *Chicago Tribune*, 1 May 1995.

24. Greene, "Wrenching Day for 'Richard.' "

25. Greene, "Wrenching Day for 'Richard.' "

26. David Finkel, "Now Say Goodbye to Diane," *Washington Post Magazine*, 4 May 1997, 10.

27. Finkel, "Now Say Goodbye to Diane," 12.

28. Viorst, *Necessary Losses*, 27.

29. Bowlby, *Attachment*, xiii.

30. Bowlby, *Attachment*, xiii.

31. Viorst, *Necessary Losses*, 27.

32. Viorst, *Necessary Losses*, 32.

33. Viorst, *Necessary Losses*, 33.

34. Barbara Latterner, "What Price Separation?" *Mothering*, 22 June 1992, 32.

Chapter Eight: The Power to Impart Faith

1. Martin Luther, "Excerpts from *Table Talk*, 'Epistle Sermon, Fourth Sunday in Advent' and 'Treatise on Good Works' in *Devotional Classics*. ed. Richard J. Foster and James Bryan Smith, (San Francisco: HarperCollins, 1990), 135.

Chapter Nine: The Power to Hone a Conscience

1. "Three Boys Could Be Charged with Murder in Baby's Beating," *Washington Times*, April 1996, A3.

2. Eugene Robinson, " 'Cunning, Very Wicked' Defendants Sentenced

to Indefinite Detention," *Washington Post*, 25 November 1993, A47.

3. Arianna Huffington, "Superpredators Overlooked?" *Washington Times*, 6 July 1996, Commentary.

4. Senator Dan Coats, "Opening Statement at the Hearing before the Subcommittee on Children and Families on Juvenile Crime," 18 July 1996, Transcript, 1-2.

5. James Fox, "Testimony at the Hearing before the Subcommittee on Children and Families on Juvenile Crime," 18 July 1996. Transcript, 7.

6. James Fox testimony, 7.

7. James Fox testimony, 8.

8. James Fox testimony, 38.

9. Ted Gest, "Crime Time Bomb," *U.S. News and World Report*, 25 March 1996, 29.

10. James F. MacArthur Jr., *The Vanishing Conscience* (Dallas: Word), 37.

11. James Q. Wilson, *The Moral Sense* (New York: The Free Press, 1993), 105.

12. Wilson, *The Moral Sense*, 105.

13. Wilson, *The Moral Sense*, 226.

14. Wilson, *The Moral Sense*, 226.

15. Wilson, *The Moral Sense*, 176.

16. William Damon, *Social and Personality Development* (New York: Norton, 1983), 160-1.

17. Damon, *Social and Personality Development*, 160-1.

18. Daniel Goleman, *Emotional Intelligence* (New York: Bantam, 1995), 196-7.

19. Goleman, *Emotional Intelligence*, 196-7.

20. Goleman, *Emotional Intelligence*, 236.

21. Patrick Fagan, "The Real Root Causes of Violent Crime: The Breakdown of Marriage, Family and Community," The Heritage Foundation, Washington, D.C., 17 March 1995, 5.

22. Goleman, *Emotional Intelligence*, 236.

23. Burton White, *The First Three Years* (New York: Simon & Schuster, 1990), 141.

24. White, *First Three Years*, 141.

25. White, *First Three Years*, 252.

26. Diana Baumrind, "The Discipline Controversy Revisited," *Family Relations* 45 (1996): 409.

27. Baumrind, "Discipline Controversy," 409.

28. White, *First Three Years*, 253.

29. Baumrind, "Discipline Controversy," 409.

30. William Glasser, *Reality Therapy* (New York: Harper & Row, 1965), 17.

31. Glasser, *Reality Therapy*, 17-8.

32. Glasser, *Reality Therapy*, 18.

33. Foster Cline, M. D., and Jim Fay, *Parenting Teens with Love and Logic* (Colorado Springs: Piñon Press, 1992), 71.

34. Cline, *Parenting Teens*, 71.

35. Cline, *Parenting Teens*, 71-2.

36. Elizabeth Dodds, *Marriage to a Difficult Man* (Philadelphia: Westminster Press, 1971), 43.

37. Dodds, *Difficult Man*, 43.

38. See 1 Samuel 2:12-36.

39. William Kilpatrick, *Why Johnny Can't Tell Right from Wrong* (New York: Simon & Schuster), 27.

40. Kilpatrick, *Right from Wrong*, 27

41. Glasser, *Reality Therapy*, 18.

CHAPTER TEN: THE POWER TO CREATE EMPATHY

1. Samuel P. Oliner and Pearl M. Oliner, *The Altruistic Personality* (New York: Macmillan, 1988), preface.

2. Heinz Kohut, *How Does Analysis Cure?* (Chicago: University of Chicago Press, 1984), 82.

3. William Damon, *Social and Personality Development* (New York: Norton, 1983), 129.

4. Damon, *Social and Personality Development*, 130.

5. Damon, *Social and Personality Development*, 130.

6. Damon, *Social and Personality Development*, 130.

7. Kohut, *How Does Analysis Cure?* 83.

8. Kohut, *How Does Analysis Cure?* 78.

9. Karen, *Becoming Attached*, 190.

10. Karen, *Becoming Attached*, 190

11. Karen, *Becoming Attached*, 199.

12. Beth Azar, "Defining the Trait That Makes Us Human," *Monitor* (November 1997), 15.

13. Karen, *Becoming Attached*, 199.

14. Mona Charen, "Showing Us How to Raise a Killer," *Washington Times*, 10 June 1997, A14.

15. Charen, "Raise a Killer," A14.

16. Oliner and Oliner, *The Altruistic Personality*, 174.

17. Oliner and Oliner, *The Altruistic Personality*, 174-7.

18. Oliner and Oliner, *The Altruistic Personality*, 198.

CHAPTER ELEVEN: THE POWER TO BUILD A BRAIN

1. J. Madeleine Nash, "Fertile Minds," *Time*, 3 February 1997, 49.

2. Sharon Begley, "How to Build a Baby's Brain," *Newsweek*, April 1997, 26.

3. Begley, "Build a Baby's Brain," 26.

4. Begley, "Build a Baby's Brain," 30.

5. Begley, "Build a Baby's Brain," 30.

6. Begley, "Build a Baby's Brain," 30.

7. Begley, "Build a Baby's Brain," 30.

8. Nash, "Fertile Minds," 51.

9. Jean Piaget, *Intelligence and Affectivity* (Palo Alto: Annual Reviews, 1981), 5.

10. Begley, "Build a Baby's Brain," 31.

11. Begley, "Build a Baby's Brain," 31.

12. Begley, "Build a Baby's Brain," 31.

13. Daniel Glick, "Rooting for Intelligence," *Newsweek*, April 1997, 32.

14. Glick, "Rooting for Intelligence," 32.

15. Glick, "Rooting for Intelligence," 32.

16. Begley, "Build a Baby's Brain," 32.

17. Begley, "Build a Baby's Brain," 32.

18. Sarah Van Boven, "Giving Infants a Helping Hand," *Newsweek*, April 1997, 45.

19. Leslie Barker, "Touched by Love: Scientists Study the Importance of Physical Contact for Premature Infants," *Dallas Morning News*, 24 June 1996, 3Cff. Retrieved from Lexis-Nexis, an electronic database service.

20. Barker, "Touched by Love," 3Cff.

21. Nicole Malec, "Babies Tickled Pink After Rubdowns," *Hartford Courant*, 23 July 1996, E1ff. Retrieved from Lexis-Nexis, an electronic database service.

22. Malec, "Babies Tickled Pink," E1ff.

23. Barker, "Touched by Love," 3Cff.

24. Barbara Meltz, "Giving Them a Little of That Human Touch," *Boston Globe*, 1 May 1992, 65ff. Retrieved from Lexis-Nexis, an electronic database service.

25. Meltz, "Human Touch," 65ff.

26. Nash, "Fertile Minds," 56.

27. Nash, "Fertile Minds," 56.

28. Begley, "Build a Baby's Brain," 32.

29. Louis M. Notkin, ed., *Mother Tributes from the World of Great Literature* (New York: Samuel Cull, 1943), 117.

30. Mabel Bartlett and Sophia Baker, *Mother-Makers of Men* (New York: Exposition Press, 1952), 44.

31. Notkin, *Mother Tributes*, 144.

32. Bartlett and Baker, *Mother-Makers of Men*, 66-8.

33. Langston Hughes, "Don't You Turn Back," *Collected Poems* (New York: Knopf, 1994), 44. Reprinted by permission of Alfred A. Knopf Inc.

34. Catherine Marshall, *Adventures in Prayer* (Old Tappan, N. J.: Chosen Books, 1975), 30.

35. Ben Carson, speech given at the National Prayer Breakfast, 6 February 1997, Washington, D.C.

36. Michael Ryan, "If You Can't Teach Me, Don't Criticize Me," *Parade*, 11 May 1997, 7.

37. Ryan, "Don't Criticize Me," 7.

38. Carson, speech at National Prayer Breakfast.

39. Ryan, "Don't Criticize Me," 7.

40. Carson, speech at National Prayer Breakfast.

41. Carson, speech at National Prayer Breakfast.

42. Carson, speech at National Prayer Breakfast.

43. Ryan, "Don't Criticize Me," 7.

CHAPTER TWELVE: THE POWER OF TIME

1. Nikhil Deogun, "Top PepsiCo Executive Picks Family over Job," *Wall Street Journal*, 24 September 1997, B1.

2. Deogun, "Family over Job," B10.

3. Deogun, "Family over Job," B10.

4. Anne Veigle, "Search for Balance between Work and Mother Love Brings Changes," *Washington Times*, 29 September 1997, B2.

5. Veigle, "Search for Balance," B2.

6. Associated Press, "Mothers of Today Don't Think They're Doing as Good as Own Moms, Poll Finds," *Washington Times*, 9 May 1997, A10.

7. Associated Press, "Mothers of Today," A10.

8. Shapiro, "The Myth of Quality Time," *Newsweek*, 12 May 1997, 64.

9. Shapiro, "Quality Time," 64.

10. Shapiro, "Quality Time," 62.

11. Shapiro, "Quality Time," 64.

12. Shapiro, "Quality Time," 64.

13. Joanne Kaufman, "Busy Signals," *Allure*, May 1997, 134, 136.

14. Shapiro, "No Place Like Work," *Newsweek*, 28 April 1997, 64.

15. Shapiro, "Quality Time," 64.

16. Kaufman, "Busy Signals," 136.

17. Shapiro, "No Place," 64.

18. Shapiro, "No Place," 64.

19. Shapiro, "No Place," 64.

20. Shapiro, "Quality Time," 64.

21. Unnamed, "Quantity Does Count When You Raise a Child," *Seattle Times*, 13 May 1979.

22. Sue Shellenbarger, "Bill Galston Tells the President: My Son Needs Me More," *Wall Street Journal*, 21 June 1995.

23. Shellenbarger, "My Son Needs Me More."

24. Laura Stepp, "Time Out for Teenagers," *Washington Post*, 28 September 1993, C5.

25. Stepp, "Time Out," C5.

26. Stepp, "Time Out," C5.

27. Stepp, "Time Out," C5.

28. Stepp, "Time Out," C5.

29. Elyse Tanouye, "Antidepressant Makers Study Kids' Market," *Wall Street Journal*, 4 April 1997, B1.

30. Tanouye, "Antidepressant Makers," B1.

31. Iris Krasnow, "Surrendering to Motherhood," *Washington Post*, 22 November 1994, D5.

CHAPTER THIRTEEN: THE JOURNEY TO THE HEART

1. Sally Quinn, "The Women's Movement Needs New Leadership," *Star Tribune*, 28 June 1992, 9Aff. Retrieved from Lexis-Nexis, an electronic database service.

2. Quinn, "The Women's Movement," 9Aff.

3. Quinn, "The Women's Movement," 9Aff.

4. Jonetta Rose Barras, "Wanted: Kinder, Gentler Women, *Washington Times*, 21 June 1996, A21.